Figuring Out People

Design Engineering With Meta-Programs .

*Deepening Understanding of People
for Better Rapport, Relationships, and Influence*

by

L. Michael Hall, Ph.D.
Bob G. Bodenhamer, D.Min.

Published by The Anglo American Book Company,
Bancyfelin, Carmarthen, Wales.

First published in the UK by

The Anglo American Book Company Ltd
Crown Buildings
Bancyfelin
Carmarthen
Wales

First published 1997.

British Library of Cataloguing-in-Publication Data
A catalogue entry for this book is available
from the British Library.

ISBN 1899836101

Printed and bound in Wales by
WBC Book Manufacturers,
Waterton Industrial Estate,
Bridgend, Mid Glamorgan.

"By Human Engineering I mean the science and art of directing
the energies and capacities of human beings
to the advancement of human weal." (p. 1)

"Production is essentially a task for engineers;
it essentially depends upon the discovery and the application of natural
laws, including the laws of human nature.

Human Engineering will embody the theory and practice—
the science and art— of all engineering branches united by a common
aim—the understanding and welfare of mankind." (pp. 6-7)

"The task of engineering science is not only to know, but to know how."
(p. 11)

Korzybski, 1921

Acknowledgments

No one gives birth to a new work without a great number of people who have supported the process. While this work came together very quickly in just a couple of months in early 1997, it grew out of years and years of study, research, and training of the meta-programs.

We especially thank the following for their support.

From Michael:

- *Wyatt Woodsmall, Tad James, and Richard Bandler* who first introduced me to the NLP meta-programs.

- *Cheryl Ann Buffa* who devotedly read every word of the text in our first drafts and provided much wise insight.

- *Jessica Hall*, my daughter for putting up with all of my computer time!

- The inventor of e-mail—through which medium Bob and I have become good friends as well as co-authors.

From Bob:

- *Richard Spencer* whose vision introduced me to NLP.

- *Gene Rooney,* my first NLP trainer and inspiration.

- *Richard Bandler* and *John Grinder* without whom NLP would not even exist.

- *Tad James* who turned me on to Time-Lining and Language and the power they offer for personal change.

- *Wyatt Woodsmall* who along with Tad walked me through Trainer's Training.

- And most importantly, to my wife *Linda*, whose love and continued support has encouraged me throughout thirty-two years of marriage and ministry.

Table Of Contents

Foreword

by Wyatt L. Woodsmall, Ph.D.

Figuring Out People: Design Engineering With Meta-Programs fills a serious void in the literature of Neuro-Linguistic Programming. Meta-programs allow us to understand human behavior and human differences. Even more importantly, they reveal to us how we may vary our own behavior and communications to become more successful in relating to and changing our own, and other people's, behavior and models of the world.

Meta-programs are probably the greatest contribution the field of NLP has made to understanding human differences. Only by understanding and appreciating human differences can we begin to respect and support other people whose models of the world differ dramatically from our own. Only by understanding human differences can we begin to replace animosity with understanding and antagonism with compassion. Only once we realize that other people are not just behaving the way that they do in order to spite us, but because that is their fundamental pattern can we begin to replace conflict with cooperation. Unfortunately until recently there has been very little written in the field of NLP on this highly important area. I am excited about the authors' outstanding contribution to this area which lies at the heart of NLP.

I was already interested in the general area of human typology when I began my NLP training in 1981. I was trained and certified in the Myers-Briggs Type Indicator® and had learned the Enneagram Personality Model from the Arica Institute before I came to NLP. I inquired curiously to see if NLP has similar personality models and felt excited to find that it did.

I first learned meta-programs in 1982 from my NLP teachers Anné Linden and Frank Stass. I also had the good fortune to attend Roger Bailey's training on his IPU Profile. I then learned the Clare Graves Value Model (1984) from Chris Cowen and Don Beck. I was excited about all of these powerful models to explain human similarities and differences and took every opportunity that I could to tell others about them.

Anthony Robbins was one of the first people I taught them to. I met Tony at a modeling training of John Grinder's in September of 1983. I got Tony involved in a modeling project that I was engaged in on pistol shooting for the US Army. As Tony and I became friends, I taught him all of the NLP Master Practitioner patterns including meta-programs and values. Later, I assisted Tony in teaching his first NLP Professional Certification Training (Feb. 1985).

During the Second Certification Training (Sept. 1985), we added a Master Professional Track. There in Colorado, I taught both meta-programs and values and met my three most senior students: Marvin Oka, Richard Diehl, and Tad James. Next, I taught a NLP Practitioner and Master Practitioner Training in Honolulu, Hawaii to a class that consisted of Tad and Ardie James, Marvin Oka, and Richard Diehl. Soon all of these people felt as excited as I did about the Myers-Briggs®, meta-programs, and the Graves Values Model.

Tad and Ardie began to use meta-programs in their business with excellent results. This led to the collaboration between the James' and myself to develop the Meta Programs and Values Inventory and the material on meta-programs and values that was published in *Time Line Therapy and the Basis of Personality.* My wife Marilyne and I have spent the last decade applying meta-programs and values in business, performance enhancement, and therapy. Marilyne and I have recently finished a book on the application of meta-programs in business, *People Pattern Power,* and a book on the applications of values to society.

I find it very gratifying to see Michael Hall and Bob Bodenhamer—who are two people I helped to train—become as excited as I am about meta-programs. It is even more gratifying to me that they have accepted my admonitions: "NLP does not end with John Grinder and Richard Bandler" and, "It is up to all of us to further advance the field." They have accomplished this in this excellent book.

The authors have immersed themselves in NLP and meta-programs and also in general-semantics and the latest developments in cognitive psychology and therapy. It is refreshing to find that the authors are not just cocooned in the field of NLP, and that they have extensively studied the origins of NLP in general-semantics as well as other disciplines that bear on NLP and its application in the real world.

I have had the privilege of knowing both authors for several years and one thing that has impressed me about both of them is their integrity, their compassion, and their dedication to applying and expanding NLP into areas of the world where it has not traveled previously. This has not come easy. Both have made major sacrifices to pursue their interests in NLP.

While all too often readers may assume that somehow books just happen, they don't. Nor is this book an accident. It has resulted from long, hard work and study and a great deal of sacrifice and dedication to the field of NLP on the part of both of its authors. For this they deserve our gratitude and thanks.

Figuring Out People is unique in several ways. First, it explains the origins of meta-programs and places them in the larger context of human growth and change. Secondly, it provides an in depth discussion of meta-programs; and thirdly, it expands on the field of meta-programs and makes a significant new contribution to the field. I will briefly touch on each of these points.

Figuring Out People has an excellent discussion on the origin and history of the development of meta-programs in NLP. It also places some very important frames around meta-programs. NLP essentially involves a process of "de-nominalization" and the authors begin their study by denominalizing both "personality" and "meta-programs." They make the crucial point that meta-programs deal not with what people *are*, but with how they *function*.

Figuring Out People presents an excellent typology of meta-programs. You can classify people in many different ways. The critical question remains, "Is the classification useful?" We only have 5-to-9 chunks of attention, and with 51 meta-programs to be considered, it would be easy to get lost. The authors help us to avoid overload by chunking meta-programs into five categories (i.e. mental, emotional, volitional, external response, and meta). This approach provides both a valuable contribution to the typology of meta-programs themselves and a very useful map to help us sort out these powerful patterns. For each of the 51 meta-programs they have provided valuable information on how to elicit and apply. The appendices to the book are extremely helpful, and I suggest that the reader familiarize himself with them at the beginning, since they serve as an excellent guide to the text. Also they are invaluable for future reference in eliciting and utilizing meta-programs.

Perhaps the most exciting part of *Figuring Out People* is the major contribution that it makes to **the development and expansion of meta-programs**. I have already mentioned the significant contribution that the authors make in their new typology for meta-programs; this book also covers more meta-programs in more depth than any other book in NLP. Its value does not just stop there, however. Its virtues are not just *expansiveness and compre-hensiveness*. Perhaps its greatest virtue lies in the creative insights of the authors into the subject of meta-programs in general and into each of the meta-programs in particular.

The authors challenge us to both understand and apply. And they continu-ally give new avenues for further exploration and study. This makes this book so valuable. It is truly *generative* and will lead to the further develop-ment, explication, and utilization of even more patterns as we strive to understand and apply its insights. This is perhaps its greatest contribution.

Wyatt L. Woodsmall, Ph.D.

Introduction

"People are not nouns, but processes."
(Richard Simons, 1997)

"I give up, I just can't *figure him out!*"

"Why in the world does she act that way? You'd have to be a psychologist to figure it out."

"Why does my supervisor have to act so secretive about office memos? He's so paranoid these days. I don't understand him."

"Go figure. I haven't a clue. When she gets into those moods of hers you never know what to expect..."

"You're doing that because you're just trying to get back at me!"

Figuring out people...we all attempt it. Living in human society pretty much demands it, don't you think? So we spend a good part of every day second-guessing people, mind-reading motives and intentions, psychoanalyzing without a license those with whom we live. We look for temperament patterns in them. We read books on "reading people." We attend relation-ship seminars. We do all kinds of things trying to *figure out people.* Yet what good does it do us? How effectively have we developed in really under-standing the strange and weird world that people live in, and out of which they come? Do you even have yourself *figured out*? Do I even know my own patterns and processes?

Beyond "Temperaments"

In this work, you will discover that we have moved far beyond all the models and instruments that try to figure people out by classifying them according to *types* and *temperaments.* Since the early Greeks with their model of the "four basic temperaments" (they called them "humours"), hundreds of models of *personality typing* have arisen. The authors base these types upon the assumption that people walk around with *permanent traits* inside them and that explains "why he is the way he is."

You will find none of that here.

Instead of beginning with assumptions of permanent inherent *traits*, we have opted for another assumption. We have opted for an assumption that Richard Simon, editor of **The Family Therapy Networker** (March/April 1997) summarized by saying, "people are not nouns but processes." Here we have looked, not at what people "are" in some absolute, unchangeable trait way, but *how people function*.

- *How* does this person think-and-emote?
- *How* does this person talk, act, behave, and relate?
- *What processes and patterns* describe this person's style for sorting (paying attention to information)?
- *What mental operational system* does this person use in remembering?
- *What human software* (ideas, beliefs) does this person use to think?

By focusing our attention on **how people** actually **function** in terms of their cognitive processing (thinking), emoting (somatizing ideas into their bodies), speaking (languaging self and others),and behaving (responding, gesturing, relating, etc.) we discover not what they "are," but **how** *they actually work in any given context* or situation. The value of this focus? Recognizing *how a person works* enables us to *figure out* their model of the world (their mental paradigm) that describes their internal "reality." This increases understanding and enlightens us about "where the person comes from."

It also increases our sense of empowerment. Why? Because in knowing how I work, or how someone else works, enables us to evaluate and match that working.

- *How effectively* does this way of thinking work?
- *How well* do I like this way of emoting/somatizing my ideas?
- *How desirable* do I find this way of talking and languaging?
- *How resourceful* does this way of sorting behaving actually work?

Dealing with **such processes** (i.e. how we sort information for relevancy) enables us to change, alter, and transform any process that doesn't work well. When you (in your mind) deal with traits, things, the way people "are," then you think-and-feel more in terms of, "Well, that's the way I am!" "I'm just stuck with dealing with him, because 'that's the way he is.'"

Wrong.

Here we start from a much more empowering presupposition, *"People are not nouns, but processes."* Count Alfred Korzybski said that when you take a word or label and stick it on a person and then use that deceptively alluring but tricky passive verb "is," you create **a primitive form of unsanity**. Linguistically, you create *the "is" of identity*. "I *am* a failure." "She *is* arrogant." "What can you expect from a bleeding-heart liberal." "Communists *are* like that." "She's heartless because she *is* a republican." "He's a Sanguine!" "They *are* sado-masochists." Etc.

Of course, our emphasis here goes against the history of philosophical labeling, psychiatric name-calling (currently called DSM-IV, Diagnostic and Statistical Manual of Mental Disorders), and psychological typing.

Yet we feel that *reducing people* to fit a category of *types, traits,* or *personality disorders* only blinds us to the rich diversity and uniqueness of the person. People operate far too complexly for us to so easily categorize, label, and classify. Nor do people tend to stay put when we put them into some word-box. They change. They grow. They learn new and different ways of functioning—of "being."

People also tend to operate differently in different contexts. Most people, in fact, experience themselves very differently in different contexts. In such, we play out different roles, take on different personas, think-and-feel according to that context or frame-of-reference.

What model therefore allows us to take *context* itself into consideration? What model of the functioning of persons enables us to take learning, development, growth, and empowerment into consideration?

Years ago (1979) **Psychology Today** reviewed the domain of **Neuro-Linguistic Programming (NLP)** in an article entitled, *"The People Who Read People."* It surveyed a brand new field within cognitive-behavioral psychology and some of the models and technologies that Bandler and Grinder had developed for "reading" people. Later we (MH & BB) entered that field. We received extensive training, and began to write about it. When we later came upon each other's writings, we decided to combine our writings about *Meta-Programs* as a way to figure out people.

This domain of "meta-programs" (software programs in people's heads about *how* to think, emote, etc.) got its initial start with Leslie Cameron Bandler as she and Richard interacted. They arose as Leslie did "textbook

NLP" (Woodsmall, 1988, p. 63) and discovered that sometimes processes didn't work. Ultimately she and Richard discovered that these "failures" brought to light the initial list of NLP meta-programs.

While Leslie invented these distinctions within the context of therapy, Roger Bailey and Ross Stewart then took them and developed them for use in business (Woodsmall, 1988, p.33). Next came Woodsmall's expansion of them as he integrated them with Myers-Briggs Personality Inventory. From that came the now classic work of James and Woodsmall (1988) in *Time Line Therapy and the Basis of Personality*. Then Reese and Bagley (1988) applied the meta-programs to profiling people and to the context of selling. Shelle Rose-Charvet (1995) used them to highlight the kind of language within meta-programs that create optimum influence.

Building upon the NLP model of "personality" (along with formulations in General-Semantics, and development in Cognitive and Perceptual Psychology), we have expanded and extended the meta-programs in this most extensive and exhaustive work (to date) on meta-programs. Here we focus not on what people "are" in some static, permanent, fated, unchangeable way, but rather, we focus entirely on **how people function.** As a model of *human functioning*, this allows us to create a "personality" profile of ourselves and others in a way that allows for growth, development, transformation, and empowerment, taking *context* into account.

So what? We now can learn to open our eyes, ears and senses, and truly *observe* people **functioning** (thinking, valuing, believing, imagining, emoting, somatizing, languaging, responding, etc.). In recognizing their *processes*, we can begin to *figure them out* in that moment of space-and-time. In doing so we can then learn to deal with them according to how they operate as how they have structured their consciousness.

Here then we have emphasized **the ongoing functioning** of people apart from getting into heavy theorizing or philosophizing about "human nature." Many will want to use this work for self-analysis and so we have provided a self-analysis check-list along with every meta-program presented. In this way, one could use this book as a tool for self-discovery and exploration, again, not to discover what you "are," but *how you work*. This model about **how people actually do think, feel, act, perceive, process information, respond, relate, behave, etc.** then informs us about how we can stop doing what doesn't work and start doing what does. Sanity sometimes beckons us in a most simple way!

For those already familiar with the NLP model, we have plowed some new ground as we have offered new distinctions: driver meta-programs, meta meta-programs, sorting meta-programs according to facets of our "states of consciousness," a meta-program sorting grid, and much more. Welcome to the adventure of discovering and figuring out—*how you operate at meta-level that affects your everyday life!*

A Quick Overview of NLP

The neuro-linguistic programming (NLP) model pre-eminently addresses "the structure of subjectivity," in describing the process of *how* we use our nervous system (neurology and brain) to create our "model of the world," which we then use to navigate life.

After our nervous system/brain inputs information from the world via our senses, we use those sense modalities of awareness for processing ("thinking") and storing ("memory"). We designate these as **Representational Systems** (RS); by them we *re-present* to ourselves information about what we have seen, heard, felt, etc. When we break down these Representational Systems of sense modalities (VAK for short), we have:

V   for Visual: sights, pictures, images, etc.
A   for Auditory: sounds, noise, volume, tones, etc.
A$_t$ —Auditory tonal (sounds)
K   for Kinesthetic: sensations, feelings, etc.
O   for Olfactory: smells
G   for Gustatory: tastes
M   for Motor: kinesthetic movements

Thus, for example, notice the VAK modes that you use when you "think" about a strawberry. What "comes to mind?" Do you have pictures, smells, tastes, touches, or sounds? In what order? How specifically do you represent the information of a strawberry in your consciousness?

How do you *represent* a bowl of strawberries? Now continue to notice your modalities as you think about a big bowl of juicy red strawberries covered with cold whipped cream.

Two additional distinctions of these Representational Systems, *external* (ᵉ) or *internal* (ⁱ), refer to the source of our data. *Remembered information* (ʳ) or *constructed* (ᶜ) distinguishes between how we constructed the information.

   ʳ Remembered information (VAK)

   ᶜ Constructed information (VAK)

   ⁱ Internal source of information (TDS, transderivational search)

   ᵉ External source of information (uptime, sensory awareness)

A moment ago you probably *remembered* an actual historical time when you saw a bowl of strawberries. So you inputted that information from *inside*. If you actually have a bowl of strawberries in front of you at this time—then you can get the sensory information in real time from the *outside*.

That gives us the *primary sensory systems.* By them we have **modes** (or modalities) **by which we can become aware of things.** *Above* **those VAK systems** we have a meta-representation system. ("Meta" refers to something "above" or "beyond," hence a higher logical level). What system of awareness occurs there? *Language.* This symbolic system of words, sentences, phrases, etc. enables us to talk *about* our sights, sounds, and sensations and to abstract at a higher logical level. We denote this meta-representational system:

   A_d — Auditory Digital (the language system, words, self-talk)

We have used *the language Representational Systems* throughout our illustration to elicit your referents for strawberry. The word strawberry itself functions as a label for the entire sensory experience. If we had used a more abstract term like "fruit," some people might call forth and represent the sights, sounds, smells, sensations, and tastes of strawberries, but that term would have elicited many other experiences as well.

The domain below, or within the Representational Systems and the meta-Representational Systems of linguistics, refer to those *qualities, characteristics,* and *components* of the modalities—hence, submodalities (SBMD). Each system has its own list of submodalities.

Visual Submodalities:
Location: close—far
Size: small—large
Focus: clear—fuzzy
Structure: 3-D or 2-D (flat)
Tone: black-and-white—Color
In/Out: Associated—Dissociated
Motion: slide—movie
Shape: contour—form
Brightness: low—high
Contrasts: many—few
Form: panoramic—bordered

Auditory Submodalities:
Location: source, direction
Volume: low—high
Tone: quality, style
Pitch: low—high
Distance: close—far
Rhythm: fast—slow, smooth—uneven
Tempo: slow—fast
Duration: short—long

Kinesthetic Submodalities:
Location: inside—outside
Nature: tactile—proprioceptive
Intensity: low—high
Weight: low—high
Duration: short—long
Size of area: small—large
Frequency: often—infrequent
Shape: configuration
Movement: none—some—much
Texture: smooth—rough
Rhythm: pattern in movement

In our illustration of strawberries, submodalities play a central role in representation. Consider your own as we ask the following questions regarding your VAK representations:

- How large of a picture do you have of the bowl of strawberries?
- Where do you see this picture? (Immediately in front of you, to your right, left, in the distance, etc.)
- Do you have a clear, sharp focus or not?
- Do you have a 3-D or a flat 2-D postcard picture?
- Do you see the strawberries in color or as a black-and-white picture?

Already you undoubtedly have experienced the shift that occurs when you change the quality of your representation. For most people, seeing a black-and-white picture of a strawberry evokes a different feeling from seeing one in color. *Distance* also plays a significant factor. If you imagine the bowl of bright red, juicy strawberries at the distance of a block away from you... that probably feels less "real" or compelling than when you put your picture one inch away from your mouth, does it not?

When a person makes a richly detailed set of representations about something, it tends to evoke more and more of one's neurology. So when you "turn up" all of your Representational Systems—so that you vividly see and feel the bowl of strawberries, do you begin now to smell them and even taste them?

Submodalities (SBMD) provides *the sub-structure* of our subjectivity—the place of "the building blocks" of human experience and the place where we code "the difference that makes a difference" (Bateson). These coding cues inform our brain and nervous system about *how to respond* to information. Change or alter the submodality coding of an image, sound, sensation, word, etc. and you can change the whole gestalt of the experience. This feels "true with a vengeance" when you find *the driving submodality.* These submodalities critically determine and effect the experience.

Consider a motivation strategy. How do you motivate yourself to read a book or study a work on human "personality?" What do you picture to yourself, say to yourself, in what tone of voice, what kinesthetic sensations do you experience, how much do you have to repeat or increase one of these steps, which do you do first , second, and third, etc.? When we sequence our Representational Systems with the appropriate SBDM qualities so that it enables us to do something—from getting up in the morning, create something, express friendliness, feel playful, communicate effectively, manage a business, eat healthily, etc.—we have *a strategy.*

What strategy do you have for *learning* as you read? Will you make internal pictures as you read along? Will you talk to yourself—repeating words and phrases, asking questions, and wondering about applications? Will you feel your hand and arm as you jot notes? What order will you do these things in order to give yourself the richest learning possible?

In addition to the sensory and language modalities of ideas, understandings, beliefs, values and decisions, and their qualities, NLP also identifies and distinguishes *syntax.* This refers to the order and sequence of these qualities—the **formula** by which we put them together to create an experience. We call this order or structure of the component pieces of modalities *a strategy* in NLP (Dilts, et al., 1980).

Once we have run a strategy to create *a mind-body state of consciousness,* then our learning, memory, perception, communication, and behavior (LMPCB) in that state will function in a *state-dependent way.* This means that while in a state of mind-body (the content and structure of our Internal Representations (IR) and the condition and quality of our physiology) we will tend to think, learn, remember, perceive, talk and act *according to the state.* The state governs and colors our processing.

If you get into a good *learning state,* then your perception, memory, behavior, and feelings will accord with that neuro-linguistic state. You will look out and see the world via that learning. And if you get into a closed-minded state, then you will find yourself thinking, feeling, perceiving, and remembering in terms of closedness and rigidity. This will make learning, curiosity, openness, etc. very difficult.

What can we do about this? We can *interrupt* (disrupt, interfere with) the state and its driving factors (our internal RS and SBMD). Then we can *shift consciousness* to redirect our brain-body toward those internal representations that enhance our state, and therefore life. We do this by using modality and submodality shifts, swishing our brain to desired outcomes giving our brain specific VAK cues of more attractive "thoughts" like *the "me"* for whom this or that would not function as a problem; reframing the meaning (significance) of an event; altering the triggers (anchors) that set the brain to go off in a certain direction, re-anchor ourselves to new directions, etc. (Check out the Glossary of terms if you find some of these terms new.)

NLP specializes in *how to "run our own brain"* so that we can take charge of the cognitive-behavioral mechanisms that control subjectivity. What **mechanisms** control subjectivity? Namely *IR* (the internal representations of modalities and submodalities that code ideas, understandings, beliefs, values, decisions) and *physiology* (quality and use of our body and nervous system). To facilitate this, NLP has invented and discovered numerous human "technologies" and methods that provide specific patterns (programs) that enable us to manage our subjectivity with greater ease and effectiveness.

Figure 1

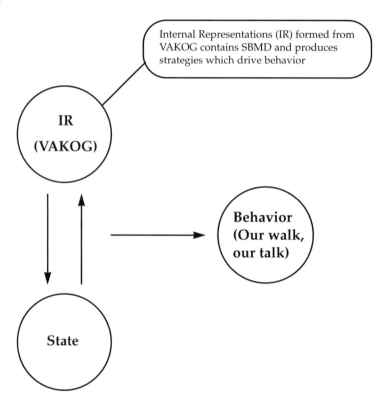

When all of these "mental," "emotional," and physiological factors combine—we end up in a holistic mind-body state of consciousness. So while we use another static nominalization ("state") for this dynamic experience of thinking, feeling, choosing, perceiving, etc., a state of consciousness ebbs and flows, moves, and expresses a gestalt—i.e., an overall configuration.

The Meta-Move to Meta-Levels/Meta-States

Within NLP, numerous models of logical level have arisen; from Bateson's (1972) logical levels of learning, to the meta-outcome model, meta-programs, and meta-states (Hall, 1995, 1996, 1997).

For a set of distinctions, or levels, to operate in *a "logical" relationship* to each other, the higher level must encompass the lower level as a class encompasses its members. A higher level also relates to, and functions as, the context *about* the lower. It sets the frame. When we "chunk up" from a primary sensory-based level to a meta-level, we call that process *"going meta,"* or making a meta-move. When we do this we *abstract* from the lower level and generate a higher order of abstraction or conception.

And as you will shortly learn, *all of the meta-programs involve this.* Therefore, they exist and function as *the frame-of-reference* out of which we think-emote-speak-and-respond. They exist as a meta-level to "regular" or primary thinking. Even right this minute—as you read this—you have various meta-level frames-of-reference working trying to make sense of this. These typically operate at that level—outside of your consciousness awareness. But you can become aware of them. And you will—as you continue in this study of *figuring out people!*

Conclusion

We trust that this basic introduction to the field of NLP will suffice for understanding the following work on meta-programs. Apart from NLP, we have derived material from Cognitive Psychology in general, Gestalt and Perceptual Psychology, and Developmental or Lifespan Psychology.

Part I

Introduction

Understanding The Patterning Of Consciousness

Chapter 1

What In The World Do We Mean By Meta-Programs?

The Operational Programs That Run Your Programs

"There's software in that thar head of yours!"
(Anonymous NLPer)

Consider your *frame-of-mind.* With what frame-of-mind have you started reading this book? Have you accessed an effective frame-of-mind? Will it support you in this reading, understanding, remembering, and using? Will it undermine your efforts?

Each "meta-program" that we describe in this book specifies a wide range of frames-of-mind. Each therefore describes a *distinction of consciousness.* You can think of them as making explicit the various and different frames-of-mind from which we operate.

Every person you meet today, that you engage in conversation, that you try to influence, or who tries to influence you, operates from some *frame-of-mind.* As such, that "program" that lies above and beyond ("meta") their specific words determines their perspective, way of valuing, style of thinking and emoting, and pattern of choosing and behaving.

Recognizing these meta-software programs in people's heads which control and run their specific frame-of-mind, enables us to know how to more effectively communicate and relate to them. It empowers us to stop getting angry at their frame-of-mind as it equips us for *how to effectively work with it!*

Origin of the Meta-Programs

The domain of "meta-programs" (software programs in people's heads about *how* to think, emote, etc.) originated with Leslie Cameron Bandler as she and Richard interacted. Woodsmall (1988) says that early in the history of NLP Leslie went about doing "textbook NLP" (p. 63). As she did, she discovered that sometimes the NLP processes didn't work. Why not? Ultimately, she and Richard discovered that these "failures" brought to light the initial list of NLP meta-programs. (This suggests the powerful role of meta-programs. They can interfere with powerful change processes!)

Leslie first presented meta-programs in Chicago during a seminar. Anné Linden, along with Steve and Connirae Andreas, participated in that seminar and first learned the model. Leslie first invented the distinctions in the context of therapy, but later Roger Bailey and Ross Stewart took them and developed them for use in business (Woodsmall, 1988, p.33).

Next came Woodsmall's expansion of them. He integrated them with Myers-Briggs Personality Inventory. Then, while conducting a master practitioner training in Hawaii, Tad James hired Wyatt to teach him the Myers-Briggs® in order to become certified to use it as a personality instrument. Later, they collaborated and co-authored the now classic 1988 book, ***Time Line Therapy and the Basis of Personality***.

Roger Bailey adapted the meta-programs as a "personality" profile (in his "LAB" profile). Later, Edward Reese and Dan Bagley III (1991) applied the meta-programs to profiling people in the context of selling. Shelle Rose-Charvet (1995) used them to highlight the kind of language within meta-programs that creates optimum influence.

The meta-programs refer to those *programs* in our "minds" that operate at a level *meta* to our content thinking and refer to **the sorting devices or patterns** that we use in perceiving, paying attention to information, and inputting and processing the stimuli around us. Jacobson (1996) refers to them as the "programs that run *other* programs," i.e. our behavior. As such they describe the *attitude* or *orientation* that we adopt in various contexts and situations.

When you think about the working of a computer, computers use some sort of *Operating System* (OS), perhaps a Disk Operating System (DOS) or more recently, "Windows," as an operating system. Without such operating systems, we would find the computer useless in processing the information we want it to process. Yet with an operating system, the computer runs a highly functional system in merging its own hardware (the materials that comprise it physically) and its software (the programs it runs) from word processing, mailing, spreadsheets, games, and the internet.

In an analogous way, *the human brain as an information processing system,* has its own **hardware** in our neurology, nervous system, brain, blood chemistry, neuro-transmitters, physiological organs, etc. (See Figure 1.1). All of these organic facets participate in inputting, processing, and outputting the energy manifestations of the world (in terms of "information" or messages). **The human "software"** consists of our thinking patterns, our ideational categories (we think and reason via "categories," Lakoff, 1987), our belief concepts, our valuational significances (or values, those ideas that we treat as highly significant), our "programs" for functioning, etc.

Figure 1.1

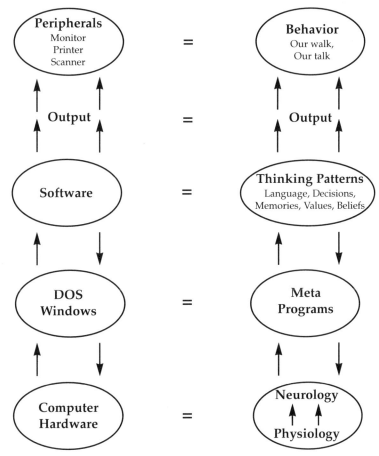

To run our thoughts-and-emotions then, we need *a software program*, so to speak, that provides instructions about **how to process thoughts-and-feelings**. Such software provides us, functionally, the equivalent of a sort of *operating system*—a system that connects hardware and software so that the neurology of brain-and-body can input, process, and output the "information" of thoughts, ideas, beliefs, etc. In this work, we call these *meta-programs.*

Defining These Meta-Programs

By definition, we define the *meta*-programs as those programs *above* the everyday thoughts-and-emotions that we experience. In terms of levels, the everyday thoughts-and-emotions operate on the primary level as the **content** that describes **what** we think-and-feel. In these *content* programs we have specific details and strategies. *Above* the content of our thoughts, we have other thoughts-and-feelings, ones that operate more out-of-consciousness. These "programs" function as the sorting and perceiving "rules" that thereby govern **how** we think-and-emote. This software, like any operating system (OS) determines **the structure** of our thoughts-and-feelings. They direct *what* we sort for.

An Illustration

For instance, consider a person's strategy (or program) for "reading." We begin with the stimulus of words in the form of a visual external. "The little brown and white cat fought furiously with the dog..." We then take those scribbles of ink on paper and use them to anchor *internal representations* of their referents. Using past referents and constructed representations we "make sense" of words by seeing, hearing, feeling, smelling, and tasting as well as ascribing language to such.

The meta-program of *chunk size* (#1. See Figure 1.4) governs whether our mind goes to trying to understand "the big picture" in a global way or whether mind goes first to receiving and inputting all of the specific details. Do you recall the color of the cat?

Recently I (BB) couldn't find the salt shaker in the cabinet. As I looked, Linda came over and picked it right out since it sat right there in front of me.

"You are sick!" she said.

"No, I just see things globally. That's why I can't see the trees for the forest! You, on the other hand, can see each and every tree as you so choose—but will tend to not see the forest!"

For years, I (MH) thought I "was" a poor speller because I would consistently and regularly mis-spell words in articles, hand-outs, books, etc. Later I learned speed reading by just reading a book and found that it came so easily. I tested at 3500 words a minute at an Evelyn Woods Reading course. I didn't understand how I could *both* read quickly and comprehensively *and* spell poorly. How could I see and recognize words *and* not see them?

When I later discovered that I operate at the global processing level—the mystery became clear. I simply don't sort for the details of spelling. I sort for the larger level meanings.

Today I can (and do) spend time proofing texts and I can shift consciousness from the forest to the trees. Yet I do find it "work." Keeping my conscious awareness down at the tree level—and sometimes at the level of the bark—takes effort. Let a slip in consciousness and an "idea" pop in— and zoom! I take off for the abstract dimension of concepts!

The meta-program of *matching/mismatching* (sameness/difference #2) governs whether we read in order to see what we find the same or matching what we already know or whether we sort for differences and look for what differs from what we already know. At a meta-processing level, matchers look to compare for similarities. Mismatchers search out differences.

For many years I (BB) would not share many of my new projects with my wife. I had learned early in our marriage that if I shared my new projects with her, she would find something wrong with them and "criticize" them. So after a number of those experiences, I just shut down. I decided I wouldn't share with her rather than get such negative feedback (not a good thing for a marriage!).

Then I learned about the meta-programs. I learned that her brain simply *sorts information this way.* Upon understanding how she processes for differences (mismatches), it totally changes my thinking and feelings. So the next time I presented some new wild idea and she sorted for how it wouldn't work(!), I just had to share my insights.

"You have to find out what is wrong with something before you can look at what is right about it, don't you?"

"Why yes, doesn't everybody?"

"Well, actually, no. But now that I know that 'sorting for differences and mismatching' simply describes how you think and process things—and that you don't mean to hurt me—I can hear it without feeling hurt!"

What a difference that made for our marriage.

The meta-program of *"Representational System"* (#3) indicates that whether we process information equally and appropriately with all of the sensory systems or we over-use the visual, the auditory, kinesthetic, etc.

Driver and Non-Driver Meta-Programs

If we think of these responses and processing styles as existing along a continuum, then we can distinguish *the degree or intensity* that a program governs our way of sorting. A *driving* meta-program refers to those software packages that we will typically and habitually over-use. We will tend to have **a structure in consciousness—yet** *above* **consciousness**, that always and inevitably gets us to think of things in a certain way (e.g. in details, matching, visual, etc.). Whenever we have a software operating system program that operates typically at one end of a continuum or the other (in an extreme form)—we have *a driver* **meta-program**.

By way of contrast, whenever our "mind" operates in the middle of a given continuum, or flexibly moves from one extreme to the other extreme of a meta-program, that meta-program will *not* operate as a **driver**. In this case, we would not feel driven by either response. We would experience a *flexibility of consciousness* that allows us to use either program structure depending upon the time, context, environment, purpose, etc. Cattell (1989) speaks to this,

> "Just as all virtues come with vices, especially when carried to an extreme, persons who score toward the extreme end on any temperament factor (even if on the seemingly more desirable pole) are apt to have adjustment difficulties." (p. 15)

De-Nominalizing *"Personality"*

What do we mean when we use such terms as "personality," "temperament," "human nature," "constitutional drives," "instincts," "traits," etc.? Do these words refer to *things* at all?

Linguistically, and neuro-semantically, these terms all take the form of a **nominalization**. This means that they look like, sound like, and therefore feel like *a thing—an actual, tangible, "real" entity of some sort.* Yet, when we apply the old 'wheelbarrow test' to such, we find that we cannot put these so-called *things* in the wheelbarrow (Bandler and Grinder, 1975).

> [The wheelbarrow test enables one to distinguish a true noun from a false noun. Because true nouns exist as tangible things (persons, places, and things), you could (theoretically) put it in a wheelbarrow. Not so with nominalized verbs. You can't put a relationship, self-esteem, motivation, etc. in a wheelbarrow!]

So in truth, "personality," "temperament," "human nature," etc. **do not exist** as "real" things. They only exist as *mental constructs* and abstract nouns. They only exist in the mind as *ideas* (ideational categories or labels). This means that they function as somebody's understandings (a mental process) about some other process. How can we understand what these words mean and what referents they point to? Using the NLP Meta-model, we begin by **de-nominalizing** the nominalized verbs. We do so in order that we can recover the actual referenced action (even a mental or "mind" action) as well as the person who created that mental map (the lost performative). Doing this allows us to examine the ideas for their merit, validity, legitimacy, and usefulness.

As we begin this work about **the functioning of consciousness** on both content levels (the primary everyday level) and structural levels (the meta-level where meta-programs exist), we want to clearly and thoroughly *de-nominalize* these terms. We want to brush away the thick mental fog that usually arises with using such terms as "personality," "temperament," "traits," etc. Then, as the fog of fuzzy definitions and vague understandings evaporate in the ever increasing morning light, we invite a sharper relief of perspective as we specify with precision the actual processes.

The result? As a behaviorist and functionist model of "mind," we will generate a set of procedures for understanding *the workings of consciousness* as it seeks to structure itself and its mapping products ("thoughts," "emotions," "beliefs," "values," etc.). In the end we will find that we have fewer and fewer "things," and more and more *processes*. Woodsmall (1988) noted that,

> "Our personality is developed as a coping mechanism. It overlies our essence and masks it. Our personality needs to be seen for what it is, i.e. an arbitrary coping mechanism, and not for what we usually take it to be, i.e. what we think is most uniquely us." (p. 11).

> "Our personality is what makes each of us different from everyone else. It is the set of patterns of behavior that we operate out of habitually..." (p. 50).

This will shift our questions. We will ask fewer nominalization questions, "What 'is' human nature?" "What kind of a person 'is' she?" "What 'is' his temperament style?" Instead, we will shift to more *process questions*. "*How* does she run her brain in this or that context?" "What style of mental structuring does he engage in—big picture or detail?" "Does that particular 'operating system' seem to work well in accomplishing that goal?"

This approach essentially moves away from "typology," and "personality" or "temperament" analysis in the old sense. Using these meta-programs, we will *not* discover what people *"are;"* we will rather discover **how they function** using their thinking, emoting, valuing, believing, perceiving, relating, communicating, etc. powers. We will discover their **operational style**.

Consequently, if we find in ourselves or another *an operational style* that doesn't work very well—we can simply shift it and go "the other way." We don't have to feel stuck, "Well, that's the way I am!" "I'm just that kind of person." "Well, what can you expect from someone with her personality traits?"

Woodsmall (1988), who brought the typology of the Myers-Briggs Personality Inventory into NLP, frequently took a denominalized attitude toward typology, one that accords with our work here. He wrote,

"Typology is the study of human differences...A type, in reality, is merely a set of characteristics that a group of people have in common..." (p. 2)

Here we primarily de-emphasize the whole concept of typology and follow Lloyd's (1989) approach.

De-Nominalizing "Meta-Programs"

In a review of a work in NLP on meta-programs, O'Connor and McDermott (1995) underlined some caveats. They simultaneously suggested a new direction that we have decided to explore,

"Metaprograms are often reified into 'things' that live inside the person, instead of a description of a set of behaviours that are evoked in a certain context—a combination of context and action. They are not completely 'inside' the person. So it is interesting to ask: 'What sort of context brings out particular ways of acting that can be coded as metaprograms?'" (p. 79)

"We would like to suggest a way to look at metaprograms and similar behavioural patterns. We tend to think of metaprograms, talk about them and write about them...as if they exist inside a person. It seems to us the *context* is equally important, and that metaprogram patterns are a combination of context and particular ways the person has of deleting, distorting, and generalizing." (p. 78)

This warns against falling into *the nominalization trap* of treating meta-programs as things. Part of the problem lies in the old typology thinking that we have all grown up with, and part lies in the fact that the term "meta-programs" itself as a noun (a nominalization) describes a nominalized process.

Realizing that we ultimately refer to *processes of "mind"* operating *in various contexts* when we talk about "meta-programs," we must continually remind ourselves to denominalize. We must constantly think of them as **behaviors**—mental, emotional, valuational, sorting, perceiving, etc. *behaviors*. Otherwise, we might fall into the same fallacy of thinking about them as things or static "traits." In this work we will repeatedly put the term back in verb-form: meta-programming, meta-processing, meta-sorting, meta-attending, meta-perceiving, etc. This will assist us in avoiding taking a wrong turn by over-using the noun, "meta-programs." When the language itself bamboozles us, we begin reifying the concept, treating these *ways of orienting ourselves in the world* as things, as entities, and internal traits, as given substances, etc.

What danger lies in that? It deludes us into thinking of the processes, not as processes, but as things. And via "thing thinking" we begin to view the reference as if totally stable, unchangeable, innate, a given, determined, and fated. To map out *the way a person processes information, sorts, orders, organizes, attends, etc.* creates a map false-to-fact.

Lloyd (1989) highlighted the learning process and the role that *context* plays in the expressions of "personality" in his dissertation,

> "Roles, norms, and rules are learned within social situations or contexts via language and relationships. Just how semantics and social rules are learned has been the continual interest for cognitive and social psychology researchers." (p. 28).

"Personality"

We will therefore think of the nominalization **"personality"** as simply *the characteristic ways that a person typically behaves* in thinking, believing, valuing, emoting, communicating, acting, and relating. We will think of "personality" as a description of the overall gestalt that emerges from all of these particular *response* styles.

Accordingly, we will work to avoid nominalizing and reifying "person-ality" as a thing, and especially not as a formulated entity **in** the person that drives them and makes them the way they "are." We ask the reader also to keep this in mind in thinking and talking about these "programs" or patterns (oops, more nounified verbs!). Though awkward linguistically, we will sometimes put the terms back into verbs, hence, programming, patterning, sorting, etc. This will assist us to avoid talking about what a person "has" or "is."

[As an aside, we have also adopted the General-semantics extension-alizing device of *E-Priming*. We do this to avoid the central unsanity disorders that Korzybski (1933/1994) consistently warned about, "the 'is' of identity" and "the 'is' of predication." So we have *primed* the *English* within this entire text (except for quoting from others) all of the forms of the "to be" verb (is, am, was, were, be, being, been, etc.). See Bourland and Johnson (1991, 1993) for the E-prime model, as well as Hall (1995).]

Accordingly, *"personality"* results from both a person's *content* programs ("strategies") that specify **what** we think, believe, value, etc. plus our meta-programs that specify **how** we engage in thinking, sorting, believing, valuing, etc. With both of these levels of functioning (what and how), any *behavior or response style* that we perpetuate and continually repeat will eventually habituate. They will habituate and then drop out of conscious awareness to become "an unconscious software program." Or, to speak in a more behavioral language, it develops as "an unconscious ongoing way of processing or structuring information." This *patterning* describes the meta-program.

We know that this habituating process occurs for our *content* programs (e.g. typing, driving a car, playing ball, expressing social skills, looking friendly, reading, etc.). It also occurs for our meta-processing styles. How we structure information also habituates as our meta-level patterning style. When this happens, the unconsciousness at the meta-level makes these "programs" even more powerful, driving, and seemingly "solid" and "real."

The end result of this? The inner-and-outer dynamic behaviors that comprise what we commonly call "personality." These solidified and stable *ways of perceiving and processing* then seem as an innate part of our "temperamental" nature (another nominalization that refers to our "temper" of mind or mental style). "Temperament" refers to the "make-up" of mind, "the peculiar or distinguishing mental or physical character" of it. Cattell (1989) wrote,

> "People respond to their perceptions of reality rather than to reality itself, and these perceptions are shaped through past experience and do not readily alter, even in responses to here and now actualities." (p. 71).

Accordingly, most people experience *a "Pseudo-Stability" feeling* about their "Self" which leads them to think that their so-called "traits" and "tempera-ments" exist as stable and real. This further explains why here-and-now actualities all so often do not (and cannot) change that person's meta-programs (and hence "personality"). Why not? Primarily because the person fails to recognize his or her *sense of "personality" stability* as the result of their perceptions and mental maps *about* the territory, rather than the territory itself.

Lloyd (1989) devoted his doctoral dissertation to this very issue,

> "While trait theory posits personality as a product of a single under-lying static disposition, state theory views personality as a multifac-torial phenomenon which is the product of the total social environ-ment."

> "In studies by Bern and Allen (1974) and Schweder (1975), it was found that people self-reported more behavioral consistency than was actually demonstrated. A conclusion that could be drawn, then, is that people have stable perceptions of their own behavioral responses even when their actual behavior is not stable." (p. 20).

What does this mean? We will argue later that at *meta-conceptual levels* (meta meta-programs) about "self" we create *stable* identity perspectives about our self, about our self "traits," about "temperament," and personality and this explains the durability of such and our pseudo-feelings of a more permanent self than actually exists. This demonstrates the Bateson (1972) principle that higher logical levels always *organize and drive* lower levels. In the chapter on changing meta-programs, we will suggest that when we change the higher level constructions, then, presto, the lower level experi-ences change!

Lloyd (1989) further noted the nature of these constructions as products of our linguistics and semantics,

> "What is being argued is that the terms used within personality research are nothing more or less than *constructs of convenience*. And it is the aim of this project to illustrate that the assessment of temperamental traits, by traditional methods, is significantly affected by specific changes in stimulus conditions." (p. 114).

For us this means that the domain of meta-programs exists as an open field. NLP and the cognitive/perceptual psychologies have only begun to identify numerous patterning sorts that people use in structuring their perceptions. The meta-programs we have identified here only exist as constructions.

The Meta-Program Lists

The lists of meta-programs in NLP have generally followed the original list by Leslie Cameron Bandler, and more recently the James and Woodsmall (1988) format. From time to time, however, individuals have added additional ones to the list. O'Connor and McDermott (1995) noted, "There is no definitive list, nor is there general agreement on criteria with which to compile such a list." As we neared completion of this work, we received Jacobson's (1996) book wherein he presented a three-fold classification very similar to what we offer here (See Appendix A and H).

We began with the James and Woodsmall list and to that list have added others that we found in NLP literature as well as in other domains. We have tapped into the rich resources of Cognitive Psychology, Perceptual Psychology, and Developmental Psychology for other structuring and patterning styles which people use in thinking-emoting.

What *criteria* have we used to determine whether to include or exclude a given patterning format? We have essentially used *the cognitive psychology question of whether "mind" can sort or pattern the stimuli of the world* in a given way and whether this style seems fairly typical for human beings. Thus we asked ourselves:

- Does this distinction describe a way that humans can process, sort, and perceive information?
- Does this distinction describe a "mental," "emotional," "volitional," "self," "communicational" response to information or stimuli?
- Does this distinction *typically* identify a way that people structure their internal mental maps about the world?
- Does this pattern assist us in understanding the different "operation systems" that people seem to use in sorting and perceiving?

In *The Spirit of NLP* (1996), I (MH) constructed a format for distinguishing these processing/sorting styles. I there suggested that these classifications arise from "going meta" to our processing. Using the traditional conceptual categories of processing information, we have designed the following categories for this work:

- **mental** (thinking),
- **emotional** (feeling),
- **conation** (choosing/willing),
- **communicational** (speaking, responding),
- **semantic/conceptual** (creating categories of meaning)
  (see Figure 1.3, at the end of the chapter).

We recognize that these five categories arise as purely linguistic and conceptual categories. From the start we acknowledge that they do not "really" exist, separate from each other. So we simply offer them as a way of classifying the multiple ways that we pattern and structure our thinking-emoting. This model also posits the meta-programs as existing as our *meta-processing levels*. In other words each of these areas of meta-programs functions as a class of meta-programs.

The first four of these categories subsume what NLP has traditionally classified as the *meta-programs.* The fifth category introduces a new distinction to NLP—*meta meta-programs.* These do not exist at the same logical level, but at a higher level. We will offer a full explanation about this distinction later.

Meta-Patterning Levels

Because these processes occur at a level **above** the primary level of everyday life wherein we do our *content* thinking and responding, they concern **the structure of perceiving itself** rather than the content of what we perceive. Thus meta-programs involve *meta-level functions.* The categories in Figure 1.2 suggests that we have a wide range of ways to pattern or structure our experience of the world. As we engage in mapping cognitively, emotionally, conatively, communicatively, and conceptually or semantically—we thereby generate our personal "style" (or "personality").

Figure 1.2
Meta Meta-Level:

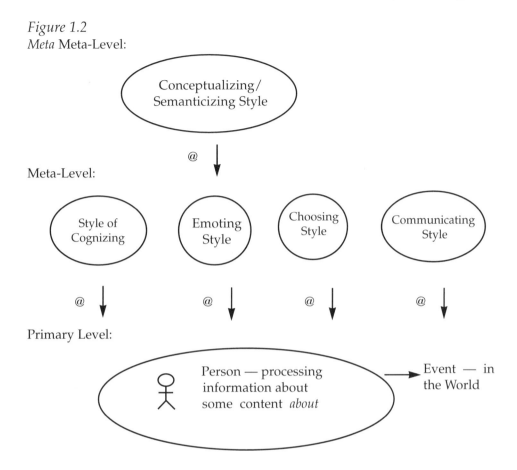

In this way **our learned and cultivated style of patterning** develops into a meta-level "reality" (constructed subjective reality) and we then *bring it to bear upon* any and all information processing (encountering and experiencing, see Figure 1.1). We also bring to bear upon all of our choices, our habituated style of choosing. At this meta-level, then, we experience this stable phenomenon that we call "personality" or "temperament." Sure it exists. It exists as *the way we have learned to typically structure our perceptions and responses.*

Why "Personality" Feels so Solid and Real

"Personality" seems and feels *permanent*, stable, inherent, and given because this conception ("self") exists at a meta-level. This also explains why it seems more difficult to change "personality" than to change some specific behavior, thought, choice, or feeling at the primary level.

What *mechanisms* generate this stability and sense of permanence? The mechanism that William James (1890) targeted—*habit*. Repetition of a way of behaving makes the behavior more solid, solidified, firm, "real" feeling and unconscious. In this model, repetition habituates the process so that it rises to a higher logical level and from there organizes and drives the lower level functioning.

Additionally, *language* generates this stability as well. As a meta-level phenomenon itself, language enables us to *encode* higher level abstractions so that, perceptually, abstract language (like the nominalizations we mentioned earlier) *seems* (and therefore feel) more solid, permanent, "real," and unchangeable.

What languaging do we specifically engage in that locks in our "person-ality" so that it seems and feels more and more innate, determined, static, and permanent? The sneaky nominalizations that arise from "the is of identity:"

> "I am a loser."
> "I'm just the kind of person who..."
> "I'm Irish, that's why I get angry so quickly."
> "I don't have much self-esteem; I never have."
> "You're just selfish."

Examine this kind of languaging in terms of how it *maps experiences*, and therefore "reality." We take a piece of behavior (losing, getting angry, not esteeming one's self, etc.) and we *identify our "Self"* with that behavior. This complex equivalence of phenomenon that exist on different logical levels (behavior and some internal thinking-feeling about it) then generates a "self" nominalization that seems so static and unchangeable.

Some of this languaging takes an evaluative quality ("selfish," "good," "charming," etc.) and then using the violation of "the is of predication," *predicates* (asserts) that the evaluative quality exists as ("is") the person's essence! Here we have lost the evaluator, the evaluator's standard by which he or she made the judgment, and the time when this process occurred. Here also we have someone then *identifying their "Self"* with the end results of that process.

We raise these concerns here because even within the NLP writings about meta-programs we find these linguistic violations. There you will read about some people *"being"* Matchers and others *"are"* Mis-matchers; some *"are"* Options, and others *"are"* as Procedures. If there exists no "is" in the territory, then such talk indicates a false-to-fact mapping (See "There is no 'is'" Appendix F).

In this work we aim to clean up such language. We aim to practice de-nominalizing continually and to adopt the General-semantics principle of E-priming to avoid the "is" of identity and the "is" of predication. We will adopt, as much as possible, a behavioral, functional, and process language by talking about people *matching* or *mis-matching* as their favorite style, as choosing to *sort for options* or *seek the right procedures* as they adapt to the world.

Contextualizing the Meta-Patterning Styles

O'Connor and McDermott (1995) also urged that we **not** think of meta-programs only as inside a person, but as *an interactive relationship* between a person and his or her encounter of the world in various contexts,

> "Metaprograms are generalizations. They may be highly context specific. In other words, just because a person is highly proactive at work, does not mean he is necessarily proactive everywhere. They may be reactive in home life. Secondly, there are no 'good' or 'bad' patterns. It all depends on what you are doing and what you want to accomplish. Metaprograms describe behaviour, not identity— what people do, not what they are. Very few people show these patterns in an extreme form, but will show a mixture not only across contexts but within contexts. As human behavior is always richer and more flexible than any generalizations coined to describe it, there are dangers (as with any psychometric test) of putting people in boxes and ignoring their ability to learn. Metaprogram patterns describe, not explain." (p. 77).

"It seems to us the *context* is equally important, and that metapro-gram patterns are a combination of context and particular ways the person has of deleting, distorting, and generalizing." (p. 78)

Accordingly, we will describe these meta-processing styles in terms of *the contexts that triggers them*. This enables us to put the lie to such static mis-mapping as, "Well, that's the way I am!" Now we can counter-example. "When do you not think that way?" "In what environment would you not process things in terms of X (matching, procedures, visual images, etc.)?" "Imagine a context in which you would shift from that style..."

How Meta-Programs Can Develop into Meta-States

While meta-programs do not involve *content* thoughts (i.e. what specific big picture or details a person thinks about), they do involve *structuring* thoughts (gestalt or detail). Accordingly, such *thoughts* tend to evoke corre-sponding emotions.

Yet the meta-programs operate at a meta-level, to the extent that one of these "sorting/perceiving patterns" initiates or induces one into a mind-body **state** (that corresponds to its structure), to that extent they can generate a meta-state.

A meta-state refers to a mind-body state of consciousness involving thoughts-feelings and physiology that transcends the primary state comprised of primary thoughts-and-emotions (fear, anger, like, dislike, calm, tense, joyful, miserable). It describes a *state-about-a-state* as in "fear of my anger," "guilty about my joy," "excited about my learning," etc. Hall (1995, 1996) developed this model from Korzybski's (1933/1994) model of second and third orders of abstractions, Bateson's (1972, 1979) levels of learning, and NLP's process of "going meta."

The *mechanism* of consciousness that enables us to build meta-states in the first place comprises our *self-reflexive consciousness*. This refers to how our consciousness *reflects back* onto itself. When it does, it then refers to (or references) its own former products. Via self-reflexive consciousness, we think-about-our-thinking, feel-about-our-feelings, etc. This mechanism of **reflexivity** endows us with the ability to make meta-moves to higher logical levels. As we reflexively move to such levels, these experiences eventually habituate and incorporate as our perceptual frames-of-refer-ence.

[Examples of self-reflexive consciousness in everyday life: fearing my fear (paranoia), feeling afraid of my anger (fear turned against oneself), feeling guilty for feeling afraid of my anger, feeling hopeless about ever changing my guilt about my fear of my anger(!).]

As they do, the next step involves these meta-structures transforming into *canopies of consciousness* so that the state, metaphorically, begins to *engulf* our primary states. As it does so, the canopy filters all incoming information and outgoing perception/understanding. Then as these **canopies of consciousness** increasingly surround us, they generate more and more state-dependency of LMPBC (Learning, Memory, Perception, Behavior, and Communication).

Eventually these develop into what we might call *"a mega-state"* within which we find all of our other states embedded. The primary state operates as embedded within the larger context of the meta-state. Perhaps also a larger order meta-state will embed another meta-state into itself. As the meta-states grow up into "mega-states"—canopies of consciousness that function as a pervasive psychic force pervading all facets of life—they seem like and feel like "reality" to us.

To flesh out these concepts, imagine embedding all of your states with *acceptance*. This largest canopy would then effect many other states of consciousness: self, negative emotions, positive emotions, fallibility. Appreciation will then operate as a primary perceptual filter as well as a permanent character trait, belief system, and dispositional style for orienting oneself in the world.

Figure 1.3
Canopies of Consciousness/Meta-Programs

M-S

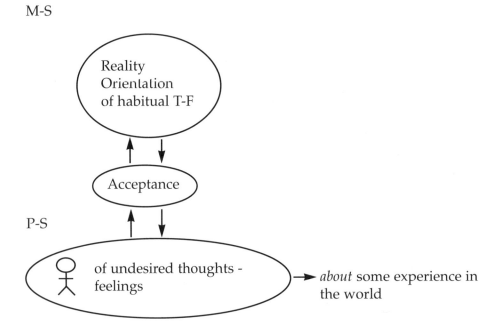

P-S

[Using our previous examples: fear of my fear generates the gestalt of "paranoia." Anger at my fear of my fear generates the gestalt of "anger turned against oneself;" Or more positively, accepting oneself, then appreciating one's acceptance of oneself, then highly esteem oneself for appreciating one's acceptance of oneself!]

If we build canopies of meta-states into the very structure of our consciousness, then we do not have to access the state of appreciation, acceptance, or whatever. *Appreciation* would then operate as so much a part of **our structure of consciousness** that it would simply function as our way of perceiving the world. We no longer have to access the state of respect for people, this canopy of consciousness simply governs all of our thinking-and-emoting. It would then operate as the largest (or mega-state) out of which we live.

Identifying Canopies

As human beings we already develop meta-states and canopies of consciousness—only we do not typically do so with appreciation, acceptance, respect, dignity, or other resources; we do it with contempt, blame, fear, anger, dread, skepticism, pessimism, etc. As self-reflexive persons, who have already generated thoughts-about-our-thoughts and inevitably experience the habituation of our thought-feelings, we already operate out of mega-states and canopies of consciousness. Given this, we need first to discover our constructions to evaluate them for ecology. Then we can decide which ones to eliminate, transform, update, or build.

This understanding about *meta-programs transforming into meta-states* explains the difficulty we have in helping someone who operates out of a primary state or a meta-state embedded in a canopy of pessimism. How do you help someone when everything you say and do gets filtered by the person through a filter of pessimism?

Optimistic, hopeful, encouraging, and helpful suggestions at the primary level inevitably get filtered out and re-interpreted. When we deal with someone in a primary state of pessimism, we will have enough difficulty interrupting the state and shaking them out of it. Their state dependent learning, memory, perception, etc. will interfere with receiving messages of optimism.

Yet how much more does this hold true with the person who operates from a meta-state of pessimism—a meta-state that has generated a canopy of consciousness? Now we will find the pessimism very pervasive and thick as a set of filters. We will experience that person has "thick-headed" and hard to get through.

Changing Meta-Programs

Can a person change his or her meta-programs? You bet! The way we have learned up to this point in our experiences to structure and pattern our thinking *only* reveals and indicates how we have learned to do so—up until now. As a dynamic, on-going process of patterning and structuring our thoughts-emotions, we can always alter that process. We have devoted an entire chapter to this after enumerating the meta-programs.

Figure 1:4
Meta-Programs In Five Categories & Meta Meta-Programs

Processing	Feeling	Choosing	Responding	Conceptualizing/Semanticizing
Cognitive/Perceptual	Emotional/Somatic	Conative/Willing	Outputting- Behaving	Kantian Categories
#1 Chunk Size *General/Specific Detail/Global/Dissociated*	#13 Emotional Coping *Passivity/Aggression*	#20 Motivation Direction *Toward/ Away From Approach/ Avoidance*	#29 Battery Rejuvenation *Extrovert/ Ambivert/ Introvert*	#40 Values *List of Values*
#2 Relationship *Matching/Mismatching Same/ Difference*	#14 Frame of Reference *Internal/ External Self-Referent/ Other-Referent*	#21 Conation Adaptation *Options/ Procedures*	#30. Affiliation/Management *Independent/Team Player/ Manager*	#41 Temper to Instruction *Strong-Will/ Compliant*
#3 Rep. system *VAKO A_d*	#15 Emotional State *Associated/Dissociated Feeling / Thinking*	#22 Adaptation *Judging/ Perceiving Controlling/Floating*	#31 Communication Stance *Blamer/ Placator/ Distracter/ Computer/ Leveler*	#42 Self-Esteem *High SE/ Low SE*
#4 Info. Gathering *Uptime/Downtime*	#16 Somatic Responses *Active/ Reflective/ Inactive*	#23 Modal Operators *Necessity/ Possibility/ Desire*	#32 General Response *Congruent/ Incongruent Competitive/ Cooperative; Polarity/ Meta*	#43 Self-Confidence *Specific Skills*
#5 Epistemology Sort *Sensors/Intuitors*	#17 Convincer/Believability *Looks, Sounds, Feels Right Makes Sense*	#24 Preference *People/ Place/ Things/ Activity / Information*	#33 Somatic Response *Active/ Reflective/ Both/ Inactive*	#44 Self-Experience *Body/ Mind/ Emotions/ Roles*
#6 Perceptual Categ. *Black-White/ Continuum*	#18 Emotional Direction *Uni-directional/ Multi-directional*	#25 Adapting to Expectations *Perfection/Optimitizing/ Skepticism*	#34 Work Preference *Things/ Systems/ People/ Information*	#45 Self-Integrity *Conflicted Incongruity/ Integrated Harmony*

#7 Scenario Thinking
Best/Worst
Optimists/Pessimists

#8 Durability
Permeable/Impermeable

#9 Focus Quality
Screeners/Non-Screeners

#10 Philosophical Direction
Why/ How Origins /Solutions

#11 Reality Structure Sort
Aristotelian/ Non-Aristotelian
Static / Process)

#12 Communication Channel Sort
Verbal- Digital/ Non-Verbal- Analogue/ Balanced

#19 Emotional Exuberance
Desurgency/Surgency

#26 Value Buying
Cost/Convenience/Quality/Time
Timidity/Boldness

#27 Responsibility
Over-Resp./Under-Respons.
Balanced

#28 People Convincer Sort
Distrusting/ Trusting

#35 Comparison
Quantitative/Qualitative

#36 Knowledge Source
Modeling/Conceptualizing
Experiencing/Authorizing

#37 Completion/ Closure
Closure/ Non-Closure

#38 Social Presentation
Shrewd-Artful/ Genuine-Artless

#39 Hierarchical Dominance Sort
Power/ Affiliation/ Achievement

#46 "Time" Tenses
Past/ Present/ Future

#47 "Time" Experience
In "Time"/"Through "Time"

#48 "Time" Access
Sequential/ Random

#49 Ego Strength
Stable / Unstable

#50. Morality
Strong/ Weak Superego

#51 Causational Sort
Causeless/ Linear CE/
Multi-CE/ Personal CE/
External CE/ Magical/
Correlational

Conclusion

We know everybody doesn't *think* the same way. This explains why everybody doesn't *feel* the same way or *value* the same things. This, in turn, explains why people don't talk or act the same way. We differ—we radically differ in these facets of human functioning.

So why don't people behave, speak, value, feel, or think the same way? Because they use different **thinking or perceiving patterns.** We call these meta-programs. These meta-programs as human *operational systems* exist at a logical level *above* our conscious level of thoughts and emotions. They speak about those sorting styles and processes that we have learned to use in thinking *about* things. This makes these programs, for the most part, outside (or *above*) consciousness.

This cognitive-behavioral model of how people **manage consciousness** provides us with not only a reason why we so frequently seem to live in different worlds—but also how we come to do so. It also offers a beacon light of insight about what we can do about it. As men and women who inevitably map out and construct the realities we live in, we *structure* our conceptual worlds and then habituate those structures into our "meta-programs." But no law exists that demands that we always, and only, structure information this way. We can choose to use different perceiving patterns. We can choose to create and live in different worlds!

Chapter 2

Meta-Programs
For Figuring Out People

*"You Can't Figure Someone Out if You Don't Know
the World They Live In!"*

In almost every area of life, whether business, personal relationships, family, children, etc., *getting along well* with others plays an important role. It plays as important a role as does intelligence, skill, aptitude, etc. in succeeding. And "getting along well" with people, in part, necessitates having some ability in *figuring people out.*

Yet what do we mean when we talk about trying to *"understand"* someone? What about them do we seek to *figure out?* Do we not search for understanding and meaning about their **style of thinking-emoting, valuing, speaking, and behaving**? When we don't understand someone (namely, their thinking, emoting, speaking, behaving, valuing) we find it most difficult to relate effectively to them.

Why not? Because we just can't *figure them out!* We can't figure out why they **think** that way! We can't figure out how in the world they could **feel** that way! As a result, we both feel *mis*understood, *dis*connected, *out of* alignment, or on *different* channels. Yet *understanding* comprises one of the central values that we all want from relating to others.

So we need a model and method for **figuring out people**, do we not?

As soon as we do *figure out people*, another problem arises. After we discover *just how different* they think, feel, value, choose, act, etc. we have to **handle our differences**. Learning to recognize how others differ from us comprises step one. Step two involves learning *how to accept, appreciate, and validate those differences.* A big job, wouldn't you say? Then comes step three, utilizing those *differences* in such a way that we don't let them get in the way of communicating and relating. This describes then the agenda for this chapter.

Figuring Out the Differences that Distinguish People

- Understanding the differences in people's sorting styles
- Accepting, appreciating, and validating those differences
- Using & working with those differences in communicating & relating

The NLP Presupposition

The meta-programs begin with the presupposition that, psychologically, we all come out of our own model of the world. We each have our own unique neuro-linguistic *Operating System* for thinking-emoting, valuing, choosing, etc. Recognizing how we inevitably bring our own *world of meaning* with us every where we go in perceiving, understanding, and experiencing the world, the meta-programs provide a model for specifically understanding *how this process works*.

After we develop an understanding of the wide range that occurs in humans in information processing and sorting, we need to appreciate these different styles. Doing so allows us to accept and validate the differing meta-programs we find in others. This will cut out the shock of "differences," and our need to fight those differences. As we do, then we can use the basic communication pattern of *pacing-and-leading* as we listen and communicate; because as we take the different meta-programs into account and dovetail them with our own, we will utilize them rather than fight over them.

Korzybski's (1933/1994) aphorism, "The map is not the territory," enables us to distinguish two dimensions of reality that we all navigate: the dimension of external reality (the world of energy manifestations) and the dimension of internal reality (human subjective thinking-emoting, believing, valuing, etc.).

We live in a very complex world. To deal with it we *delete* hundreds of thousands of bits of stimuli. We *generalize* the stimuli we process into general categories, and we *distort* other stimuli to create our own private internal worlds or understandings. These three processes (deletion, generalization and distortion) occur at both the sensory level (what we sense) and the linguistic level (how we talk about it to ourselves and others).

As you read this you have deleted lots of auditory and visual stimuli around you, have you not? Take a moment...right now and notice...all of the sights, sounds, smells, tastes, internal dialogues, body sensations around, and in, you. *How* did you selectively *tune out* all of that stimuli? Equally interesting, how do you now tune into it when you so choose? Neurologically you have the capacity for selectively hearing, selectively seeing, and selectively feeling. Can you now shift awareness of the toes on your left foot? That stimuli existed there the moment before I mentioned it—but did you have consciousness of it?

This *selective seeing, hearing, and feeling* explains how we can live in the same world with each other and yet each have differing experiences, under-standings, feelings, and models about that world. It explains why two witnesses to the same event can have completely different stories. Their stories, in fact, may tell as much about them, and their own meta-programs, than about the event.

This understanding reveals a crucial factor about people. *We all operate out of our own model of the world.* This **world-model** consists of our mental map about things beyond our nervous system. It consists of our belief system and perceptual system. It identifies our internal subjective world—that inner reality.

We do not deal with "reality" (the actual energy manifestations "out there") but with the transforms of those energies. Our nervous system abstracts again and again to create our *map* **of** the territory, and that map consists of the only thing that we can know and deal with. These maps comprise our understanding *of* reality—our individual truth. *First level reality* (the external and "objective" world) differs from *the second level reality*—our subjectivity. From *that* reality we operate as we do in the world.

To the extent that we can *identify another person's map of reality*, then to that extent can we begin to understand him or her. We can then use that under-standing to enhance communicating and relating. This entails conscious-ness of language patterns, belief/value filters, and style of thinking. In doing this we *enter into* their world and *pace* their reality. When we can do that, we can then more profoundly motivate, persuade, understand, and relate.

The second dimension involves our *neuro-semantic world*. We refer to this when we analyze the difference between ourselves and someone else as, "Well, the difference is just semantics." *The world of semantics* (words, meanings, etc.) exists purely on *the verbal level* of our inner subjectivity (hence, neuro-semantic, a product of our brain and nervous system). It does not exist externally. It exist as "semantic reality." Yet this neuro-semantical reality has led to not only arguments that create confusion, push buttons, and lead to unproductive states and ruined relationships, it has also led to wars between nations. When we confuse the territory (reality) and our map (subjective reality) of it we fail to recognize how differing processing styles influence experiences and emotions.

Rational-Emotive Behavior Therapy (REBT, formerly RET) presents a cognitive schema of *the ABC's of Emotions and Personality*. This model asserts the same neurological fact, that the **A**ctivating events can only trigger **C**onsequences of emotion and behavior within us. They do so as they activate and get processed through our **B**elief Systems (understanding, interpreting, meaning, appraisal, perspective).

Out of this area of personal subjective reality we live our everyday life and understand (or fail to understand) each other. If you work from the assumption that others process information, emote, value, perceive, respond, and experience reality in just the same way as you do, you will fail to realize the wonderful uniqueness of others. You will also tend to *project* your own model or map of the world onto them. This will, in turn, blind you to the many other ways that people think and emote. This problem describes the key "reading" problem most of us have and struggle with when we try to figure out someone. We tend to "read" them through the filters of our own patterns. Yet in doing so we see precisely only what we have the ability to see—we see only what we tend to typically see within.

Understanding Differing Processing Styles

The ways people pay attention, code, and process information ("think") describe their *"model of the world,"* and create it. The ways people do this falls into predictable patterns—**meta-programs**.

By learning these thinking, feeling, choosing, communicating "programs" that run the way we interact and communicate (the Operating System in our bio-computer), we can identify *patterns*. In doing so, this assists us in developing professional communication and relational skills. This improves our ability to understand, connect, influence, persuade, etc. It empowers us to reduce conflict and misunderstanding. It enables us to meet others *at* their model of the world rather than wait around until they learn our language and patterns.

Meta-Programs as "Channels" of Awareness

Whenever we communicate we say words using our entire physiology. This generates the two primary communication channels: verbal and non-verbal. This *output* of information also involves both *the content details* of our message, and *the process style* of how we package that message. So as we communicate any given message, we do so (inevitably and inescapably) at many meta-levels. At these process levels, we develop various patterns for how we process.

These patterns operate as filtering processes that distort, delete, and generalize information. It does this because we can only handle so much information at a time. In a now classic paper, Miller (1956) said that typically, we can consciously only attend to five to nine variables (7+-2) at any given time. As our thinking-perceiving style habituates into our meta-program Operating Style, it operates as our unconscious filtering sort and thereafter structures or patterns all incoming data.

When we go beyond the five to nine variables, our conscious mind overloads. No wonder our structuring and patterning of information so easily "goes unconscious." Consciousness cannot handle it. So we habitualize it into an out-of-awareness (meta) pattern. We learned the alphabet one small chunk at a time, then habitualized it. The same occurs with typing. When you try to recall the location of certain letters on the keyboard, do you think of them consciously? Not if you type well. Your "fingers" "know," but your conscious mind does not.

Bagley and Reese (1989) explain,

> "Everywhere we look we see patterns. Patterns are so important to us that they form our reality. Perhaps you have gone through a formal receiving line where the protocol and patterning is so rigid that if you say anything other than the obligatory 'Hello' 'How are you?' 'I'm doing fine' you probably won't even be heard. The information won't sink in....we also make decisions based on certain predictable patterns. In other words, we tend to make decisions in the same way we have made similar decisions before.

All this pattern talk lays the foundation for this important premise: people buy within their own predictable patterns. These patterns are principally based on how they mentally sort information. Therefore, when you are able to recognize these mental sorting patterns you are in a position to understand the required steps they go through to arrive at decisions. *If what you offer aligns with how they decide, then you have rapport and you are on your way toward satisfying their pattern needs as well as their outcome needs."* (our italics)

Our meta-programs function as unconscious *perceptual filters* that structure messages and information. Each generates a "channel" of awareness—awareness of the chunk size, its relationship to other information, representational system, etc. (see Figure 2.1).

This now allows us to ask each other while we communicate, "What channel of awareness have you tuned into?" "Have you tuned in to the Global Channel? The Mismatching Channel? The Other Referent Channel?" Not knowing *what channel* a person speaks from, or to, or how to *channel surf* through the various possible meta-program (i.e. channels of awareness), causes one to miss the program the other person broadcasts!

These unconscious filters as sorting mechanisms, however, eventually take on a life of their own. They habituate. As they do, we have less and less awareness of them. We take them for granted. We assume them as "the right" and "real" way to perceive. We may even come to think it "wrong" to do otherwise! By these meta-programs we formulate our representations and map out our reality.

Figure 2.1
Channels of Awareness

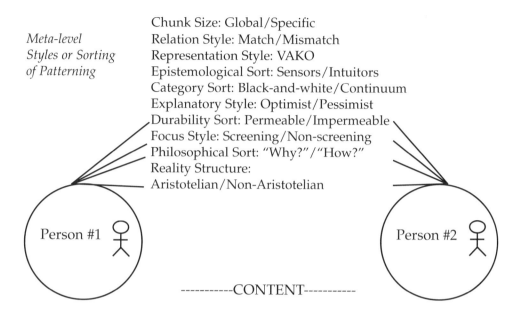

Meta-level
Styles or Sorting
of Patterning

Chunk Size: Global/Specific
Relation Style: Match/Mismatch
Representation Style: VAKO
Epistemological Sort: Sensors/Intuitors
Category Sort: Black-and-white/Continuum
Explanatory Style: Optimist/Pessimist
Durability Sort: Permeable/Impermeable
Focus Style: Screening/Non-screening
Philosophical Sort: "Why?"/"How?"
Reality Structure:
Aristotelian/Non-Aristotelian

Person #1

Person #2

-----------CONTENT-----------

Meta-Programs as a Means to "Reading" People

What specific **patterns** determine the way people think, value, feel, speak, gesture, behave, and respond? *How* can we learn to more effectively "read" these unique and personal patterns in others? *How* can we "read" people *and* do so accurately?

Actually every day we all engage in this business of "reading" people. We do it incessantly! We want to *figure others out*! So we constantly make guesses about what others think, value, want, and feel. And we do so based on our assumptive beliefs and understandings about "human nature." We do so because *if* we can figure out the motives and intentions of others, the possibility of them tricking or hurting us, lessens, and this will help us to avoid a lot of unnecessary pain and trouble. We also make second-guesses about what they will do in the future, how they will respond if we make this or that response. We do all of this second-guessing based upon our prediction of what we believe about the person's inner nature underneath his or her roles and manners. We mind-read their deeper motives.

Also, every day we *mis*guess and *mis*read! Why? Because of the complexity, layeredness, and multi-dimensional functioning of people. After all, how well do you "read" your own thoughts, emotions, values, motives, beliefs, etc.? How well do you know your own structuring processes—your own thinking and emoting styles?

Ultimately, the art of figuring people out by reading their patterns involves a very imperfect art. Yet we can improve and develop our skills in this area. We can learn how to improve our calibration to the patterns at meta-levels (the meta-programs).

The Target of Reading People's Patterns

How do you attempt to *figure people out?* **What** specifically do you pay attention to in order to make your evaluations? Do you focus on the clothes they wear? Their behaviors and gestures? Their style of eye contact? Your feelings about them?

"Reading" people also involves *meaning attribution*. What meanings do you give to these items? What serves as the basis of your appraisals? (Inevitably when we read another person we do so in terms of our own history, meanings, emotions, etc.)

This list of things to "read" suggests reading levels. I can start outside at *your persona*—the roles and positions you play in society and in relationships. Yet such roles also suggest driving thoughts and feelings. So I can go deeper—to *your "personality" style*—your characteristic thoughts and emotions.

Figure 2.2

Persona	"Personality"	Inner Person	"Person"
Roles	Style	Truer Thoughts	One's "Self"
Positions	Surface Thoughts	& Feelings	beyond
Clothes	Emotions	Values	Thoughts &
Outward style	Presentation	Beliefs	Emotion,
			Speech & Behavior

Yet that only represents another level. I can go deeper. I can go deeper than just your surface thoughts and feelings to deeper levels that include *your deeper or higher values and belief*, into you as a "person." What comprises you as a "person"? Certainly your cognitive-emotive style. "Reading" those patterns provides a more profound sense of having reached a fairly deep core level.

In day-to-day life we often live quite blind to each other. More often than we might suspect, we fail to truly realize what another experiences. How does this occur? In part it occurs because we operate from the presupposition that others think-and-feel *as we do*. We use ourselves as models for how others think, feel, speak, value, gesture and behave (or should!). We call this psychological mechanism "projection."

The things we notice about others fall into two main categories, *verbal and non-verbal* responses. The verbal category includes words, language style, predicates, and other facets of the linguistics that form someone's inner world. The non-verbal category includes such things as eye accessing cues, gestures, breathing, sense of space, behaviors (roles), context, etc. While learning how to figure out people, we also learn to more accurately predict the responses of others. Thereby, we learn to predict their behavorial, communicational, and emotional responses more accurately. In such "reading," we want to move beyond the external roles and masks until we truly see the person in all their uniqueness and specialness.

Distinguishing **Content** *Programs and* **Meta**-*Programs*

We all have lots of operational programs in structuring our map of the world and these programs run our mental, emotional, choosing, communicating, and semanticizing and operate at two levels: content and process. Together they operate as our *strategies* that specify the structure of our subjective experiences.

A good example of how content and process programs interface shows up in our strategy for reading. Consider your own *reading strategy* as you, even at this moment, read this. Notice how that you quickly and unconsciously look at the ink marks on this page and via those marks perceive English letters and words which, in turn, evoke various VAKO (Visual, Auditory, Kinesthetic, Olfactory-Gustatory) representations and meanings. Amazing! Somewhere inside you you have some kind of a "reading program."

Yet you didn't have this program as a newborn. Your language development and use arose over time as a learned phenomenon. Unfortunate feral children who grow up apart from human culture not only do not know how to read, they also don't know how to speak or process human language. "Knowing how to read a book" operates as *a learned strategy*, not an innate skill.

Consider the complication of this task. We have to translate ink marks into meaningful symbols and then let those symbols evoke appropriate representations and meanings. In spite of this complexity, this eventually habituates so that we run this program unconsciously. Then we can engage in reading *without* consciously noticing the process. We just do it.

Our neurologically stored *reading program* now operates at a level outside of conscious awareness (we typically use the spatial metaphor of *below* consciousness). Once upon a time we had to slowly and meticulously learn the eye-scanning patterns and associations between letters, words, meanings, etc. We had to learn to start on the left side and move to the right.

Yet over time, repetition made such eye-scanning programs drop out of awareness. Now, whenever we pick up a paper or book (a stimulus), we activate the existing program. This holds true for a great many other behaviors e.g. riding a bike, skating, shaking hands, adding, subtracting, etc.

To "read" anything we have to know *the patterns* that govern the structure of what we wish to read. *Patterns* provide this key. We can't read anything without knowing the organizing patterns. Reading means "to receive or take in the sense of by scanning, to study the movements of" (as in reading lips), "to understand the meaning of words or symbols, to interpret." If we want to learn to read **Hebrew**, first we have to identify and learn the characters. Then we have to recognize and reorganize our expectation that the pattern will move from right to left, that words consist of consonants (and in some Hebrew writing—little points and dots above and below the consonant letters consist of the vowel sounds).

Figure 2.3

בראשית ברא אלהים את השׁמים זאת הארץ

Can you read *that*? Even after you learn the pronunciation of these letters and words, you then have to ask, "What does it mean?" This demonstrates our need for knowing *patterns* in order to read something. Without the patterns, such ink marks on paper make no sense at all. It conveys no "meaning" even to a searching receptive mind. With patterns, however, we can both articulate the expression and understand the significance. Via pattern recognition we bring order out of chaos. So with reading or figuring out a person—we come to understand a person by means of recognizing their patterns.

Figure 2.4

בראשית ברא אלהים את השׁמים זאת הארץ

the earth	and	the heaven	God	created	the In beginning

This holds true for medical doctors who learn to "read" symptoms of pain or distress in the human body. It also holds true for auto mechanics who learn to "read" the mechanical cues of cars. These professionals have developed a familiarity with how a body or a car operates (or should optimally operate) and the significance of various symptoms. So they learn to calibrate their attention to specific expressions as cues, and have learned what meanings to attribute to them.

"Reading" People to Figure them Out

This principle holds true for developing proficiency in *figuring out people*. When we face the chaos of the many cues in a person's communications and expressions, we need a comprehensive knowledge of human *information processing* (their patterns), and the significance of such cues.

A *meta*-program then functions at a level above or beyond the specific learning program. It does not deal with *content*, but **process**. Meta-programs operate as *"about"* the content level. They function as messages or processes *about* that lower level. *The meta-programs prescribe the various ways we can pattern or structure the lower thought.*

For instance, in a reading program, when some people read words (a visual external stimuli) they *hear* the words in their head. So they "make sense" of the marks by "representing" the auditory information by hearing an internal voice saying the words.

Others *see* images of the words or the referents of the words. They internally represent the information using the visual modality.

Still others get *sensations* about the words or their meanings. They use kinesthetic representations (body sensations).

Which system do you favor? If you know which representation system you primarily use, you know one of your meta-programs which we will shortly cover (#3).

Further, when some people read, they look for things that *match* what they already know. They pattern their attention to *matching* known knowledge. As others read, they look for what they do not know and what stands out as different (they *mismatch*). Again, if you know your style in this area, you know another one of your meta-programs (#2).

Meta-programs then describe the structure and form of our information; and sometimes this plays a crucial distinction in learning and developing.

I (MH) once had a young adolescent as a client who had failed three grades and whose parents had become convinced that their son had a very low IQ. When his parents brought him in, they brought in a three-inch stack of psychiatric reports indicating a trail of "learning disabilities" all the way back to the first grade. He had been diagnosed as having half-a-dozen different problems.

As I began working with him, I asked about the color of his room. He didn't know. I asked about the room's shape. He didn't know. "What does your dad's voice sound like?" He didn't know. "Can you imagine what Donald Duck's voice sounds like in your mind—can you hear him quacking out, 'Are you dumb or something?'" He couldn't—although he snickered about that line.

This big boy, 6'1" and 205 pounds and, of course, on the football team, simply *had no sights or sounds in his head*. No wonder he didn't "learn" academic information very well!

Turning to one area of skill and resourcefulness that I knew he had, I asked, "How have you learned to play football?"

It turned out that his coach also had lots of trouble with him. Jim never seemed able to "get it" (the football plays) when the coach drew out the moves on the blackboard. The coach had to take him out to the field and actually *walk him through the moves*.

Ah! Jim's learning strategy (and representational strength)—kinesthetics! So I gave him some homework. He had to go home and make **mental snapshots** of his room, the house, the classrooms, his mom's face, etc. I also asked him to begin to make **auditory snapshots** of his dad's voice, Donald Duck, two of his favorite songs, etc.

Thereafter week by week for two months, our sessions consisted of his reports of the sights and sounds in his world. My questioning simply gave him the opportunity to begin noticing—noticing as he had never before. And as he began to "snapshot" and encode visual and auditory information—he grades "mysteriously" began to improve. It turned out that Jim didn't have a low IQ, he had simply not developed his visual and auditory modalities.

Accepting and Appreciating the Meta-Programs

So what? What values accrue when you know meta-programs? How can meta-programs help us appreciate all of the differences that we find in others?

1. **Conflict reduction.** As we recognize that people radically differ in their *patterns* for sorting, attending, processing, and making sense of the world, we *accept* this fact as a given, and no longer need to fight it! Further, when we stop wasting energy on fighting their meta-programs, we can use this understanding of a person's style to more fully *understand* them in terms of their own model of the world. Grasping the patterning style provides us insights into what they value, *how* they think, feel, value, etc. This describes a much more sane approach to inter-personal reality.

What can we appreciate specifically about differences? **The explanatory power they provide.** They provide us explanations as to *how* others can see and feel so differently. In reading and with familiarizing yourself with many of the meta-programs, you will probably experience what most do— a sudden awareness about a particular person, "Oh, that explains why they think that way!"

This *accepting and appreciating* stops us from needless conflicting with people. Instead, we can *pace (or match) their processing style*, which, in turn, facilitates them feeling understood; and that generates a sense of rapport.

2. **Moralization reduction.** Accepting differences in meta-programs further stops all of the energy and conflict that we waste on moralizing about the "right" way to think. "You shouldn't be so detail minded!" "Why do you always have to have a procedure? What's wrong with you?" "Me, me, me—you always reference off yourself. You shouldn't do that!"

As we more fully *accept and appreciate* another's "structure of subjectivity," we don't have to "demonize" their style of processing information. Rather than fight their style, we can appreciate its values, and then simply match it in communicating and relating. This, by the way, will cut out most of the "resistance" that we encounter from people.

3. *Communication flexibility.* The result of adopting more acceptance and appreciation of differences leads to expanding our communicational flexibility. Understanding and pacing a person's way of knowing, perceiving, etc. empowers us to communicate in a way that optimally fits the other person's style. This empowers our message to have maximum impact for that person.

4. *Empathy development.* Such acceptance and appreciation also expands our abilities of empathizing because it frees us up from an imprisonment in thinking that our way of thinking exists as the only right way to think. Recognizing and learning to appreciate other frames of mind and thinking styles increases our empathy for other viewpoints.

5. *Prediction accuracy.* Finally, with expanded empathetic understanding of others, we have a means for more accurately "reading" and *predicting the person's responses.* We will be able to figure others out because we will have greater access to the kind of thinking that creates their reality.

Using the Meta-Programs to See Patterns

If the ways we code information, pay attention, and process thoughts both *describe* our model of the world and *create* it, then the ways people perceive and sort, fall into predictable patterns. We can now look for such systematic and regular patterns in ourselves and others. First we need to develop conscious awareness of how people attend the world.

1. *One at a time.* If you look at the full list of meta-programs and try to learn them *all at once* you will overwhelm yourself. Instead, *aim to learn them one at a time.* We have provided several diagrams (Figures 1.1 through 1.3) to assist in organizing our thinking and remembering of them. We have also designed a Sorting Grid (Appendix F) to assist learning. Begin by using it as a tool to make a psychological profile on yourself, and then others that you know well. This will help you think about such processing patterns. As you take the meta-programs *one* at a time, **practice** it until you feel proficient in recognizing and using it.

2. *Give yourself permission.* Do you have permission to "go meta" and notice people's operational style? If not, give yourself permission to do so. Do you have permission to "go meta" *while talking* with them? Do you fear that will seem rude or uncaring? If you get that kind of internal objection, then reframe it as representing a truly caring and considerate approach because it empowers you to understand them more fully.

3. **Use lots of open-ended questions.** Open-ended questions especially encourage a person to express his or her meta-programs. As the classic question, "Does this glass look half empty or half full to you?", invites a person to indicate a typical way of perceiving, as do the elicitation (questions) that we have included with each meta-program.

4. **Use lots of downtime questions.** These play a valuable role in eliciting meta-programs inasmuch as they require a person to go "inside" to access the required information. When we don't have certain information "on the tip of the tongue," we will tend to demonstrate our meta-programs. Downtime questions obviously depend upon both the content and the context. Examples of such include the following: "As you think about your childhood home, what color was your room?" "How many stop lights do you go through when you drive from home to work?" "Name the sixth number in your telephone number." "When you think of the tune of 'Mary Had a Little Lamb' and the tenth word of that song, describe the tonality at that point."

5. **Elicit fully associated states.** Don't make the mistake of trying to elicit meta-programs with a person not fully accessing their experience.

6. **Prioritize the meta-programs and look for the drivers.** Remember that the meta-programs do **not** all carry the same weight of importance. They will differ according to how a person uses and values them. So in *identifying* the meta-programs, also *prioritize* them in terms of importance *to that person* in that given context. Identify the person's meta-programs which seem the most important and impactful (the person's driver meta-programs). Continually wonder, "What meta-program seems to exercise the most significance for this person?"

7. **Practice writing pacing statements.** When you feel ready to use the information you have gathered about someone, practice writing *pacing statements* to match their processing style. This may do more to increase your communication skills than anything else.

Thus, if the person sorts by self in a strong way and mismatches with counter-examples (or with polarity responses), he will typically feel inclined to challenge you with "prove-it-to me" statements. This can spiral into a pointless matching of wits. Counter that with a pacing statement. "You seem so good at knowing your needs that only you can truly decide what's ultimately right." A communication like that will pace his meta-processing style that structures his very thinking and emoting. It will also *validate* his style. Then, instead of fighting his style of thinking and deciding, you will utilize it.

With a visual and general sorter, keep your details at a minimum as you describe future possibilities vaguely. The person will then shape it into his or her own image: "With your great eye you can see how you could use this in your business to improve production." The person will also feel respected because you didn't bore him or her with details.

As you learn to match a person's sorting patterns, you will not have to swim against the current of that person's basic inclinations. In this way you will add a turbo charger to your communication skills. We recommend that you first get acquainted with your own meta-programs. Doing so will deepen your own understanding of how you operate at this psychological level. It will also give you an appreciation for the value of these meta-programs. Then you will know just the right way to sell yourself on something you want. This will provide you with a custom-made self-motivation program that will fit your own personality just right.

Using and Working with Meta-Programs in Communicating and Relating

If we understand meta-programs as *sorting patterns* then how do we specifically work with these sorts?

James and Woodsmall (1988), Rooney (1990), and others also describe meta-programs as "sorts" or "neuro-sorts." This term *sort,* coming from *computer terminology,* describes how a computer organizes information. Using this metaphor, the meta-programs create our "mental" functioning that then determines **how** we notice, organize, formulate, maintain, and chunk data (messages) as we make sense of things. Meta-programs thus provide unconscious parameters, guidelines, and general rules that organize perception and thinking.

Phenomenologically we experience our consciousness as simple and direct. Our thoughts seem so "real" and concrete to us. Our representations, values, beliefs, and memories seem so much "the way it is." Yet behind our experience of this phenomenon there exists great complexity with regard to consciousness. Bateson (1972, 1979) repeatedly asserted that we have no consciousness of the neurological mechanisms that give rise to our phenomenological sense of our consciousness of reality (phenomenology refers to our sense of and experience with phenomena at the sensory level). Quoting studies in perception, he showed that we usually cannot become aware of the mechanisms that create or cause perception—which explains how various perceptual "illusions" can so fool our nervous system. We only know what we "sense" on the screen of our consciousness as it ebbs and flows.

As the meta-programs describe *patterns* for sorting out the stimuli that impacts us, it provides awareness of *how* a person processes information at unconscious levels to create his or her subjective reality. What then? We can then *match* the meta-programs in communicating to access the person's neurological circuits for processing information in the way that seems "real" to that person. Since one cannot *not* respond to one's own way of making sense of things—this makes the communication impactful indeed.

Rooney (1990) writes,

> "... although the current state of research on **Neuro-Sorts** (meta-programs) has not been extensive enough to be able to say how they originate, where they come from neurologically, or why each individual has the particular sorts they do, there are a few things that are known about them."

In the following sections, we have specified some of these things that we know about meta-programs, and suggested ideas about working with them.

How do We Work with Meta-Programs?

1. **By accepting meta-programs as creating a general direction for consciousness.** Meta-programs differ from beliefs because they typically function in a far more general way than do beliefs. They function as a focus of consciousness rather than specify the content of a specific belief. Rooney writes,

> "They operate more as a direction, a tendency, a general guideline by which we select, or through which we funnel and channel the incoming information that will later be formed into beliefs."

2. **By accepting them as contextually dependent.** A person may operate in a very *internal* way in one context of life (i.e. spiritually, going inside to find meaning regardless of what others say or do), while very *external* in another (i.e. in one's job, seeking direction and instructions from others). The contextual dependency of meta-programs suggests that while we will find them operating consistently within a given area, they will often operate very differently in another arena. While exceptions occur, expect *meta-program consistency* within a given dimension. We need to always inquire about *the context* within which we use a given meta-program, and the contexts wherein we don't use it.

Meta-programs also depend on the cultural contexts. A style of sorting can habitualize for a whole group of people so that certain meta-programs may predominate for various racial, religious, familial, or political groups. This means that the percentages of people in a given country, society, area, generation, economy, educational institution, etc. may favor a certain meta-program style for thinking, emoting, etc. When examining meta-programs, take this into consideration. Does this thinking-emoting structuring style typically characterize any larger groups with whom this person associates? For example, the fundamental mindset, whether political or religious fundamentalism, operates from a perceptual category sort (#6) of black-and-white thinking. An extreme "liberal" will similarly use that kind of thinking. Moderates, by definition, operate somewhere in the middle and hence sort by using continuum thinking.

3. *By thinking of meta-programs as operating on a continuum.* We do not exist as necessarily *either* this pattern *or* that one (either/or). While some people do process in a polarized way in one or two of the meta-programs, we generally fall somewhere in between on the continuum. So we need to ask, "To what extent" or "how much" do I or this other person structure thinking or emoting in this or that pattern?

4. *By expecting meta-programs to operate in a "state" dependent way.* This means that our use of a meta-program greatly depends upon our mental-emotional state a given time. A meta-program can differ according to our internal state (internal context), the situation (external) in which we find ourselves, and the amount of stress we experience. Thus we need also to ask about the person's state. How do we perceive in a stressful state versus a calm and relaxed one? How do we think-feel when in a social group versus working alone? When resourceful or unresourceful?

Typically, most people in a "stress" situation will experience it associatedly (#15). When this happens, you can count on the person taking things personally and engaging in other cognitive distortions such as Awfulizing, Catastrophizing, Blaming, etc. Such association into the state of stress involves sending messages of "danger" or "overload" to the brain which then activates the fight/flight mechanism. When that happens, the autonomic nervous system goes into high activation of defense. Yet in most modern situations, this response pattern does not serve us well! Yet if a person uses that as their meta-program—this will result. Knowing how to "read" this provides us with the ability to choose to dissociate and to invite others to sort that way as well.

5. ***By refusing to moralize about meta-programs.*** Meta-programs have nothing to do with morality (i.e. "correct or incorrect," "good or bad," "right or wrong"). No ethically "correct" way exists to filter information. Some of the meta-programs will, in certain contexts, work much more productively than others. Yet these styles merely provide us with choices about how to process information and respond. They do not prescribe "the way things are," much less "the way things should be."

They operate as *sets of distinctions* we can make about information. Therefore **we do not view them as "true or false," but useful or not useful in a given context at a certain time.** The human brain works in a far too marvelously complex way for us to neatly categorize its functioning in such ways. The meta-programs simply provide us a useful tool for thinking of human behavior (e.g. information processing with our neurology). Nor do we, in NLP, use them as simply a new way to label and categorize people. If these distinctions enable us to more productively understand ourselves and others, then they have value for us.

6. ***By expecting consistency, but not permanence.*** When we structure information at a meta-level it endows our "sense" of self and reality with a consistency. It does this by creating ongoing coherent patterns. Though flexible and alterable, meta-programs do endow our everyday experience with a sense of stability. This may create the pseudo-sense of having an unchangeable "personality" or "temperament." Rooney wrote about this,

> "If we operate as *internals*, spiritually, we will consistently function that way in all spiritual matters and at all times."

It becomes a habit.

Habits, for all the bad press they get, do keep us consistent and regular. So with our meta-habits of mind. We inevitably follow patterns in how we process and code information. This *form of patterning* gives us a way to discover the patterned ways people think.

7. ***By anticipating that they will change over contexts and time.*** As we grow and mature, the way we pattern our thinking as we sort for meaning changes. These do **not** function as permanent, static "traits." They operate much more as states.

For example, during a "normal" and healthy maturation from a child to an adult experience in life, we typically can expect a person to change from referencing off of Others (external) to referencing off his or her own understandings, values, and beliefs (internal). This generally describes a healthy personal "centering."

Lloyd (1989) devoted his research to this subject. His dissertation, "The Impact of Role-Expectation Cognitions upon Test-Taking," describes his exploration into *the trait hypothesis* behind the construction of several psychometric tests (Taylor-Johnson Temperamental Analysis etc.). He tested the trait theory presupposition that the way a person "is" will **not** change over the years and **would not** change if you ask a person to take the test while in different states.

Yet the test-taking experiments showed the very opposite. People's scores move all over the place when they imagined taking the test as "my eighteen year old self," "as my current self," "as myself at sixty," etc. In other words, the state (even accessed by imagination) determined the "trait."

In summary, since meta-programs describe our mental-emotional categories of internal patterning, they determine what information we will use and how we will formulate both our "world view" and "self-view." Knowing this empowers us to work with others calmly, thoughtfully, respectfully, and patiently. We have no need to take offense or anger about someone's particular meta-programs. This knowledge can also assist us in more accurately predicting the way another person will act.

Remembering that these programs do not exist as things or permanent traits enables us to **not** put people into conceptual boxes. Instead they enable us to empathetically understand others in our relating and communicating. Remembering that people "are" *not* their programs, but merely express styles of thinking and emoting in various contexts at various times and can sometimes develop some really entrenched habits of mind-and-emotion.

Tools for Figuring Out People

Developing people-reading literacy skills necessitates several tools. What tools will you specifically need to figure out people using this model?

1. ***Sensory awareness.*** Opening up your eyes and ears, and other senses, to the input that others constantly offer. Come into "uptime." Put all of your "downtime" thoughts, emotions, and filters on hold and shift awareness to only the stimuli before you. The more skill you develop at attentive listening, the more skill you will develop in figuring out people.

2. ***Distinguish between descriptive and evaluative terms.*** This will prevent you from "reading" others through your patterns and filters. As you distinguish between what you actually see, hear, sense in sensory awareness (*description*) and between the values and meanings which come from memories, values, traumas, beliefs, (*evaluative*), you can read without projecting (mind-reading). Ask yourself, "What does this descriptive element (language, gesture, behavior, emotion, etc.) mean to me?" to access your own meaning system so that you know it. Since all evaluative words and processing arises from our own model of the world, we need to constantly go meta, get out of content, and move into a descriptive mode.

3. ***Pay attention to linguistic markers.*** These identify the cues that **mark out** how a person represents and formats their experience. Use this to gain insight into the person's operating model of the world. Many of the meta-programs have cue words and terms that will alert you to their presence.

A visual processor (#3) will use visual words (see, look, color, etc.) a kinesthetic processor will use feeling and sensation words (feel, heavy, smooth, impact, etc.), and one processing auditorially will use words of sound (hear, rings a bell, sounds right, etc.).

4. ***Develop a comprehensive knowledge of the patterns.*** These provide you with the key to your "reading" as you figure out people. They enable you to organize the input offered you in making sense of them. Learn, drill in, memorize, utilize, practice until you make them "second nature." Do so until you make them part of your own processing, until you organize them as your intuitions. As we must learn how to make auditory discriminations to appreciate music and visual discriminations in order to appreciate art, so must we train our senses to note discrete meta-program distinctions.

5. ***Develop clean kinesthetic channels***. One of our tools for "reading" people involves the felt impact that another's words, gestures, and behaviors make on us. Yet to utilize this capacity necessitates putting ourselves into a calm state so that we can cleanly note the impressions that stir our senses and emotions. Mere kinesthetic awareness will not suffice. We must have kinesthetic channels *uncontaminated* from our own emotions, emotional filters, and predispositions.

When people generally talk about taking a feeling approach to others, they usually refer to feeling sensitive about *their feelings*, rather than those of another. Yet that leads to mind-reading, projection, and outright hallucination about others! The emotions they think they hear, see and feel in others, arise from within themselves. This ability to distinguish between what we receive as *input from the outside* and *what we generate within ourselves* separates effective communicators from mind-readers.

6. ***Go meta.*** Move to a meta-level, to the person's meta-levels of temperament, mental, emotional, relational, etc. processing. Continue to inquire, "What does this way of talking, acting, emoting, etc. tell me about this person's operational meta-programs in this context?" "What does this reveal about me and my meta-programs?"

7. ***Keep your "reading" always tentative***. Test your conclusions and assumptions. Ask the person about their thinking, emoting, choosing, etc. Invite more information, and test it against the person's overall configuration of traits.

Conclusion

NLP first offers us a way to *manage our own mind* and then it offers a model for *figuring out others*. Starting from the presupposition that we all inhabit unique and different worlds of thought, emotion, meaning, experience, etc., we seek to understand others in terms of their mental maps of the world. This also involves their meta-mapping style (the meta-programs). Accepting and appreciating these differences empowers us to pace their model of the world rather than fight with them about it. What a much more enhancing process!

In the following chapters, we have presented the most extensive list of meta-programs to date. Yet this certainly does **not** exhaust the subject. In fact, we feel that it just barely begins to address this domain about how we sort, pay attention, and perceive.

Part II

The Meta-Programs

Template of Meta-Programs

The "Mental" Meta-Programs
#1. **Chunk Size:** *General/Specific; Global/Detail;*
Deductive, Inductive, Abductive

#2. **Relationship Sort:** *Matching/Mismatching;*
Sameness or Difference/Opposite;
Agree/Disagree

#3. **Representational System Sort:**
Visual/Auditory/Kinesthetic/Auditory-digital

#4. **Information Gathering Style:**
Uptime/Downtime

#5. **Epistemology Sort:** *Sensors/Intuitors*

#6. **Perceptual Categories Sort:**
Black-and-white vs. Continuum

#7. **Scenario Thinking Style:**
Best vs. Worst Scenario
Thinking; Optimists/Pessimists

#8. **Perceptual Durability Sort:** *Permeable/Impermeable*

#9. **Focus Sort:** *Screeners/Non-screeners*

#10. **Philosophical Direction:**
Why/How; Origins/Solution Process

#11. **Reality Structure Sort:**
Aristotelian/Non-Aristotelian (Static/Process)

#12. **Communication Channel Preference:**
Verbal(Digital)/Non-Verbal(Analogue), Balanced

The "Emotional" Meta-Programs
#13. **Emotional Coping or Stress Response Pattern:**
Passivity/Aggression/Dissociated

#14. **Frame of Reference or Authority Sort:**
Internal/External; Self-Referent/Other-Referent

#15. **Emotional State Sort:**
Associated/Dissociated; Feeling/Thinking

#16. **Somatic Response Sort:** *Active/Reflective/Inactive*

#17. **The Convincer or Believability Sort:**
Looks, Sounds, or Feels Right; Makes Sense

#18. **Emotional Direction Sort:** *Uni-directional/Multi-directional*

#19. **Emotional Intensity/Exuberance Sort:** *Desurgency/Surgency*
Timidity/Boldness

The "Volitional" Meta-Programs
#20. **Direction Sort:** *Toward/Away From, Past Assurance/Future Possibilities; Approach/Avoidance*
#21. **Conation Choice in Adapting:** *Options/Procedures*
#22. **Adaptation Sort:** *Judging/Perceiving, Controlling/Floating*
#23. **Reason Sort of Modal Operators:** *Necessity/Possibility/Desire; Stick—Carrot*
#24. **Preference Sort:** *Primary Interest—People/Place/ Things/Activity/Information*
#25. **Goal Sort—Adapting to Expectations:** *Perfection/Optimization/Skepticism*
#26. **Value Buying Sort:** *Cost/Convenience/Quality/Time*
#27. **Responsibility Sort:** *Over-Responsible/Under-Responsible*
#28. **People Convincer Sort**: *Distrusting/Trusting*

The External "Response" Meta-Programs
#29. **Rejuvenation of Battery Sort:** *Extrovert, Ambivert, Introvert*
#30. **Affiliation & Management Sort:** *Independent/Team Player/Manager*
#31. **Communication Stance Sort:** *Communication Modes*
#32. **General Response:** *Congruent/Incongruent/ Competitive/Cooperative/Polarity/Meta*
#33. **Somatic Response Style:** *Active/Reflective/Both/Inactive*
#34. **Work Preference Sort:** *Things/Systems/People/Information*
#35. **Comparison Sort:** *Quantitative/Qualitative*
#36. **Knowledge Sort:** *Modeling/Conceptualizing/Demonstrating/ Experiencing/Authorizing*
#37. **Completion/Closure Sort:** *Closure/Non-Closure*
#38. **Social Presentation:** *Shrewd & Artful/Genuine & Artless*
#39. **Hierarchical Dominance Sort:** *Power/Affiliation/Achievement*

The Meta Meta-Programs

#40. **Value Sort:** *Emotional "Needs," Beliefs*

#41. **Temper to Instruction Sort:** *Strong-Will/Compliant*

#42. **Self-Esteem Sort:** *Conditional/Unconditional*

#43. **Self-Confidence Sort:** *High/Low*

#44. **Self-Experience Sort:** *Mind/Emotion/Body/Role*

#45. **Self-Integrity:** *Conflicted Incongruity/Harmonious Integration*

#46. **"Time" Tenses Sort:** *Past/Present/Future*

#47. **"Time" Experience:** *In "Time"/Through "Time"; Sequential vs. Random Sorting*

#48. **"Time" Access Sort:** *Random/Sequential*

#49. **Ego Strength Sort:** *Unstable/Stable*

#50. **Morality Sort:** *Weak/Strong Super-ego*

#51. **Causational Sort:** *Causeless, Linear CE, Multi-CE, Personal CE, External CE, Magical, Correlational*

Chapter 3

The "Mental" Meta-Programs

Meta-Programs in Thinking, Sorting, Perceiving
(#1-12)

These meta-programs pre-eminently describe our Operational System for human processing of information. They describe how our *attention* functions in terms of *how* it attends and processes information cognitively (mental understanding) and *what* it attends. In this chapter we focus on those meta-level styles of inputting, processing, and outputting of information (messages, "differences") that have to do with what we call "mind" or cognition. These facets of our operating system indicate *how* we have learned to "run our brain" and offer an understanding of the many thinking patterns that we can use to "run our own brain."

In the following, we will offer a brief description of each meta-program pattern with an elicitation question or process. In our seminars we typically devote lots of time for multiple examples, demonstrations, and experiential laboratories so that learners can develop skill in recognizing and utilizing such. Here we offer the model with some applications.

#1.	**Chunk Size:** *General/ Specific; Global/ Detail; Deductive, Inductive, Abductive*
#2.	**Relationship Sort**: *Matching/Mismatching; Sameness or Difference/Opposite; Agree/Disagree*
#3.	**Representational System Sort:** *Visual/ Auditory/ Kinesthetic/ Auditory-digital*
#4.	**Information Gathering Style:** *Uptime / Downtime*
#5.	**Epistemology Sort:** *Sensors/ Intuitors*
#6.	**Perceptual Categories Sort:** *Black-and-white vs. Continuum*
#7.	**Scenario Thinking Style:** *Best vs. Worst Scenario Thinking; Optimists/Pessimists*
#8.	**Perceptual Durability Sort:** *Permeable/Impermeable*
#9.	**Focus Sort:** *Screeners/ Non-screeners*
#10.	**Philosophical Direction:** *Why/ How; Origins/ Solution Process*
#11.	**Reality Structure Sort:** *Aristotelian/ Non-Aristotelian (Static / Process)*
#12.	**Communication Channel Preference:** *Verbal/ Non-Verbal; (Digital/ Analogue), Balanced*

#1. Chunk Size/Reasoning Style:
General & Global/Specifics & Details
Deductive, Inductive, Abductive

Concept: With regard to the size of the "chunk" of information that people prefer when thinking, communicating, learning, etc. we generally move from one of two basic positions, with a third position taking a lesser role. Deductive thinkers start *globally* and move downward, inductive thinkers start *specifically with the details* and move upward, and abductive thinkers use metaphors and analogies to think "on the side."

Elicitation: "When you pick up a book or think about attending a workshop, what do you pay attention to first—the big picture, book cover, or specific details about its value?" "If we decided to work together on a project, would you first want to know what we generally will do or would you prefer to hear about a lot of the specifics?"

Description:
1. Some people prefer to *start with specific information* in very small chunks and then to **induce upward** to general principles. They go for *details* and feel most comfortable with this level and size of data. They prefer to "chunk" their processing of information in sequences that enable them to then induce up *the scale from specificity to abstraction.* As inductive thinkers, they say, "Give me the details and let me see what it means to me." This describes the technical and scientific attitude par excellence. A person who sorts in a highly specific way sees the trees, but not the forest.

2. By contrast, other people prefer to *start with the big picture* that encapsulates a more *global* outlook. They make sense of the world in terms of their overall frame. They want "the forest" first, not the trees. They want a *gestalt* configuration (the whole or overall pattern) in their information processing and then they can **deduce** downward to the small chunks. These deductive thinkers will say, "Give me your general concept or idea and let me see what that rationally implies." This describes the philosophical and artistic mind par excellence. A person who sorts globally will see the forest, but not the trees.

Consider **a vertical continuum** that goes from the smallest and tiniest of specific detail to the highest and most global perspective. The ability to move from specific to abstract describes the scientific form of intuition. Here a person *chunks up* to larger levels of information. The ability to *chunk down* to specifics describes the philosophical form of intuition. It enables one to apply abstract concepts. James and Woodsmall (1988) have created a chart that provides a model for this vertical continuum which they have designated as "Hierarchy of Ideas." We have adapted that chart to the one that we have renamed "Hierarchy of Language on the Scale of Specificity and Abstraction" (Figure 3.1 p.60).

3. Bateson (1972, 1979) described a third style, **abduction.** This refers to *not* moving up or down the scale of specificity to abstraction, but reasoning **"on the side"** by means of indirect thinking models: analogies, metaphors, stories, etc. As thinking laterally, or "on the side," rather than going up (induction) or down (deduction) the scale of abstraction/specificity, Bateson (1979) used *abduction* to talk about how we sometimes think about one thing *by thinking about something else.* He put it in contrast (or addition) to induction and deduction. Abduction shows up when one uses slogans, proverbs, icons, koans, riddles, stories, metaphors, poetry, myths, etc. to language their new high level abstraction (pp. 149-153). In lateral (abductive) thinking, we move (conceptually) to the side and think about examples. A person can do this before or after chunking up or down as well. (See "Marketing managers—Managers—Finance managers in Figure 3.1 as an example of abduction).

Identification:
1. *Global sorting/Deductive.* Those who sort in a general way easily recall times they felt bored and frustrated by someone who seemed compelled to feed them detail upon detail they really didn't want or need. These who think more abstractly do so in contradistinction to those who think more concretely and specifically. They begin with high level abstractions (principles, ideas, concepts, beliefs, etc.) and *deduce downward* to specific. Those who sort generally will often believe, "If you keep your eye on the dollars, the pennies will take care of themselves." In global processing, we think in terms of the big picture, our overall vision, the principle induced, etc.

2. *Detail sorting/Inductive.* Those who sort via specifics can recall the frustration of dealing with someone who seemed to talk "up in the air," vaguely, and did not supply them important details of reality. People who sort specifically often believe, "If you keep your eye on the pennies, the dollars will take care of themselves." They begin with specific details and *induce upward* to general principles and global conclusions.

3. *Lateral sorting/Abductive.* Not only do we reason through induction (the scientific mindset) and deduction (the philosophical mindset), but we also reason via analogy, metaphor, story, narrative, etc. (the poetic mindset). Here we think about one thing in terms of another. Bateson explained that much of his creativity arose from his abductive thinking.

James and Woodsmall (1988) estimate that 15% of people operate from the Specific category, 25% from Specific with some Global, and 60% from the Global.

Languaging: We can discover this pattern by asking, "What do you want first when you hear something new—the big picture or the details?" By just listening to someone giving lots of specifics, details, and sequences, usually indicates a specific processor. If someone talks in terms of overviews, principles, and concepts—you probably have a global sorter on your hands. Knowing **how,** and **at what level,** a person processes information gives us important information about how to package our communication to that person in an effective manner. Yeager (1985) describes the language at the top of the scale as "meta-words" (p. 153).

Pacing: To pace and communicate with someone who needs and wants details, give him or her lots of specific details, break things down into specifics. Use lots of modifiers and proper nouns. To communicate with someone who needs a more gestalt understanding first, talks in concepts, principles, and the larger ideas first. Skip the details when you start; you can go there later.

If you approach a gestalt processor with specifics you will likely bore and/or frustrate him in the communication interchange. If you approach a detail processor with generalities you will likely create distrust and confusion because your communication seems too vague and unrealistic to that person. To develop into a top-notch communicator, notice where the person starts on the **specificity/abstraction scale** and chunk your information at that level.

The model and questions in two NLP models, the Meta-Model and the Milton Model, provide language patterns for moving up and down the hierarchy continuum in terms of chunk size.

REBT Cognitive Distortion:
Ah! Jim's learning strategy (and his "representational" strength in that he favors and over-uses a particular representational system)—By global sorting, we may over-generalize too quickly using too many fluff words, non-referencing nouns, verbs, labels, etc., or draw inadequate conclusions too quickly. "I failed to make the team! I'll always be a failure. I can't ever do anything right!" By over-using the inductive reasoning pattern we may get so lost in details that we may lose our way in terms of our direction.

Contexts of Origin: These patterns can arise from modeling parenting figures who demonstrated either global or detail sorting; parenting figures who misused either style so that the child learned to value the opposite; trauma experience with a teacher or authority figure who forced a child to "go global" or "look at the details."

Further Reading: Bateson (1972, 1979) Bandler (1985).

Self-Analysis:
__ **S**pecific Inductive Sorting/**G**lobal Deductive Sorting (Detail/General)
__ **L**ateral Sorting or **A**bducting

Contexts:
    __ Work/Career   __ Intimates
    __ Relationships   __ Hobbies/Recreation
    __ Sports   __ Other:_____
    __ **High/Medium/Low** level   __ Driver MP: **Yes/No**

Figure 3.1
Hierarchy of Language on the Scale of Specificity & Abstraction

High-level Abstractions control lower-level ideas,representations, understandings

The Chunking Up Process

World of Meta-Level Abstractions
(the Kantian Categories)
(The Meta Meta-Programs & Meta-States)

Agreement Frame-of-Reference

↑

"What does that meaning mean to you?
What idea, example describes this?"

"For what purpose...?"

"What intention do you have in this...?"
"What does this mean to you?"

↑

When mediating, chunk up to get agreement.
Chunk-up until you get a nominalization.

The Structures of Intuition.
Deductive Intuition: the ability to take a general principle & chunk down to apply & relate to specific situations.

Inductive Intuition: the ability to chunk-up to find meanings, connections & relationships between the small pieces.

The Chunking Down Process:

↓

"What examples/references? "

"What specifically do you mean...?"
(Use any meta-model specificity question)

↓

More and More Specific Details & Distinctions

The World of Submodalities

The Big Picture
The World of Abstractions

↑

The language *mechanism* that moves us upward into higher level abstractions—*the Milton Model.*

Using intuiting to gather/process information live here in the world of the big chunks and into "Trance"

Existence
↑
Economy
↑
Business
↑
CEO

Marketing Managers—Finance Managers
↑
Managers
↑
Unit Managers
↑
Supervisors
↑
Administrative Support
↑

The language *mechanism* that enables us to move down the scale into Specificity—*the Meta Model* Those who gather information by Sensing live here. We come out of trance when we move here.

(Edited from Hierarchy of Ideas
Copyright 1987-1996, Tad James)

#2. Relationship Sort:
Matching/Mismatching
Sameness or Difference/Opposite

Concept: We generally have one of two basic ways of mentally operating in *how we work with and compare data* when we first confront new information. We can either look for what **matches** what we already know—what we find as **the same** as our existing knowledge, or we can look for what **differs** or mis-matches our knowledge. This meta-program plays a dominant role in determining our overall style of thinking as well as our world-view.

Elicitation: "What relationship do you first see between what you do now and what you did last year?" "What do you pay attention to first when you walk into a room?" Or, put four similar pens on a table, two in the same pattern and two in a different order. Then ask, "What relationship do you first notice when you view these four objects?"

Identification: How do you "run your brain" when you first attempt to understand something new? Do you look first for similarities and match up the new with what you already know? Or do you first check out the differences? Or do you first do one pattern and then immediately do the other?

1. *Sorting for sameness.* People who match, focus their attention on how things match up in a similar way to previous experience. They tend to value security and want their world to stay the same. They will not like change very much and may even feel threatened by it. Sorting for sameness creates a conservativism within. They like regularity and stability and so can stay on a job for several years without feeling bogged down. As the rapid growth and change of information and technology speeds up, sorting for sameness can create stress and difficulties. (Estimated at 10% of the USA population).

2. *Sorting for differences.* Those who mismatch will first notice the things that differ. They value change, variety, and newness. They will not like situations that remain static, but find them boring. When overdone, they will only notice differences, problems, and things that do not fit. This represents a fresher style of thinking in contrast to the more stable style of sameness. Difference sorters will notice the incorrectly hung picture. They also love change almost as a constant diet. "Change for change sake—if for no other reason!" Use terms about change, "re-engineering," for example, and it sounds like music in their ears. People who extremely mismatch will get excited about revolutionary changes. (Estimated at 5-10%.) Imagine someone who mismatches in an extreme way marrying someone who sorts for sameness at an extreme level!

3. *"Matching with Exception"* describe those who first notice similarities, then send their consciousness to differences. They like things to remain relatively the same, but allow change that comes about gradually. Generally, they prefer a little change in life every two or three years and can endure a major change every five to seven years. Such people live quite stable lives and tend to adapt well (most people fall here, estimated at 55-65%).

4. *"Mismatching with Exception"* describes those who first notice differences, and then send their mind to similarities. Such individuals tend to enjoy change and variety, but not revolutionary change. They enjoy rearranging things. This may lead to changing relationships, jobs, homes, etc. fairly frequently to satisfy the desire for variety (estimated at 20-25%).

5. *Sorting for sameness and differences equally.* This describes a fairly equal sorting for both of these distinctions. Such people frequently say, "The more things change, the more they stay the same." They will seek both change and diversity in a pretty equal way (estimated at 5-10%).

Figure 3.2

Matching	Matching	Balanced	Mismatching	**Mismatching**
Sameness	W/Exception	◄— Equally —►	W/Exceptions	**Differences**

Languaging: People who match will tell you how things look the same to them. They will focus on the things that remain stable. Mismatchers will talk about how the things differ. You will hear them talk about the "new, changed, different and revolutionary." People who *match with exception* and people who *mismatch with exception* will discuss how things gradually change over time. Listen for comparatives: "more, less, better."

Pacing: With those who match, emphasize areas of mutual agreement, security, what you both want, etc. and ignore differences, especially at first. With people who mismatch, emphasize how things differ, the new, the different, the distinctions, even the revolutionary. Talk about adventure and development. With those who have a bit of both (either pattern with exceptions) alternate your talk between things that match and those that mismatch.

Emoting: In communication, we often find those who mismatch difficult to deal with. This arises because they will think in mismatching ways to whatever we say! So their consciousness will constantly go to counter-examples of our statements. When we present an idea, suggestion, belief, etc., they will swish their brain to a mismatch representation and come back with a list of *"Yes, buts..."* to demonstrate why the idea will not work, or lacks validity. Used continually, this can feel very frustrating! So present the idea as something that probably won't work... They will then mismatch that. They will more likely give you a list of reasons why it will! "I have some serious reservations about whether we can get this project out on time..."

Polarity: Sorters describe those who have extreme patterns of mismatching. These people will respond automatically with *the opposite response* from whatever you desire. When this happens, congruently and sincerely *play their polarity*! In Uncle Remus, Brer Rabbit did this by begging Brer Fox to not throw him into the briar patch (the outcome that he actually wanted).

Languaging: When you offer a matching person something new they will typically respond with a similarity comparison, "Isn't this just like...?" They process first for similarities. Matchers generally feel quite comfortable with the tendencies to perceive similarities more than differences. When persuading them, play to their comfort zone and emphasize the similarities between your proposal and their familiarities.

Statistics: More people use a matching sort than a mismatching which explains the success of standardized franchises across the USA. James and Woodsmall (1988) say that 5-10% use Sameness, 55-65% use Same with Exception, 20-25% use Difference with Same, and only 5-10% use Difference.

Contexts of Origin: Conditioned from the parenting figures who modeled matching or mismatching. If parenting figures misused either style, the child may have learned to value the opposite. Trauma experience with parent, teacher or authority figure who totally forbade child to disagree may lead a child to develop a fear of mismatching, or to make a decision to always mismatch!

Further Reading: James & Woodsmall (1988).

Self-Analysis:
__Sameness Matching/Difference Mismatching

Contexts:
__ Work/Career	__ Intimates
__ Relationships	__ Hobbies/Recreation
__ Sports	__ Other:_____
__ High/**Medium**/Low level	__ Driver MP: **Yes**/**No**

#3. Representational System Sort:
Visual/Auditory/Kinesthetic/Auditory-digital

Concept: Brains "think" or create "thoughts" via the process of *re-presenting* sensory data (information) the "mind" that we process via our external senses. Thus we "see" images and pictures, we "hear" sounds, noise, music, words, we "feel" sensations, movements, etc. NLP describes these *sensory systems* of information inputting and processing of **the representational systems.** They comprise the essential components of "thought."

Bandler and Grinder (1975) also noted that people tend to develop *a "most highly favored" representational system* and use this for most of their "thinking." Thus, some people operate more in the **visual system**, others in the **auditory system**, others in the **kinesthetic system**, and yet others in the **auditory digital** (language) system. (Too much reading, higher education, etc. can initiate one to mentally live more and more in a "world of words.") After Bandler and Grinder designated the sensory channel a person relies primarily on as one's most favored representation system, they identified the system one most uses to *access or reaccess stored data* as the Lead System. They frequently will differ. As a result, a person could *see* a scene and recall it visually (lead system), but not realize that they use that process or have awareness of such—only have *a feeling* of such (using their kinesthetic Representational System).

Elicitation: "When you think about something or learn something new, which sensory channel do you prefer?" "Which channel do you use most commonly?"

Identification: We can discover this pattern of human processing in two primary ways: (1) by listening for the kind of *predicates* (verbs, adverbs, adjectives) a person uses and (2) calibrating to *eye accessing patterns*. We can listen for visual, auditory and/or kinesthetic predicates. We can also observe a person's eye scanning movements wherein eyes moving up generally indicates visual access, down to the right for kinesthetic access, eyes moving horizontally on a level plane and down to the left as auditory access (see Appendix C).

1. Visual representers: People who process and organize their world visually usually sit up erect, move eyes upward when visualizing, breathe high in chest, use high tones, move quick, and use visual predicates (see, imagine, clear, picture, etc.). Visuals look at people and want others to look at them when they talk. In terms of body types, many visuals appear as thin and lanky.

Those who sort by seeing tend to want "space" that they can see. So when you communicate with them, back off and give them room for seeing.

2. Auditory representers: People who process and organize their world with sounds move their eyes from side to side when accessing information. Their respiration comes from the middle of the chest in a regular and rhythmic way. Many will have a gift of the gab, enunciate clearly, demonstrate a sensitivity to tones and volumes, sub-vocalize, not look at the person talking so that they can point their ear to hear better. In body type, they typically have a moderate form between the skinny visual and the heavy kinesthetic, sometimes a pear-shaped body. These processors will use more auditory predicates (hear, loud, soft, clear as a bell, sounds right, etc.).

3. Kinesthetic representers: People who process and organize things with their body sensations will move their eyes downward when assessing and use kinesthetic predicates (touch, feel, grab, warm, moves me, impact, etc.). They breathe deeply, talk and move slower, gesture a lot, etc.

4. Auditory-digital representers: Laborde (1984) describes them as "the cerebrals" because they can "live in their heads" and can develop "a thick filter of language between their sensory perceptions and their experiences." Such people can live so much "in a world of words" that they have little awareness of pictures, sounds, or sensations. This puts them in "computer mode" in the Satir Categories (#31). Woodsmall had noted that such persons love lists, criteria, rules, meta-communication, etc.

Pacing: To match a person communicationally, use the kind of predicates that fit their favorite representational system. This enables one to "get on another's channel" and talk in that person's language. Expect confusion and responses as if you speak a foreign language when you mismatch someone's style. If the person over-uses one system, they will often respond as if amnesic and literally will not hear what you say.

Languaging: Listen for specific visual, auditory, and kinesthetic predicates. Auditory digital language involves lists, rules, criteria, abstractions, nominalizations, etc.

Contexts of Origin: One's home of origin may have put more value on seeing, hearing, feeling, or saying words. The most significant persons may have valued one of these over the others. Trauma experience involving the tabooing of one of these, "Be seen and not heard!" may lead a person to over-value the visual channel to the auditory. Frequently, a child over-exposed to traumatic experiences will become overly associated into the kinesthetic mode. As a result, they may even shut down their visual and auditory inputting.

Further Reading: Bandler and Grinder (1976).

Self-Analysis:
__ **Visual**/**Auditory**/**Kinesthetic**/**Auditory**-digital (Language)

Contexts:
__ Work/Career	__ Intimates
__ Relationships	__ Hobbies/Recreation
__ Sports	__ Other:_____
__ **High**/**Medium**/**Low** level	__ Driver MP: **Yes**/**No**
__ Cross Modalities: V-A, V-K, K-V, etc.	
__ Drivers	

#4. Information Gathering Style:
Uptime/Downtime

Concept: In processing data, a person can notice and focus on the internal world of his or her own subjectivity, which we designate as in *"downtime,"* or can notice and focus primarily on the external world, which we designate as in *"uptime."*

Elicitation: "When you listen to a speech or conversation, do you tend to hear the specific sensory-based data (VAK) or do you go inside (downtime) and listen for what the speaker means?" "Do you want to hear proof and evidence from the outside or do you take more interest in your internal thoughts about it?"

Identification: **Uptime** refers to having full sensory awareness of things in the environment and paying attention to what we receive from the outside. When listening, we process by *attending descriptively* to the other person's responses (posture, eye contact, gestures, etc.) rather than by our assumptions of those cues. When we operate from an uptime state, we generate little information from within, from out of our model of the world.

Downtime, by contrast, refers to going "inside" of ourselves, so to speak, and taking cognizance primarily of our own thoughts and emotions. To do this makes us "blind and deaf" to the external world. To do this means that we have accessed a "trance" state (*transitioned* from the waking state to an internally focused state) of internal awareness wherein our own images, sounds, words, sensations, etc. provide the most compelling data. In downtime, a person doesn't seem present. The person has "zoned out" and gone somewhere else. So we will see a minimum of eye contact, perhaps a staring off into space, a defocusing of the eyes, etc.

You can expect uptime and downtime patterns to constantly alternate. If you try to listen to someone from a downtime state, you will make assumptions based on your own internal thinking and feeling and will more likely project onto the other rather than receive from the other. This represents, obviously, a fantastically poor listening strategy!

Pacing: Match your words to either the external or internal world depending on the person's state.

Languaging: Listen for the difference between descriptive language of the outside world versus the evaluative language of the inside world.

Emoting: Uptime emotions will tend to correspond with the immediate environment. Downtime emotions will tend to lack correspondence to the environment.

Contexts of Origin: The frequency arises from modeling of parents or emotionally significant persons, or dis-identification from them if they used one of the patterns. Trauma experience of chaos, violence, and distress so that child escaped via the inscape of Downtime fantasies, dreams, hopes, etc. or went into hyper-alert state, always in Uptime.

Further Reading: Dilts, Bandler, and Grinder, DeLozier (1980).

Self-Analysis:
__ Downtime/Uptime

Contexts:
__ Work/Career	__ Intimates
__ Relationships	__ Hobbies/Recreation
__ Sports	__ Other: _____
__ High/Medium/Low level	__ Driver MP: **Yes/No**

#5. Epistemology Sort:
Sensors/Intuitors

Concept: There exists two key ways for gathering information from things: by either using one's *senses* or by *intuiting* (This meta-program simply expresses a further development of #4). Those who use their *senses* primarily gather information about the world through empirical means—the sensory modalities. They use their capacities for seeing, hearing, feeling, smelling and tasting to deal with concrete and factual experiences. Using the uptime access state, they tend to function primarily as empiricists and pragmatists (even positivists).

Those who use their *intuitions* gather information through non-sensory means—by their in-knowing of things. They look for possibilities, make assumptions about the meanings of things; look for relationships, and appraise larger significances of things. And because they approach things abstractly and holistically, they tend to function as rationalists and visionaries (even as phenomenologists and constuctivists). They will tend to do more downtime accessing.

Elicitation: "If you began to study a subject, would you take more interest in facts and their applications for the now or would you find more interest in the ideas and relationships between the facts and their application for the future?"

Identification: We can discover this pattern by asking, "When you listen to a speech or conversation, do you tend to hear the specific data given or do you intuit what the speaker must mean and/or intend?" "Do you want proof and evidence or do you find it more interesting to explore your intuitions about it?" "Which do you find more important—the actual or the possible?" "Upon what basis do you make most of your decisions—the practical or abstract possibilities?"

1. By *intuiting*, we gather information but primarily trust our intuition in determining the meaning. In so doing, we may not pay much attention to external observation. We may pay more attention to it later when it "pops up" in consciousness. *Intuiting* moves us to use *meaning* to determine facts, not vice versa; 25% of the USA population operates in this manner. The danger arises in *intuiting*—we may end up ignoring or disregarding sensory data that may conflict with internal intuitions! Intuiting leads one to think of oneself as imaginative, ingenious, and in touch with one's unconscious. Intuitors often think of sensors as dull and boring. *Intuiting* leads to possibility thinking, tolerance of complexity, appreciation of aesthetic and theoretical, autonomy, pattern thinking, loving to work at a symbolic level, creative level, etc. The intuitive style will involve more evaluative language and labeling.

2. By *sensing (sensors)*, we primarily prefer to work with facts and known meanings. 75% of the USA population use this style of perceiving the immediate, real, and practical facts of life's experiences. The danger that arises from *sensing too much*—we may disregard hunches, creative intuitions, dreams, wild ideas, etc. Sensing leads to thinking of oneself as practical, down-to-earth, real, etc. often think of intuitors as unrealistic,

having their head in the clouds, impractical. *Sensing* leads to factual and empirical thinking, valuing authority and pragmatism, appreciates realism, order, goal-oriented tasks, etc. The sensing style will focus primarily on descriptive, sensory-based language.

Languaging: Listen for sensory based words in those who primarily operate from the sensor position, and for "intuition, possibilities," and concepts in those who operate from the intuitor position. Accordingly, you may find (as we have) that more often than not intuiting persons will sort globally and sensing persons will sort specifically.

Pacing: With sensors you communicate more effectively by using the sensory modalities, by being specific, detailed and explicit. With intuitors communicate with more abstractions, intuitions, and talk about possibilities as well as your overall frame.

James (1989) makes this interesting observation about intelligence tests,

> "Intelligence tests that are currently in use in the United States tend to be biased toward Intuitors, since a *sensor* needs to weigh all of the answers for a specific question in the test, while an *intuitor* can often see at a glance which is the right answer. So on the Myers-Briggs, there tends to be a direct correlation between the score of the individual on the intuitor scale and his level of intelligence."
> p. 103).

RET Cognitive Distortions: The evaluative thinking and intuiting pattern, when over-done, can lead to Labeling and to Mind-Reading. Labeling arises from using too general, vague, and unspecified language that fails to keep the evaluation index to person, place, time, event, etc; mind-reading attempts to intuit another person's internal states, intentions, motivations, and thoughts without checking with the person for validation. When so intuiting, we should make our guesses tentative, avoid using "you" language, invite feedback, and present our assumptions gently.

Contexts of Origin: Same as #4. Valued, appreciated, and rewarded for either Sensing or Intuiting.

Further Reading: James and Woodsmall (1988).

Self-Analysis:
__ **S**ensor Inputting/Intuitor Inputting

Contexts:
    __ Work/Career   __ Intimates
    __ Relationships   __ Hobbies/Recreation
    __ Sports   __ Other: _____
    __ **H**igh/**M**edium/**L**ow level   __ Driver MP: Yes/No

#6. Perceptual Categories Sort:
Black-and-white vs. Continuum

Concept: Some minds operate more skillfully, and/or have received more training, in discerning broad categories while others operate with more sophisticated discernment within the gray areas in between the polar ends of a continuum.

Elicitation: "When you think about things or make decisions, do you tend to operate in black-and-white categories or does your mind go to the steps and stages that lie in between?" "Which do you value most?"

Identification: Black-and-white thinking enables a person to make clear and definite distinctions. It motivates one to make quick decisions and to adopt a more "judgment" perspective. Continuum thinking, by contrast, enables one to discriminate at much finer levels, motivates one to make fewer judgments, and to adopt a more indecisive style.

Languaging: Continuum thinkers will talk about the gray areas, use lots of qualifiers in their language, and typically continually correct themselves about other possibilities. When over-done, they will "yes, but" themselves and end up continually in a state of indecision. Black -and-white thinkers will speak in a far more definite and definitive way, express far less toler-ance, will feel tempted to speak dogmatically, and will typically talk in perfectionistic terms.

Emoting: Everybody tends to go to the black-and-white style of thinking when they experience a strong stress state. When we get to our stress threshold, the fight/flight syndrome kicks in as our autonomic nervous system withdraws blood from the brain and stomach and sends the blood to our larger muscle groups for fighting or fleeing (See #13). This consequently seems to bring out the all-or-nothing (survivalistic) thinking pattern—thinking most appropriate for extreme situations of danger or threat.

Pacing: After identifying the dominance of one style or the other, match the perceptual style that you find.

RET Cognitive Distortion: When the black-and-white categorical thinker over-does this pattern it can result in All-or-Nothing Thinking. The dichotomizing style of thinking sorts the world of events and people in to polarities (good-bad; right-wrong; mind-body, etc.) which may not map out the territory with any accuracy at all. Frequently such things totally delete all choices in the middle.

Contexts of Origin: All children begin their cognitive processes in terms of separating out and distinguishing the larger distinctions first (black-and-white, either-or). Piaget identified this as the *concrete thinking stage.* Over time a child may learn to make finer and finer distinctions and so develop the continuum thinking mode. Some physiological conditions of brain functioning can inhibit, even prevent, a person from moving into the operational and post-operational thinking stages. Trauma experiences can induce a person frequently into a fight/flight mode (#13). This causes a regression to more survivalistic thinking in a black-and-white mode.

Further Reading: Piaget (1954). Korzybski (1941/1994).

Self-Analysis:
__ **Black-and-white/Continuum Thinking**

Contexts:
__ Work/Career	__ Intimates
__ Relationships	__ Hobbies/Recreation
__ Sports	__ Other: _____
__ **High/Medium/Low level**	__ **Driver MP: Yes/No**

#7. Attribution Style:
Best vs. Worst Scenario Thinking
Optimists/Pessimists—Helpless/Empowered

Concept: Whether a person first looks at the problems, dangers, threats, difficulties, challenges of a situation or the opportunities, possibilities, wonders, excitements, and thrill determines whether their mind goes first to worst or best case scenarios. Sorting for the best case scenario orients one in an optimistic, hopeful, goal-oriented, and empowered way. Sorting for the worst-case scenario orients one in a pessimistic, negative, and problem-focused way. When overdone, pessimistic thinking generates feelings of hopelessness.

Elicitation: When you look at a problem, do you tend first to consider the worst case scenario or the best? Does your mind go to problems and difficulties or to opportunities and positive challenges?

Identification:
1. *Pessimists.* Those who first have their minds conditioned or trained to go to worst case scenario types of situations turn into "pessimists" who think "negatively." Yet as their consciousness entertains problems and difficulties, they develop expert skill at quality control analysis, technicians for trouble-shooting problems, and proof-readers. When over-done, they can quickly and automatically attribute the "helpless" format on things. Seligman (1975) summarized this in **three "P"s:** *personal, pervasive, and permanent*—the problem relates to me personally ("I'm flawed."), operates pervasively ("It affects everything in my life!"), and will do so permanently ("It can't change.").

Seligman's research focused around two concepts: *controllability and predictability*. When animals or humans conclude from a particular context that they have no ability to effect or control a result, and cannot predict results, they learn "helplessness."

Sheila had an ideal family—a husband who loved her and three children. Then one day her husband left her and the family for another woman. These events triggered in Sheila old memories of her own father deserting her and her mother during her childhood. Three years later, her mother died of cancer. At that time, her uncle took her in. The divorce, her mother's death, and now her divorce all contributed in Sheila locking her mind into the worst-case scenario style of thinking. It fit her feelings about life. But then that style of sorting motivated her to look for the worse in everything! And that, in turn, lead to a severe depression, dependency on others, and anti-depressants.

To experience healing from this, I (BB) worked with her to help her recode her painful memories so that she could then undo the decision to see the dark side of things. Then we worked to empower her to look through the eyes of optimism.

2. *Optimists.* Those who have their minds conditioned or trained to go first to the best case scenarios operate as the "optimists" who move through life with golden perspectives of visions and dreams. They can skillfully catch and present a vision, keep people motivated with a long term dream, etc. In contrast to the negative and helpless frame, thinking optimistically activates an "empowerment" frame-of-mind. When over-done, this style can lead to viewing everything with "golden glasses" so the person lacks the capability to face a difficulty directly and honestly. Too much of this sorting and a person becomes motivated to deny problems.

Languaging & Pacing: Those who think pessimistically first will speak about problems, dangers, threats, difficulties, etc. Meet them at that model of their world. Those who think optimistically will first talk about dreams, visions, solutions, ideas, suggestions, etc. Pace where they begin, then lead to the other side of the continuum. This develops *flexibility of consciousness*.

Emoting: This pattern will obviously generate corresponding "positive," pleasant, and "up" emotions for the optimists and "negative," unpleasant, even painful and distressful emotions for pessimistic sorters.

RET Cognitive Distortion: Those given to the problem-orientation mode of perceiving, when over-doing it, can end up *filtering out the positive* to their own detriment and that of others. When this occurs in times of high levels of stress, distress, and upset, it can lead to a tunnel-vision that views the world through dark glasses. When a person does this, he or she will then disqualify and discount solutions, positive ideas, suggestions, resources, etc. as illustrated in the example with Sheila.

Contexts of Origin: Modeling of and identification with parents and others can lead to the development of either style, Optimism or Pessimism. Overly sheltered and protected in childhood may lead to extreme development of rose-colored optimism; trauma experiences may lead to fatalistic pessimism. Physiological sensitivity to stimuli may lead to the "worst case scenario" type of thinking—more awareness of what may go wrong (see #13 also).

Further Reading: Seligman (1975, 1991).

Self-Analysis:
__ **O**ptimists (Best Case, Empowerment)/**P**essimists (Worst Case, Helplessness)

Contexts:
__ Work/Career	__ Intimates
__ Relationships	__ Hobbies/Recreation
__ Sports	__ Other: _____
__ **H**igh/**M**edium/**L**ow level	__ Driver MP: **Yes/No**

#8. Perceptual Durability Sort:
Permeable/Impermeable

Concept: This meta-program addresses the *quality* of our mental constructs in terms of their *permeability or impermeability*. What kind of mental constructs do you create or build? Some people process ideas, thoughts, beliefs, values, etc. in ways that generate strong, solid, firm, and impermeable constructs (both as ideology and representation) while others process such with much more permeability. This means that other influences (ideas, emotions, experiences) can permeate to effect the person's thinking.

Elicitation: "As you begin to think about some of your mental constructs, your ideas of success and failure, of love and forgiveness, of relationships and work, of your personal qualities... do you find the representations of what you know as permanent or unstable? How can you tell?" "Think about something that you know without a doubt—about yourself. Now think of something that you know but you know with doubts and questions... How do these sets of representations differ?"

Identification: Some people, in building their mental constructs, build impermeable ones, such that they seem,

> "not capable of being revised or replaced, no matter what new experiences are available... a person can tolerate a number of subordinate inconsistencies without discarding or modifying the overall construct" (Schultz, 1990, pp. 390-1).

These *impermeable construct people* typically move through life with rigid and ungiving beliefs and belief systems.

Others build constructs that have the quality of high permeability. Such permeable constructs "are capable of being revised and extended in the light of new experiences." Cade and O'Hanlon (1993) describe this distinction about the range of permeability of constructs as *cognitive complexity*,

> "...this may be defined in terms of the large number of independent dimensions available to be used in the drawing of distinctions at any time, can arguably be equated with flexibility, responsiveness, tolerance, understanding, creativity, etc." (p. 27).

I (MH) met a client once who suffered from extreme fluctuations in emotions about herself. In response, I first elicited a full description of several repeated events in which she felt especially resourceful. Then I amplified and anchored those states. But as soon as we had finished, she couldn't *hold on to or maintain* those representations or feelings. Other thoughts, memories, and feelings from other events would immediately permeate them and thereby contaminate her sense of resourcefulness.

This lead me to question her *Perceptual Durability Sort.* Once she realized that she had habitualized this permeability sorting pattern (a meta-level awareness on her part), she ran an ecology check on it. Upon realizing how it sabotaged her, she decided to develop more flexibility of consciousness so that she could choose to create impermeability of his resourceful state. She then made that change. Thereafter, she began to experience more solid representations and feelings about herself so that she could live and maintain a more solid sense of herself.

Languaging: Listen for terms and words of hesitation, doubt, questions, shiftingness, etc. to detect permeable constructs. Listen for terms and words of sureness, definitiveness, "no question," "undeniable," "absolutely," etc. to detect impermeable constructs. Look also for the modal operators (#23) of necessity ("must") and impossibility ("can't") connected with impermeability and those of possibility ("can," "will") connected with permeability.

Contexts of Origin: Degree of intrusion and respect for personal boundaries, including privacy, right to think-feel and respond as separate and autonomous person may lead one to creating solid representations in consciousness that persevere. Chaotic and rushed environments may have provided too little time for a child to consolidate representations. Taboos against thinking in certain ways, intrusive models who ripped up thoughts, ideas, ways of thinking may lead to over-permeable style.

Further Reading: Cade and O'Hanlon (1993) *A Brief Guide to Brief Therapy.* Schultz (1990) *Theories of Personality.*

Self-Analysis:
__ Permeable Sorting/Impermeable Sorting

Contexts:
__ Work/Career	__ Intimates
__ Relationships	__ Hobbies/Recreation
__ Sports	__ Other: _____
__ High/**Medium**/Low level	__ Driver MP: **Yes**/**No**

#9. Focus Sort:
Screeners/Non-screeners

Concept: The term "stimulus screening" refers to how much of the environment a person characteristically screens out. When they do, they thereby reduce the environmental load of input stimuli as well as a person's arousal level to it. In this regard, people typically fall somewhere along a continuum between screening out *none* of it to screening out *a great deal* of it.

Elicitation: "When you think about the kind of places where you can study or read, can you do this everywhere or do you find that some places seem too noisy or have too much of other stimuli that prevents concentration?" "Describe your favorite environment for concentrating on something?" "How distractable do you find yourself generally in life whether reading, playing, talking, thinking to yourself, etc.?"

Identification: This meta-program relates to how long it takes for a person to experience stimulus overload and therefore neuro-semantic "stress." Because we all have stress limits, none of us can endure frequent and extremely high states of arousal levels without going into overload. In chronic stimulus overload our nervous systems reach their limit and fatigue sets in. Not only does physical tiredness result, but other defense mechanisms also begin to kick in.

1. *Non-screeners.* We call people who characteristically do little stimulus screening, non-screeners. Their attention to the environment tends to operate in a diffuse way. They typically see, hear, smell, and otherwise sense a great deal of what goes on around them. They will also tend to *not* rank the various elements of a situation and so fail to shut out unimportant or irrelevant stimuli. As a result, they often experience places as complex and over-loaded with triggers for distraction. Mehrabrian (1976) notes,

> "Low levels of stimulus screening simply indicate less selectivity and therefore amplified arousal to different situations whether pleasant or unpleasant. We can say that non-screeners have a more delicately or finely tuned emotional mechanism. They are relatively sensitive to small variations in stimuli and may be put out of whack by gross ones." (p. 60).

Since I (BB) operate primarily from the auditory sensory mode (#3), I find noise distracting and, at times, annoying. While teaching, if a student ruffles papers or click a pen, I will typically tactfully ask him or her to stop. It bothers me that much. This sort even has affected me while sleeping—when I haven't screened out barking dogs.

2. *Screeners.* People who, more typically, operate in a selective way as to what they notice we designate as screeners. They automatically and unconsciously rank facets of a complex situation so as to reduce the need to attend to everything in a diffuse way. They move into an environment in a focused way by screening out the less relevant elements. A high level screener can screen out so much that he or she may come across as non-attentive, zoned out, and even uncaring. Autism describes an extreme state of screening.

By way of contrast with Bob, I (MH) screen so much that I can totally ignore all noises, voices, sounds, etc. while studying in a busy airport. I even missed a plane one time having become so totally engrossed in some book!

During my very first training with Richard Bandler, I innocently clicked away on my lap top computer while sitting on the front row. It didn't bother me! Richard attempted several tactful hypnotic (embedded) commands to get me to stop—I didn't "hear"this. Finally, he had to stop, look at me, and in his typical manner, tell me in no uncertain words to cut it out! Screener or non-screener?

Emoting: In the same environment, those who do not screen will feel much more aroused (even stressed) than those who screen. Mehrabrian (1976) notes also,

> "What is more, the non-screeners' reaction to novel, changing or sudden situations lasts longer than that of screeners." (p. 59).

Typically, passives will tend to screen less than aggressives inasmuch as they sort for danger signals in the environment (see #13). Look for signs of distractibility in those who do not screen and un-disturbability in those who do,

> "Non-screeners reach the maximum tolerable arousal levels more quickly and more often than screeners. This means that prolonged exposure to high-load environments tend to overwork the non-screeners' physiological mechanisms. Thus, stressful settings, which are often unpleasant as well as loaded, take a heavier toil among non-screeners than among screeners." (p. 60).

Non-screeners also show a higher degree of empathy for others inasmuch as they feel sensitive to the emotional reactions of others. Mehrabrian says that "there is a slight tendency for women to screen less than men."

Languaging: Listen for the non-screener to value and talk more about "quiet, peace, comfort," etc. They will complain about noise preventing them from thinking, smells overwhelming them, etc. The screener will value and talk about "excitement, adventure, novel experiences and places," etc.

Neurological indicators: For non-screeners who experience high physio-logical arousal, they also have peripheral vasoconstriction—namely, the capillaries in the hands and feet contract. This means that the skin temper-ature of these organs have a lower temperature than one's body tempera-ture,

> "Highly aroused people are likely to have cold feet or cold hands."
> (Mehrabrian, 1976, p. 60).

Contexts of Origin: Very similar to #8 with regard to contexts of intrusion or non-intrusion, time for thought and meditation or lack of it. Children begin life with seemingly little ability to screen out and so learn how to selectively attend. Most children need permission to screen, and adults can easily prevent them from doing so.

Further Reading: Mehrabrian (1976).

Self-Analysis:
__ Non-screening Sort/**S**creening Sort

Contexts:
__ Work/Career   __ Intimates
__ Relationships   __ Hobbies/Recreation
__ Sports   __ Other: _____
__ High/**Medium**/Low level   __ Driver MP: **Yes**/**No**

#10. Philosophical Direction:
Why/How
Origins/Solution Process (Philosophical/Practical)

Concept: How "minds" think in terms of philosophical direction alternate between "why" did this or that happen and "what" does this or that mean in terms of origins and source.

Elicitation: "When you think about a subject (whether a problem or not), do you first think about causation, source, and origins (why), or do you think about use, function, direction, destiny (how)?"

Identification:
1. *Why* people tend to sort for the philosophical past and so value (or over-value) understanding its origin and source. The assumption that drives this mental software goes like this, "If I can understand where something came from, I gain mastery over it." In psychology, this shows up in what Bandler and Grinder have designated, "psycho-archaeology" as manifested in the Freudian and Jungian styles. (Glasser, 1965, has provided portraits of this.)

When those who sort for *why* go to therapy—guess what they want to know? The why—the cause and origin of the problem! People who have experienced traumatic experiences frequently get themselves "stuck" in their trauma state and then generate PTSD (post traumatic stress disorder) because they loop around and around asking about "the why."

2. *How* people tend to sort for the use and purpose of things. They devote little attention (but some) to origins, they care more about the "so what?" The *how* philosophical direction moves them into a more solution focus rather than problem focus. "What can I do about it?" "How can I use or respond to this?"

Languaging and Personality: The why orientation turns a person into a philosopher (#21 perceiving) whereas the how orientation turns a person into a pragmatic who takes action in changing things (#21 judging).

Contexts of Origin: Which philosophical orientation predominated in the minds of one's parents and teachers? Did one identify and model it or dis-identify from that style of orientation? Trauma experiences tend to encourage people to look for reasons, origins, etc.

Further Reading: Learning-Style Inventory, Kolb (1981).

Self-Analysis:
__ **Why** - Origins/**How** - Function

Contexts:
__ Work/Career	__ Intimates
__ Relationships	__ Hobbies/Recreation
__ Sports	__ Other: _____
__ **High/Medium/Low level**	__ Driver MP: **Yes/No**

#11. Reality Structure Sort:
Aristotelian/Non-Aristotelian (Static/Process)

Concept: How "minds" think about the territory of "reality"—whether in terms of something static, permanent, things, solid, eternal, etc., or changing, processes, movement, etc., determines the kind of map they use in navigating life.

Elicitation: "When you think about reality, do you tend to think about it as something permanent and solid made up of things or do you think of it as a dance of electrons, fluid, ever-changing, made up of processes?"

Identification:
1. *Aristotelian.* People who think of reality as static adopt **the Aristotelian view of things** which enables them to view life from a macroscopic or microscopic perspective of physics. They live (mentally and conceptually) in a world filled up with Things, Objects, People, etc. and so then talk primarily in terms of Nouns and Nominalizations. This leads them to reify

processes into Things (nominalizations). They tend also to use Aristotelian "logic" that shows up in the "is" of Identity ("He *is* a failure") and the "is" of predication ("She *is* stupid"). Talking about the "ises", they live in a pretty solid and "frozen universe" wherein they can feel stuck and view things as unchangeable.

2. *Non-Aristotelian.* People who think of reality in terms of process have adopted **a more non-Aristotelian mindset** and so view life primarily from a sub-microscopic perspective of physics. This enables them to appreciate and use the quantum level. They conceptually think about reality as "a process reality" full of energy manifestations, hence processes, actions, etc. so that "things" represent a larger level macroscopic illusion of the nervous system, a workable and usable concept, but only that—a concept. In talking, they use more verbs, functional language, behavioral descriptions and so live more in a process world.

Languaging and Personality: The language of nouns and nominalizations generates for the Aristotelian mind a solid black-and-white world (#6), encourages more concrete thinking (#1), and so leads to more judging (#21). The language of verbs and processes leads to more continuum thinking, how thinking (#10), more perceiving, fluidity in personality (flexibility).

Our public education system has powerfully contributed to the Aristotelian type of thinking. Such also permeates our culture even at the end of the twentieth century. The psychological community still labels using the DSM IV. If a person gets labeled as having "a panic disorder" and goes on the public dole, then tax dollars supports that style of living in fear. Korzybski (1933/1994) posited what a Non-Aristotelian way of thinking-feeling and talking would look like. NLP has built upon this foundation. Thus the NLP response to a "panic disorder" turns it back into a process by asking, "How do you know when to panic yourself? How do you get your body to become filled with fear? What do you see, say to yourself, etc.? If you didn't do that, what would you experience?"

Contexts of Origin: Our nervous system induces us all first into the Aristotelian way of perceiving and thinking. So to shift this meta-program depends entirely upon education out of the Aristotelian set of perceptions that characterizes the "common sense" at the macro-level. That level defines the child's mind and the mind of the primitive. The Non-Aristotelian mindset arises from the world views encouraged by quantum mechanics, quantum physics (non-Newtonian physics), Einsteinian thinking, etc.

Further Reading: Korzybski (1941/1994).

Self-Analysis:
__ Aristotelian Static/Non-Aristotelian Process Sorting

Contexts:
__ Work/Career	__ Intimates
__ Relationships	__ Hobbies/Recreation
__ Sports	__ Other: _____
__ High/**Medium**/Low level	__ Driver MP: **Yes/No**

#12. Communication Channel Preference:
Verbals/Non-Verbals; Analogue/Digital

Concept: Information comes to us along two primary channels—the verbal and the non-verbal channel. *The verbal channel* contains all of the symbolic systems that we have developed to communicate: language, music, math, art, computer languages, etc. *The non-verbal channel* contains all of the sign cues that arise from our physiological and neurological state: breathing, posture, muscle tone and tension, gestures, eye scanning, etc. Bandler and Grinder (1976) described the verbal channel as containing *content* messages and the non-verbal as *analogical* and *relationship* messages (p. 34). While both "channels" provide a multitude of messages and data, some people tend to favor one channel or the other,

"...in any set of simultaneously presented messages, we accept each message as an equally valid representation of the person's experience. In our model, no one of these paramessages can be said to be more valid—or truer, or more representative of the client—than any other. No one of a set of paramessages can be said to be meta to any other member of its set. Rather, our understanding of a set of paramessages is that each of these messages represents a portion of the client's model(s) of the world. When the client is communicating congruently, each of the paramessages matches, fits with, is congruent with each of the others. When the client is communicating incongruently, we know that the models of the world which he is using to guide his behavior are inconsistent." (pp. 37-38).

Elicitation: "When you think about communicating with somebody, what do you tend to give more importance to—*what* they say or *how* they say it?" "When you communicate, do you pay more attention to the words and phrases that you use or to your tone, tempo, volume, eye contact, etc.?" "When you hear someone say something that seems incongruent with how they express it, and you don't know which message to go with, which do you favor as the more 'real' message?"

Identification:
1.   *Verbal.* People who sort primarily for *what* another says, their language, terms, phrases, etc. hear and operate more on the verbal channel than the non-verbal. The more a person uses the Auditory-Digital representation system (#3), the more likely he or she will also favor the verbal channel. Certain professions obviously overload this channel: lawyers, writers, beaurocrats. Those with the Emotional coping style of "aggression" (the "go at" stress response, #13) may also more likely favor the verbal channel than those who use the "go away from" stress response. The latter, with their focus on danger signals, will typically pay more attention to the non-verbal channels.

2.   *Non-Verbal.* People who sort primarily for *how* others talk will sort for tone, tempo, volume, pitch, breathing, etc. They will tend to value and care more for the neurological state that the person's physiology demonstrates than what the person actually says. More typically such individuals will distrust the verbal channel knowing how easily others can "just say words" to cover up some reality. Some professions obviously favor the non-verbal channels (e.g. acting, nursing, sales, etc.). When over-done they can jump to conclusions in mind-reading and even telling others what the "really" think and feel. These individuals may also tend to favor the Intuitor's sort (#5).

3.   *Balanced.* Those who take both channels as equally valid expressions of information and data (communication) will treat both categories as para-messages without favoring one over the other.

Languaging and Personality: Those who favor the verbal channels want words and will tend to distrust their "senses" and intuitions when they pick up messages and signals from the non-verbal channels. You may hear them saying things like, "Just tell me what you think or feel." "Just take me at my word." They may over-talk and trust talk and "talk" devices: debate, logic, discussion, etc. Those who favor the non-verbal channel will say things like, "Those are just words, I want to see actions." "Your words say one thing, but your tone another."

People who consider that the highest quality information comes from behavior will develop a strong interest in their *people watching skills* whereas those who assume the highest quality information comes in language will develop more linguistic skills.

Accessing Meta-Programs: How does this meta-program effect your accessing of the linguistic markers (verbal) and physiology (non-verbal) that inform you about meta-programs?

Contexts of Origin: One's favorite Representational System will play a role in the development of this meta-program. Also if one could trust parents and teachers to back up their words with appropriate and congruent actions, one may come to favor the verbal channel. Disappointment and trauma surrounding the talk of adults may lead one to distrust that channel and prefer to "read" the non-verbal channels. Thus one's learning and experiencing history with the role of language accurately or deceptively representing interpersonal reality, plays a crucial role.

Further Reading: Bandler and Grinder (1975, 1976).

Self-Analysis:
__ **V**erbal/**N**on-Verbal/**B**alanced

Contexts:
__ Work/Career   __ Relationships
__ Intimates   __ Hobbies/Recreation
__ Sports   __ Other: _____
__ **H**igh/**M**edium/**L**ow level   __ Driver MP: **Yes**/**No**

Summary

As we move through life we *mentally* learn to make discriminations. We learn to first process either globally or in detail; to match for sameness or mismatch for difference; to favor either the visual, auditory, kinesthetic, or language system; to gather information from the world or intuitively from inside; to consider solutions or problems; to endure or fade away; to focus or distract; to wonder why or wonder how; to process things as static at the macro-level or as processes at the micro-levels, and to pay more attention to the digital language system or the analogue system. In these "mental" categories (as well as others), we learn to sort and pay attention to the information around us.

These first meta-programs—now give us a dozen distinctions that we can make with regard to how our brains (and the brains of others) can process information cognitively. Before proceeding to the next chapter, take some time to think through the following questions. Even better, get out a notebook and do some writing.

- What have you learned about your own style of "thinking" as you read through these descriptions?
- Which meta-programs have you discovered most powerfully drive your subjective experiences? How well do they serve you?
- How much *flexibility of consciousness* do you have with these first twelve meta-programs?
- Have you learned to over-do any of these first meta-programs so that a given processing style creates problems or difficulties for you?

Take some time to go through this list of the cognitive meta-programs and imagine using the other side of the continuum to sort and process information. As you do that notice what kind of a mental world that would put you in. Identify two or three people in your life that you know well. Now go through the list and identify their cognitive meta-programs. What does this suggest in terms of communicating with them?

#1.	**Chunk Size:** *General/ Specific; Global/ Detail; Deductive, Inductive, Abductive*
#2.	**Relationship Sort:** *Matching/Mismatching; Sameness or Difference/Opposite; Agree/Disagree*
#3.	**Representational System Sort:** *Visual/ Auditory/ Kinesthetic/ Auditory-digital*
#4.	**Information Gathering Style:** *Uptime / Downtime*
#5.	**Epistemology Sort:** *Sensors/ Intuitors*
#6.	**Perceptual Categories Sort:** *Black-and-white vs. Continuum*
#7.	**Scenario Thinking Style:** *Best vs. Worst Scenario Thinking; Optimists/Pessimists*
#8.	**Perceptual Durability Sort:** *Permeable/Impermeable*
#9.	**Focus Sort:** *Screeners/ Non-screeners*
#10.	**Philosophical Direction:** *Why/ How; Origins/ Solution Process*
#11.	**Reality Structure Sort:** *Aristotelian/ Non-Aristotelian (Static / Process)*
#12.	**Communication Channel Preference:** *Verbal/ Non-Verbal; (Digital/ Analogue), Balanced*

A Brief Metalogue

Meta-programs—as the Meta-Formats or Mind-Codes
informing Consciousness how to process/format information

My (MH) daughter Jessica asked me why I wanted to read the computer book, **WordPerfect Workbook**.

"To learn how to run the brain of my computer." I said, "The more I can *figure out* its brain and its program formats, the better relationship I can have with it(!) and the more I can get it to obey my every command!"

"What does 'format' mean?" she asked.

"It indicates the form or style that the computer will put a document into— the form or shape of the paper size, the print size or shape, bold or italic."

"Well, what if you don't format, dad?" she asked.

"Then the default settings run the show."

"Default settings?"

"Yes the settings that the designer built into the computer's brain so that if you don't make a choice, you essentially choose to go with the designer's choices, the default choices."

"See, when you push Shift-F8, the computer shows you all of the options about formatting the document's information."

"But when I look at the screen I don't see any format commands."

"No, you don't. You have to push F11 to have the codes revealed. Shift F11 and we get the Reveal Codes screen. You remember I talked about the meta-programs in NLP?"

"Yes."

"Well, the Shift-F8 in WordPerfect as the Format command operates as do the Meta-Programs operate in human consciousness. It moves one to a level where he or she can format and pattern their information in a document form at whatever level (word, page, document) of specificity they choose. So via the Shift-F8, you can install new meta-programs for the computer's head."

"Neat!" she said, and then added, "Do people have a Shift-F8 button that reveals their codes?"

"Well, no, not exactly." I said.

"What do you mean with those hedge words 'not exactly,' dad?"

"Well, if you know the formatting options available to the human brain like general or gestalt, match or mismatch, visual, auditory, kinesthetic, etc. then when you look at the way a person has formatted their information, you can easily recognize what default choices they work from in their formatting information."

"Neat."

"Could you ask questions, kind of *formatting questions*, to get a mind to format in a certain way?"

"You just jumped way ahead of me, you little sneak!...Yes, you could. Suppose you asked, 'What would the big picture about that idea look like?' Or, 'What specific detail would you like that would enable you to under-stand that better?' Or, 'If you matched this with what you know, what thoughts would come to mind?' 'If you played devil's advocate and mismatched what I just said, then what?' Each question would invite the mind to format in a certain way, or move to a particular meta-program."

"Neat. So, dad, when you look at the big picture of what you want to do for me this evening, and see what you really feel great about in fulfilling your values of being a good father..."

Chapter 4

The "Emotional" Meta-Programs

Meta-Programs in Emoting and Somatizing
(#13-19)

In this chapter we focus on another set of meta-programs, those that describe **how** our cognitive (or mental) processes *emote* as it creates our "emotional" states of consciousness. These operating system patterns similarly affect the way we attend, input, process, and output information which, in turn, affect our "emotions."

"Emotions" differ from mere body sensations (our kinesthetics or feelings) in that they *involve some cognitive evaluation or judgment*. At the mere feeling level ($K^{+ \text{ or } -}$), fear, anger, excitement, lust, joy, etc. all pretty much involve the same kind of physiological arousal, bio-chemical "juices," neuro-transmitters, and neurology. What separates these as "emotions" involve *the evaluations* within them.

Thus, "emotions" (Kinesthetic-meta, K^m) arise from and involve a valuational process. "Positive" emotions indicate that we *feel the validation* of our values whereas "negative" emotions indicate that we *feel the discounting, violating, and disconfirmation* of our values.

Here we fully accept the neuro-linguistic understanding that Korzybski (1941/1994) developed in hyphenating of "mind-emotion," "thought-feelings," "neuro-linguistics," etc. "Mind" and "body" do not, and cannot, operate separately. Such elementalism maps out a false-to-fact correspondence with the human nervous system. This relationship involves processing information in the cerebral cortex (and other places) and somatizing those evaluations throughout the whole organism.

[*Elementalism*—a term in general-semantics that describes treating a holistic phenomenon like mind-emotions as if made up of separate parts or elements. *False-to-fact* in general-semantics refers to a mapping result. A mental or linguistic map inaccurately sketches out a feature.]

Thus in "thought" we always have body sensations and neurology, and in "emotion" we always have "thought" as awareness, understanding, ideas, concepts, etc. Always and inevitably we have, and can only have, *mind-body thoughts-and-emotions*. When the cognitive facet predominates, then we have *thoughts*-emotions and when the somatic, feeling, neurological part predominates, then we have thought-*emotions*.

Ellis (1976) developed this holistic understanding of mind-body in these words,

> "Human thinking and emoting are not radically different processes; but at points significantly overlap. Emotions almost always stem directly from ideas, thoughts, attitudes, beliefs... and can usually be radically changed by modifying the thinking processes that keep creating them."

So as a person thinks—so he or she emotes. And when a person alters their thinking, he or she changes their emoting. This describes the cognitive-behavioral mechanism in change.

#13. Emotional Coping or Stress Response Pattern:
Passivity/Aggression/ Dissociated

#14. Frame of Reference or Authority Sort:
Internal/External; Self-Referent/ Other-Referent

#15. Emotional State Sort:
Associated/ Dissociated; Feeling/ Thinking

#16. Somatic Response Sort:
Active/ Reflective/ Inactive

#17. The Convincer or Believability Sort:
Looks, Sounds, or Feels Right; Makes Sense

#18. Emotional Direction Sort:
Uni-directional/ Multi-directional

#19. Emotional Intensity/ Exuberance Sort:
Desurgency/ Surgency

#13. Emotional Coping Style or Stress Response Pattern:
Passivity/Aggression/Dissociated

Concept: This sorting style specifically relates to "stress" whether that stress takes the form of threat and danger (chronic or acute) or whether it takes the form of overload (chronic or acute). How does a person *process* and/or *sort* for such stressors? Does the person move toward in order to confront and "take it on," or does a person move away from it in order to avoid it?

The fight/flight or *General Arousal Syndrome* describes a neurological process, cued by the conscious mind (via messages of "danger" or "overload"), but runs entirely by the "unconscious" mind (the autonomic nervous system). It prepares physiology and neurology to access *a high level energy state* for fighting or fleeing. Via repeated experiences of fight/flight, trauma, distress, etc. we can learn to "turn it off" from consciousness. People who do this and make this their "driver program" for so responding access *a dissociated state,* and when over-done, can create dissociative disorders of personality (See #15 Associated/Dissociated.)

Elicitation: "When you feel threatened, or challenged, by some stress...do you immediately respond, on the emotional level, by wanting to get away from it or to go at it?" Invite the person to tell you about several specific instances when he or she faced a high stress situation. Do you detect a "go at" or "go away from" response to it?

Identification: The "go at" and "go away from" *emotional coping* responses arise from the fight/flight syndrome built within our very neurology. Consider these response styles of the General Arousal Syndrome on a continuum from one extreme of passivity to the other extreme of aggression. Consider also how the person responds in various arenas: work/career, home, relationships, hobby, sports, etc.

1. *Those who respond aggressively* **go at** *their stressors.* More often than not, they actually *like* challenges, stress, pressure, and adventure. Look for the automatic and immediate response of wanting to take on the challenge or stress. When over-done or when given way to with little thought, aggressive responders can turn into violent, dangerous, and out-of-control persons. At high levels, people find them intimidating, threatening, and manipulative.

2. *Passive responders,* on the other hand, forever attempt to **get away** from stresses, confrontations, threats, and dangers. They want more than anything to make peace, to create harmony, and to make things pleasant and nice for everybody (Satir "Placator, #31). When over-done, they transform into people-pleasers and door-mats and reinforce the "go at" responses of others (what we generally describe as "co-dependency").

Both styles of responding operate as *a function of stress and insecurity.* Messages cued to the brain of "danger" or "overload", activate the autonomic nervous system to go into these fight/flight responses. In long-term intimate relationships, we have found that perhaps as many as 90% of marriages involve opposites. This suggests that we typically value and adore the behavioral traits of the opposite style and want to "marry" it.

3. In the middle of such a continuum, we would have the tempering quality of *assertiveness.* Here a person has **learned** to stop fighting or fleeing and has learned how to cope with the internal sense of stress by thinking and talking the stress out rather than acting it out. We will still experience the emotion of feeling an urge to either fight or flee, but we will control (or manage) that urge, and not act on it. Consequently, we can maintain enough presence of mind in order to think and talk out our stresses—a description of an emotionally healthy person.

Pacing: To pace and communicate with an aggressive responder, take his or her idea and wrestle with it. Explore it, ask questions about it, have the person future-pace it. A person with the "go at" style wants you to confront it, deal with it, and grapple with the ideas. Such people appreciate directness, forthrightness, confrontation, etc. So affirm these qualities in that person.

To pace and communicate with a passive responder, hear his or her ideas out fully and completely, and never interrupt. Give verbal and non-verbal "go" signs that essentially say, "Tell me more, I have a lot of interest in what you've got to say. I want to understand you and your point of view." Don't disagree directly or vigorously. Talk about the importance of finding harmony, peace, pleasantness and niceness.

Languaging: Aggressive responders will tend to use the modal operators of possibility, while passive responders will use those of necessity. Those with the approach style (go at) think and talk in terms of possibilities, ideals, and hopes. They focus on what they want. People who primarily avoid (move away from), will tend to think and talk more in terms of what they want to avoid, and about laws, rules, protocols and necessities that they feel upon them (shoulds, musts and have tos).

Emoting: The Fight/Flight stress responses also relate to whether we typically associate or dissociate emotionally. Fight/Flight responses experienced in emotional association will show up in overt and obvious ways. We will see changes in breathing, skin color, eye dilation, etc. When we see a dissociated fight/flight response to high stress, the person will seem cold and unfeeling, unemotional, unaffected and not accessing his kinesthetics. Such a person may have accessed the "computer mode" (#31). If the person gets stuck in that mode, then he or she will continually push awareness and expressiveness of the emotions away.

An assertive person may choose to go to computer mode and dissociate. The difference occurs in the area of choice. When you ask about the stress state, the person can access the kinesthetics and then make a choice to dissociate.

Contexts of Origin: This meta-program operates primarily neurologically in terms of the nervous system's sensitivity to stress. Nobody "is" a passive or aggressive. Each of us rather functions in a passive-aggressive way or in an aggressive-passive way. Physiological nervous system sensitivity (those who tend to move away from stress, conflict, distress, etc.) may have a more finely tuned and sensitive set of sense receptors, whereas those who move toward such do not find the sensory impact significant until much later. Modeling of and identification with significant persons plays a role in modifying these styles. Trauma experiences that induce states of stress can habituate and become chronic that a person moves to one extreme or the other of passivity and aggression. I (BB) have noticed that clients who struggle with what feels as "uncontrollable anger" inevitably have a history of some kind of abuse. And more often than not, it occurred during the imprint period within the first seven years, although I have found a few who learned it during the modeling years (8-13) or the socialization years (13-17). Childhood experiences of permission and/or taboo about anger and fear can influence a person to one side or the other of this continuum.

Further Reading: Hall (1987).

Self-Analysis:
__ **P**assive/**A**ggressive

Contexts:
__ Work/Career	__ Intimates
__ Relationships	__ Hobbies/Recreation
__ Sports	__ Other: _____
__ **High/Medium/Low level**	__ Driver MP: **Yes/No**

#14. Frame of Reference or Authority Sort:
Internal/External
Self-Referent/Other-Referent

Concept: We have two fundamental ways in evaluating a person, situation, experience, or idea. We can do so *from within* our own frame-of-reference (internal) or *from without* our reference (external). This sorting filter concerns how we posit our *locus of judgment*, which means where we put the authority of our judgment for taking action and making evaluations, whether from inside ourselves or outside? *Who* (or what) do we use as a reference?

Elicitation: "Where do you put most of your attention or reference, on yourself or on others (or something external to yourself)?" "What do you rely on for your authority?"

Identification:
1. *Self-Referencing.* Those who operate *Internally* evaluate things on the basis of what *they think* as appropriate. They motivate themselves and make their own decisions. They choose and validate their own actions and results. They may gather information from others, but they always decide on their own. Thus they live "from within" (notice similarity to #4). Such people operate in *a self referent* way and this enables them to decide within themselves and know within themselves what they want, need, believe, feel and value.

2. *Other-Referencing.* Those who operate *Externally* evaluate things on the basis of what *others* think. They look to others for guidance, information, motivation, and decisions. They have a greater need for feedback about their actions and results, and they can feel lost without guidance or feedback from others. They live "from without" and often opt for a style of "people pleasing." Some feel so dependent on others they live their life totally in reference to the values and beliefs of some other. These *other referent* persons need feedback and information from others to decide on what they know, understand, want, believe, feel and value.

Languaging: One linguistic cue to listen for involves the use of the word "you" by *other referent persons* when they talk about themselves. Self-referencing people tend to more directly use the personal pronoun, "I."

We can discover this pattern by asking, **"How** do you know that you have chosen or acted right or that you have done a good job, chosen the right bank (right car, etc.)?" "When it comes to decision making, how do you generally go about it?" "What kind of information do you want in making decisions?" Listen for whether the person tells you that *he or she* decides or whether they get information from some *outside source*. As an excellent follow-up question, ask, "Do you just know inside or does someone else have to tell you?"

Self-referencing people will say, "I just know. I feel it. It feels right." Other-referencing people will say things like, "My boss tells me. I look at the figures..." Those coming from their own internal state will speak of their own values, beliefs, and understandings. They will come across in an assertive and forthright manner. Those coming from some external source will speak of placating and pleasing others.

Pacing: In pacing and communicating with the self-referencing, emphasize that he or she will know inside. "You must make the decision—it belongs to you." "What do you think?" Help the person to clarify his or her own thinking. With the other-referencing, emphasize what others think. Give statistics, data, and testimonials from significant others. "Most people find this product or service very useful."

The self-referencing use their internal frame-of-reference to decide which stereo to buy as they identify their own personal inclinations. The other-referencing who use an external frame-of-reference care about the inclinations of other people and information from other sources (i.e. mass media, consumer reports, advertising). People who use an internal frame with an external check or an external frame with internal check provide a more challenging pattern to discern.

Emoting: Those who do *self-referencing* also do lots of independent thinking and don't need the opinions of others for confirmation. They trust their own understandings, values, beliefs, desires, tastes, etc. This results in the emotions of independence, autonomy, confidence, clarity, self-motivation, proactivity. Those who do *other-referencing* feel more insecure and trust others for validation. They feel more dependent upon confirmation by others. They generally appreciate clear-cut guidelines, prizes, feedback, recognition, etc. They can enjoy and participate as a team player more readily as well.

Statistics: The self-referencing frequently end up as entrepreneurs, leaders, and pioneers. They blaze new trails. Managing these self-regulating people involves communicating with clarity, about goals, procedures, or criteria, and then turning them loose. They dislike tight supervision. The other-referencing, in areas where external checks play a crucial role, excel because of their "program" to "go external" to get the facts and figures. Managing someone who uses an external frame-of-reference goes much easier. Such persons generally take feedback and information from an outside source well. But they also need more praise, affirmation, and commendations.

Maturity: Through the process of maturation, we begin as babies and children by entirely using an external frame of reference—referencing off our parents. As we grow, we develop more and more of an internal frame of reference as we come to feel more and more sure of our thoughts, values, beliefs, skills, tastes, etc. The majority of personality models views a mentally-emotionally healthy person as moving more and more to self-referencing without losing the ability to do other-referencing as needed.

Contexts of Origin: Modeling and identification with early models either grants permission or forbids (taboos) it. Levels of rewarding for one or the other style: self or other referencing. Cultural norms in the West tend to encourage and condition females to do other-referencing while encouraging males to do self-referencing. McConnell (1977) quoted research on regional contexts (the north versus the south in the USA) as having more internalizers versus externalizers (pp. 298-302).

Further Reading: James & Woodsmall (1988). Woodsmall (1988).

Self-Analysis:
__ **O**ther Referencing/**S**elf Referencing (External/Internal Frames)
__ **B**alanced in both other-referencing and self-referencing
__ Other-Referencing with Self-referencing check
__ Self-Referencing with Other-referencing check

Contexts:
__ Work/Career	__ Intimates
__ Relationships	__ Hobbies/Recreation
__ Sports	__ Other:_____
__ **H**igh/**M**edium/**L**ow level	__ Driver MP: **Yes/No**
__ If Other-Referencing:	

Referencing off of who or what? Reference person or group?

#15. Emotional State Sort
Associated/Dissociated
Feeling/Thinking

Concept: As we process data, we can do it in one of two ways—associatedly or dissociatedly. With **dissociation** we think and process the data with a degree of "psychological distance" from the emotional impact of the material. In a dissociated representation we will see our younger self in the picture rather than seeing things out of our own eyes. We will see, hear, smell, and feel representations as if they stand "over there." We have stepped outside of the image so that we can think "about" things.

With **association** we think and process the data by experiencing the full emotional impact of our emotions. When we create an associated represen-tation, we see what we would see if we stepped into the movie. Then we will hear what we would hear if actually there, smell, taste, and feel it as immediately present. By stepping into the picture, we entertain the thoughts "of" the experience.

Elicitation: "Think about an event in a work situation that once gave you trouble..." "What experience surrounding work would you say has given you the most pleasure or delight...?" "How do you normally feel while at work?" "When you make a decision, do you rely more on reason and logic, personal values or something else?"

Identification and Emoting: As we observe the eye-accessing cues, note to what extent a person engages in any kinesthetic access (see Appendix C). If a person accesses the kinesthetic mode and stays there, you can assume that they have entered into an associative mode. If he or she accesses kines-thetic awareness but does not stay, assume dissociation.

1. *Dissociation.* To identify dissociation note the emotional affect of the person—it will be mild, dull or bland. The person will have accessed the Satir communication category of the "Computer Mode" (#31). He or she will talk *about* an experience rather than *of* it. The person will operate more from reason and logic than emotion. This corresponds to William James' (1890) "tough-minded" category and associated corresponds to his "tender-minded" category.

2. *Association.* In associated representations we will feel (or re-feel) from a full body state as if re-experiencing the sights, sounds, and sensations. This can range from a very light and mild emotional state to an extreme and exaggerated one. The more intense the emotional associating, the more changes will occur in skin color, breathing, muscle tension, and all of the other physiological signs.

3. *A Chosen Balance.* While we all tend to have our favorite way of experiencing data (associatedly or dissociatedly), a person can get stuck in one or the other and lose or not develop the flexibility of consciousness to choose whether to associate or not.

Pacing and *Languaging:* Use the language of association if you want to pace someone already there and the language of dissociation for someone not psychologically in an experience.

50% of the USA population makes up those who primarily orient themselves associatedly and dissociatedly. In terms of gender use, 45% of women use Thinking or Dissociation, in comparison to 50% of men. A level of objectivity arises from this style and often arises from taking the third Perceptual Position, or a meta-viewpoint.

The thinking style of dissociation leads to a theoretical orientation, skepticism, empiricism, reality-testing, an experimental style, a good handling of intellectual realms (lectures, examinations, science, technology), and the values of order, achievement, dominance, and endurance. The emoting style of association leads to a more social, spiritual, nurturing, affiliating, and tender-minded style of life, with the values of caring, empathy, understanding, and supporting.

RET Cognitive Distortion: When we experience a lot of distress, pain, trauma, and upset, *and* stay there so that we experience the state as chronic, we will almost inevitably fall into the cognitive distortion that Ellis (1976) made popular of *Awfulizing* and *Catastrophizing.* We use these non-referencing words (they refer to nothing real or actual in the world!) and thereby amplify our emotional pain. In Awfulizing we over-exaggerate a negative undesirable experience. We may also fall into the distortion called Emotionalizing. Ellis describes this as over-estimating the importance of emotions and moods, assuming that if we feel something, it must "be real." "I feel like a rotten miserable failure, therefore 'I am' a rotten miserable failure." Emotionalizing leads us to victim thinking-and-feeling, disempowerment, impulsive and reactiveness, and impatience.

Contexts of Origin: This arises chiefly from modeling, identification, dis-identification with models, from the number and levels of traumatic experiences, skills or lack of them, for coping, cultural norms, permissions and taboos for either pattern. In the West, females tend to receive much more permission for feeling or associated processing while males receive more permission and encouragement for thinking and dissociated sorting.

Further Reading: Ellis (1976).

Self-Analysis:
__ Associated/Dissociated (Thinking/Feeling)

Contexts:
__ Negative Emotions	__ Positive Emotions
__ Present	__ Past
__ Future	__ Work/Career
__ Work/Career	__ Intimates
__ Relationships	__ Hobbies/Recreation
__ Sports	__ Other:_____
__ High/Medium/Low level	__ Driver MP: **Yes/No**

#16. Somatic Response Sort:
Inactive/Reflective/Active (Low to High Action Style)

Concept: Some people process information in a very active, quick, immediate, and impulsive way—the Active style. Others engage in the handling of information much more reflectively, thoughtfully, slowly, etc.—the Reflective style. Others do not seem to engage in information processing much at all, or at least with much reluctance—the inactive style.

Elicitation: "When you come into a new situation, do you usually act quickly after sizing it up or do you do a detailed study of all the consequences before acting?"

Identification:
1. Active people orient themselves as doers. They make things happen. Often they act first, and think later! As entrepreneurs and go-getters, they certainly shape the world. And while they will more likely make lots of mistakes, they also get things done, and make many more successes.

2. Reflective people tend to study and ponder than to act. This makes them more passive as they sit back to contemplate before acting. The belief that motivates them says, "Don't do anything rash!" Those who have more of a mixture of both of these styles have a more balanced and healthy approach. Look for them to operate primarily in the A_d and Computer (#31) mode.

3. Those who respond inactively neither study nor act, they attempt to ignore and avoid.

Pacing and Languaging: Pace in your communication to each by appealing to the values of each.

Contexts of Origin: These include physiological wiring and predisposition, the extent to which the motor cortex has been conditioned to act increased by certain psychoactive drugs. Also from modeling, identification, and dis-identification with models. Children, generally wired for immediate "acting out" of cognitive awareness, must learn to slow down that process, "think," etc. Trauma experiences inducing fight/flight (#13) may lead to reactive style.

Further Reading: Woodsmall (1988).

Self-Analysis:
__ Active/**Reflective**/Inactive

Contexts:
__ Work/Career	__ Intimates
__ Relationships	__ Hobbies/Recreation
__ Sports	__ Other: _____
__ High/**Medium**/Low level	__ Driver MP: **Yes/No**

#17. The Convincer or Believability Sort:
Representation of Acceptance of Persuasion
Looks, Sounds, or Feels Right and/or Makes Sense

Concept: As we process information, we learn to value different qualities and experiences. This leads us to have different strategies for feeling convinced about the value, importance, or significance of something. **What** specifically leads us to *accept* the believability of a thing? Some people will believe in something and therefore make decisions to take action about it because it *looks right* (V^+), others need it to *sound right* (A^t), others believe when it *makes sense* (A_d) and yet others when it *feels right* (K^+). What makes something believable to you? What convinces you?

Elicitation: Ask questions that presuppose decision-making. *"Why* did you decide on your present choice of car?" *"What* helps you decide where to vacation?" "As you make a decision about where to vacation, *how* do you think about such? Do you see, hear, or create feelings about it?" "What lets you know that you can believe that a product feels right for you?"

Identification: Consider all of the different facets that go into the structure of persuasion around a major purchase like a new car. *How* do we go about gathering information in the first place for making this decision? *What* information do we need? *What sensory systems* do we use to think about it? *How often* do we have to think about it before the information seems "right?" We here distinguish two sub-categories: convincer *representation* and convincer *demonstration.*Two factors play a critical role in this meta-program. (1) Which mode of awareness do you (or another) use (VAK and A_d) and (2) the *process* of moving from mere thought to a feeling of conviction and persuasion. How many times does it take in order for you to believe something?

Languaging: Listen for the sensory-system predicates used and the process of time, quality, and repetition that the person refers to.

People who use *visual convincers* do things because their representations look right. When the visual qualities seem compelling, then they act. Accordingly, visual aids, diagrams, pictures, etc. assist the process (estimated in the USA population between 50 to 75%).

People who use *auditory convincers* have a representation that sounds right. They hear it as clear as a bell. What volume, pitch, voice quality, speed, style, etc. does the person find most convincing? Here modeling the voice quality of one who they find most convincing really helps (estimated between 15% to 35%).

People who use *an auditory digital convincer* have a strong language representation (or self-talk) which produces their feelings that a choice seems logical, reasonable and makes sense. They like data, facts and reasons. What specific ideas, words, values, expressions, etc. most effectively elicit persuasion? Here books, reports, pamphlets, letters of recommendation, etc. significantly contribute (estimated as low as 3% and as high as 15%).

People who use *a kinesthetic convincer* have a visceral representation of their choice that triggers the right tactile or internal sensations—it feels right. Here hands-on experiences have a significant impact (estimated between 12% to 15%).

When communicating, present your information in the corresponding sensory channel, use appropriate predicates to "juice" up your descriptions, and to match their convincer strategy.

The Process Factor: Next, identify the factor(s) in the process that demonstrate the quality of *believability* to the person. Ask, "*How often* does someone have to demonstrate competence to you before you feel convinced?" "How many times do you typically have to see, hear, read, or do something before you feel convinced about your own competency at it?" Does the convincer (or believability) occur (1) automatically, (2) over a number of times, and how many times (3) over a period of time and how long a time or (4) by consistency.

1. *Automatically.* People with an automatic convincer comprise easy sells and need little convincing inasmuch as they just assume believability unless proven otherwise. With their "program" of already tending to believe, they will gather some information and imagine the rest(!). The problem here lies in sometimes trusting too much and too quickly. (Estimated at 8% to 10%).

For years I (BB) operated in the automatic mode. Eventually, however, after purchasing too many products I didn't need and signing up for too many MLM programs, I have altered my meta-program to "a number of time." Experience has a way of encouraging us to change our meta-programs, doesn't it?

2.   *Repetition.* Many people only trust and believe when they have had a certain amount of exposure to information, experience, etc. It seems as if it takes so many neurological "exposures" (thinking-feeling the information inside) in order for the idea to solidify enough to seem "real" and believable. Such a person has a number of times (3, 5, 17, etc.) and will not feel persuaded until that number of presentations have occurred. This raises the question, "How many?" *Pace* by using repetition. Speak to him or her the number of times that they require.

Consider this frightening thought—the great majority of people can come to believe almost anything if repeated often enough in compelling representations! (Estimated at 50%.)

3.   *Time Period.* Unlike the amount of exposure to an idea (as in Repetition), others need the exposure to occur over a period of "time." And this quality of "endurance over time" describes the factor that allows an idea to solidify in their mind. So for someone with a period of time convincer, you will find that their sense of "time" plays the crucial element in their convincer. If it holds up over time and/or if a certain amount of time passes. Tad James (1988) has suggested that we wait 10% of their "time" (6 days if 60 days represents their period) and then say, "I've been so busy since the last time we talked, it seems like it's been two months, do you know what I mean?" (Estimated at 25%.)

4.   *Never (or almost never, consistently never!).* Some people almost never *accept* something as believable. As the reverse of the automatic truster, this person automatically almost always never believes. This person almost never gives anyone the benefit of the doubt. This kind of person hardly ever feels convinced. You have to prove something to him or her every single time! Alluding to previous experience will not work with this one.

My the stories I (BB) can tell about this one! I married a lady with this meta-program. Linda can give any salesperson a run for their money!

(Put this person to work in doing quality control on things that you want to always check out afresh each and every time—like airplane maintenance!) *Pace* your language to him or her accordingly, "I know you'll never feel convinced that this represents the right time for you to do this, so the only way to know is to get started and find out." (Estimated at 15%.)

Contexts of Origin: Same as #3. Significantly impacted by experiences of coming to trust as a child as well as by experiences of belief in emotionally significant persons. Trauma experiences can undermine this process so that a person builds a belief system of categorically never believing in anyone.

Further Reading: James & Woodsmall (1988). Woodsmall (1988).

Self-Analysis:
__ Looks right/Sounds right/Feels right/Makes Sense

Contexts:
__ Work/Career	__ Intimates
__ Relationships	__ Hobbies/Recreation
__ Sports	__ Other: _____
__ High/Medium/Low level	__ Driver MP: **Yes/No**

Process:
__ Automatic	__ Repetition
__ Time Period	__ Never (almost never)

#18. Emotional Direction Sort:
Uni-directional/Multi-directional

Concept: This meta-program relates to *the focus and diffusion of emotions*. It refers to directional quality of a person's consciousness in the experiencing of emoting. When some people emote, they do so in a uni-directional style, others do so in a multi-directional style.

Elicitation: "When you think about a time when you experienced an emotional state (positive or negative), does that bleed over and affect some or all of your other emotional states, or does it stay pretty focused so that it relates to its object?"

Identification:
1. *Multi-directional.* When some individuals have a "down" day at work, their "down" emotions immediately and powerfully (associatedly, #15) affect every other area of life. The emotional state that relates to one facet of life has *a multi-directional way* of working out. When over-done, that pattern leads to moodiness, instability, displaced emotions, and other forms of emotional instability. The person seems unable to keep the emotions **about** that one facet limited or contained to that area.

2. *Uni-directional.* Other individuals do contain their emotions so that they emote in a direct and singular way *(uni-directional way)*. If such a person feels upset, down, angry, joyful, contented, etc. at work, then they *keep* those feelings *contextualized* to that referent and do not let them bleed over into their relationships. The person will feel and associate into their emotions in the area of reference of their thoughts-and-feelings, but they will not associate them into other areas.

When balanced, this enables them to keep their emotions appropriate and contextualized. When over-done, this pattern leads to rigid ego boundaries, even multiple "personality" disorders.

Language and Emoting: The multi-directional sorter will tend to displace emotions from context to context and allow a strong negative (or positive) emotional state to collapse onto other states. Their emoting style operates in a diffuse way, without boundaries or constraints. The uni-directional sorter segments and sequences their emotional states so that this or that emotion *about* a particular situation stays contained.

Jane never seem to know *what she felt* about anything in particular. Her feelings about work, her children, a friend, Bill, her aging parents, her health, etc. seemed to entirely depend upon *the emotion of the day.* And, depending on that emotion, she seemed to color everything else by it.

By way of contrast, her husband Bill never experienced his emotions in a multi-directional way. He could easily and quickly tell you what he felt about work, about his marriage, his hobbies, his children, etc. So if he had a bad day at work, he would feel upset, frustrated, angry, confused, or whatever *about* work, but then he would leave it there and come home and have a delightful time.

Jane didn't know how to think or feel about Bill's uni-directional focus and diffusion of his emotions. "How can we have a tiff and then he go out and enjoy the kids riding bikes? He acts like nothing is eating away at him." Bill similarly didn't understand Jane. "How can she treat me and the kids so bad when she's had a falling out with her mother? Can't she leave that there, take a break from that and quit fuming and fussing about it?"

Contexts of Origin: Determined by permission (or taboo) for experiencing and registering emotions according to which areas we view as acceptable and which as forbidden. A child may experience a home context where parents accept his/her fear, but rejects anger, etc. Modeling and identification with how parents and others separate or fail to separate facets of their emoting to keep them separate.

Self-Analysis:
__ Uni-directional/**M**ulti-directional/**B**alanced

Contexts:

__ Work/Career	__ Intimates
__ Relationships	__ Hobbies/Recreation
__ Sports	__ Other: _____
__ High/**M**edium/Low level	__ Driver MP: **Yes**/No

#19 Emotional Intensity/Exuberance Sort:
Desurgency/Surgency—Timidity/Boldness

Concept: Cattell (1989) describes this as the boldness/timidity factor in emoting and notes that it involves more of a constitutionally determined factor. It shows up in surgency and desurgency. It measures the emotional exuberance of a person from shy, timid, restrained, threat-sensitive to adventurous, thick-skinned, and socially bold.

Elicitation: "When you think about a situation at work or in your personal affairs that seems risky or involving the public's eye, what thoughts-and-feelings immediately come to mind?"

Identification: On a continuum between low and high exuberance and emotional intensity, people can attend and value high levels and low levels.

1. *Surgency.* People who sort for high emotional intensity seek out and enjoy dangerous types of experiences (rollercoasters, haunted houses, horror movies, etc.). They often enjoy feeling fearful. They enjoy the limelight, center stage, attention, and receiving recognition, and so engage in more risk taking. They often think and act in very creative ways. Cattell (1989) writes,

"Their physical underactivity provides immunity to physical and social threats that others find noxious." (p. 136)

When over-done, this pattern can lead to antisocial behavior. When combined with concrete thinking, many behave like the "fools who rush in where angels fear to tread."

"Their bold inattentiveness to danger signals and the press for excitement, in combination with low intelligence, inevitably resulted in poor and rash judgment. This combination often found in prisoners." (p. 141).

2. *Desurgency.* People who sort for low emotional intensity cling to certainty and predictability and develop neither criminal-like thinking nor that which characterizes creativity. With their low tolerance for fear and arousal, they protect themselves by going into a shell, fear attracting attention, avoid risks, secure themselves with routinized lifestyles, etc. When over-done, one can feel fear and anxiety driven, act like a doormat for others, and experience a body full of nerves.

Languaging and emoting: The timid and fearful tend to talk and feel in silent introspective ways, full of cares and worries, reflective of danger and risks, cautious, negative, and avoidant. The bold and risk taking tend to move forward in a cheerful, happy-go-lucky style, frank, expressive, quick, alert, talkative.

Contexts of Origin: Probably due to physiological factors and nervous system functioning. Yet also conditioned by experience that allows, permits, reinforces surgery or not. Long-term chronic trauma experiences can alter thinking-emoting, acting, blood-chemistry, and habitual way of experiencing life.

Further Reading: Cattell (1989).

Self-Analysis:
__ Desurgency/Surgency/Balanced

Contexts:
__ Work/Career   __ Intimates
__ Relationships   __ Hobbies/Recreation
__ Sports   __ Other: _____
__ High/Medium/Low level   __ Driver MP: Yes/No

Summary

We all use our "body stuff" of kinesthetic sensations and evaluative emotions as we move through life. We "go at" and "move away from" experiences, information and people. We feel confident or insecure about doing so, we reference from what we think-feel or care more about what others think-feel. We have an action style from low to high activity. We have a strategy for trusting or distrusting. And when we emote—we do so in a focused and directed way—or all over the place! All of this emoting comes out of a basic style of exuberance or lack thereof.

Now take some time to review and contemplate your "emotional" meta-programs. Which function as *drivers* for you? Which *drive* you too much so that you lack the flexibility of consciousness to shift to the other side of the continuum? What thoughts, beliefs, or values *drive* your "emotional meta-programs?

As you take second position to somebody with a different "emotional" meta-program, try it on fully and notice the different world it generates. What would you experience if you used this meta-program more often?

Finally, contemplate how you exist as so much more than your emotions. You *have* emotions and you emote, but you "are" not your emotions. These body correlations of your thoughts and values simply indicate what meanings you have attached to things, positive and negative. To what extent, however, have you *identified* yourself with your emotions? Do you now have permission to know yourself as a person who exists as *more* than your emotions? What stops you from giving yourself that permission even now?

#13. **Emotional Coping or Stress Response Pattern:**
Passivity/Aggression/ Dissociated
#14. **Frame of Reference or Authority Sort:**
Internal/External; Self-Referent/ Other-Referent
#15. **Emotional State Sort:**
Associated/ Dissociated; Feeling/ Thinking
#16. **Somatic Response Sort:**
Active/ Reflective/ Inactive
#17. **The Convincer or Believability Sort:**
Looks, Sounds, or Feels Right; Makes Sense
#18. **Emotional Direction Sort:**
Uni-directional/ Multi-directional
#19. **Emotional Intensity/ Exuberance Sort:**
Desurgency/ Surgency

Chapter 5

The "Volitional" Meta-Programs

Meta-Programs Involved in Willing, Choosing, Conation
(#20-28)

We now move to those meta-programs that have to do with another focus of the attention of consciousness—*conation*. This term refers to choosing, willing, and attending our intending. We commonly speak about such in terms of our *"will"*—what we *intend* to think, perceive, feel, and do, and what we then follow up with *attention*.

How we "think-emote" not only involves our *representations* ("mental," "cognitive") and somatic body sensations ("emotional")—but also our **choices**. How do we *direct* our thoughts-feelings? **In what *direction* have we learned to typically send our consciousness?** How have we learned to *adapt* ourselves in terms of our various life contexts (home, relationships, work, career, recreation, etc.)?

What *"rules"* have we chosen to live by? Have you *decided* that the world operates by compulsion or desire? What facets of life do we find most pleasure in? *How* do we go about moving ourselves forward in fulfilling our desired outcomes (goals)? How do we relate to choosing our choices? How have we chosen to trust or distrust people in choosing to believe them or not? *How we "run our brain" in terms of our choices describes our operational system for deciding, opting, preferring, and focusing attention?*

#20. **Direction Sort:** *Toward/ Away From, Past Assurance/ Future Possibilities; Approach / Avoidance*

#21. **Conation Choice in Adapting:** *Options/ Procedures*

#22. **Adaptation Sort:** *Judging / Perceiving, Controlling/ Floating*

#23. **Reason Sort of Modal Operators:**
Necessity/ Possibility (Desire); Stick / Carrot

#24. **Preference Sort:**
Primary Interest— People/ Place/ Things/ Activity/ Information

#25. **Goal Sort—Adapting to Expectations:**
Perfection/ Optimization/ Skepticism

#26. **Value Buying Sort:** *Cost/ Convenience/ Quality/ Time*

#27. **Responsibility Sort:** *Over-Responsible/ Under-Responsible*

#28. **People Convincer Sort:** *Distrusting / Trusting*

#20. Direction Sort:
Toward and Away from Past Assurance/Future Possibilities
Approach/Avoidance

Concept: With regard to *the direction* we move about the things we value, we have two general orientations and we can come to specialize in one or the other. Some people have a basic orientation of moving *toward* their desired values. Others adopt a basic orientation of moving *away from* undesired values. Thus, *pull values* motivate some people first and foremost while *push values* primarily motivate others. *Pull values* consist of the positive benefits that will result and so they *attract* a person into the future. *Push values* consist of the negative values that a person does *not* want. They create a sense of *aversion away from* the undesired.

Elicitation: Ask "What do you want?" "What do you want from a relation-ship, or a job, etc.?" "What will having this do for you?" "What do you value of importance about...?" After you get an answer (usually in the form of a nominalization: e.g. love, peace, happiness, etc.), move to a meta-level and ask for the meta-outcome of that. "When you get love, peace, and happiness, what does that mean to you?" (In doing this, we seek to discover the complex equivalence between behaviors and values.)

Listen for *toward* and *away from* values. "It means respecting each other and taking care of each other." "It means not fighting and arguing with each other, not feeling bad."

Identification: People who move *toward what they want* have a *toward* motivation strategy in their consciousness. They move toward their desired outcomes so that their goals *pull* them into their future. In other words, they use a *go at* response style toward goals and values. They feel motivated to achieve, attain, and obtain. While they can set priorities regarding these desired values, they have more difficulty in recognizing what they should avoid. They feel best motivated by carrots or incentives, not aversions.

People who *move away from* what they dis-value, on the other hand, have a *move away from* strategy that energizes them to avoid things that they do not want. They operate with a consciousness, orientation, and focus on what they want to *avoid* rather than what they want to approach. They primarily use a *go away from* response style. They feel motivated to move away from, avoid, steer clear of, and get rid of disvalues and aversions. Accordingly, they have more difficulty with goals and managing their priorities. They can get easily distracted by negative situations. They feel best motivated by the stick (e.g. threats, negative aversions, pressure).

What we move toward or away from consists of our **values**. Accordingly, we all have both toward values and away from values. For some, one direction or the other will operate more predominantly.

Languaging: In those who *move toward values*, we will hear goals and specific wants. We will hear avoidances, aversions, disvalues, etc. from those who *move away from* things. People will communicate their values and disvalues in **nominalizations** (e.g. process words that they have turned into static nouns). Listen for and distinguish **inclusive** and **exclusive** language. *Toward* language tends to *include* (i.e. gain, have, get, attain, achieve) while *away from* language *excludes* (e.g. stay clear of, get rid of, stay away from, avoid, and don't need).

In responding to a question like, "What do you want in a good relationship?" those who take *toward* orientation will say, "I want peace, love, and happiness." Those with an *away from* orientation will say, "I don't want any fighting or trying to manipulate each other." Those who *move toward but with some away from* would say, "I want us to consider each other's feelings so we don't fight." Those who *move away from with a little toward* will say, "We won't feel hurt by each other because we will have more of a sense of harmony."

Pacing: To pace and communicate (e.g. negotiate, manage, relate, etc.) with a person who moves **toward values,** talk about what you can do that will help the person achieve his or her outcomes. Mention the carrots, bonuses, and incentives inherent in your plan or idea. With those who *move away from*, talk about what and how you can help them avoid, the problems they can minimize or put off, and the things that won't go wrong. Emphasize how easy your idea or plan will make their life.

Emoting: Those who *move away from* will tend to sort for past assurances and look for security, safety, and protection. Provide them with a history of evidence inasmuch as they want to rest assured about their choice as already proven over time. They seek more to solve problems than move toward goals. They don't feel moved by rewards and goals as much as by avoiding evils. Those who *move toward* values tend to sort for future possibilities and so will think and feel more in terms of possibilities, opportunities, excitements, passions, dreams, etc. They enjoy the possibilities that lie within open-ended opportunities. They feel attracted to bigger risks for greater potential payoffs.

This Approach/Avoidance sorting category allows us to make some distinctions regarding what a person will look for when seeking to buy or purchase something. Avoidance responders want to know what problems the product will take care of. Goal-oriented people will experience the problem-avoidance approach as negative. They will want to know how a product will help them *attain* their goals.

Since everybody moves away from some things and toward other things— everybody has a *propulsion system away from "pain" and toward "pleasure."* What do you (or someone else) specifically move away from? What registers neuro-semantically as "pain" for you? What registers neuro-semantically as "pleasure" for you? That your "pains" may comprise another's "pleasures" alerts us to the fact that we have much plasticity in human nature regarding what we condition in ourselves as pain and pleasure.

Statistics: 40% of the USA population uses the *toward* orientation whereas 40% use the *away from* direction. Another 20% have both directions operating simultaneously.

Contexts of Origin: This emotional meta-program of Toward and Away From closely relates to the conational meta-program of Toward and Away from *stress* (#13), yet it differs in terms of its reference. In the other meta-program, the energies moved toward or away from *danger and threat*, here it moves toward or away from *values*. Modeling significant persons greatly affects this, as does permission and taboos to do so. Trauma experiences can reorient a person into an avoidance mode.

Further Reading: Woodsmall (1988), Robins (1991), Hall (1996).

Self-Analysis:
__ **Toward**/**Away** From (Approach/Avoidance)
__ **Toward** & **Away** from Equally
__ **Toward** with some **Away** From
__ **Away** from with some **Toward**

Contexts:
__ Work/Career   __ Intimates
__ Relationships   __ Hobbies/Recreation
__ Sports   __ Other:_____
__ High/Medium/Low level   __ Driver MP: **Yes**/**No**

#21. Conation Choice in Adapting:
Options/Procedures

Concept: When it comes to dealing with instructions or getting something done, we have two broad responding styles—the *Procedures* style or the *Options* style.

Elicitation: Ask *why* questions. "Why did you choose your car?" (or job, town, bank, etc.).

Identification:
1. *Procedures.* People who orient themselves via procedures like to follow specific and definite procedures. They may not know how to generate such procedures if no one provides them. They work well at doing procedural tasks "the right way." They feel motivated when following a procedure and may have an almost compulsive need to complete a procedure. Thus the sense of closure (#37) typically will operate as an important value to them.

2. *Options.* Those who orient themselves via options, on the other hand, work much better at developing new procedures and at figuring out alternatives to a strategy. More typically, they will not work very well when it comes to following procedures they have already performed. If it works, they would prefer to improve it or alter it. Valuing alternatives and creativity, they would rather search for an innovative and different approach.

Languaging: After asking a "why" question, listen to the reasons given. If the person talks about choosing and expanding *options*—they express an options orientation. Listen for "possibilities, choices, reasons, other ways, alternatives, why tos." If the person tells you a story and/or gives you lots of facts, but doesn't talk about choosing—that person has expressed a procedure orientation. They answer the "why" question as if you had asked them a "how to" question. The story they tell will explain "how" they came into their situation. Listen for such linguistic markers as "right way, proven way, correct way, how to..."

Pacing: As you pace and communicate with someone who uses the options program, talk about possibilities, options, and innovations. "We'll bend the rules for you to get this done." Avoid giving fixed step-by-step procedures. Rather, play it by ear and emphasize all of the alternatives available to them. Allow them to violate procedures.

To pace and communicate with someone who uses the procedures program, specifically detail a procedure for them that clearly takes them from their present state to their desired state. Give them ways of dealing with procedural break downs. Use numerical overviews, "five steps to effective negotiation."

Contexts of Origin: Possibly the brain physiology involved in the specialization of right or left hemisphere can predispose one to left brain sequential tasks over right brain holistic and visual processes. Modeling and identifying with someone who effectively uses either style certainly plays a role as does dis-identifying with someone who uses a style that brings hurt and pain.

Further Reading: James and Woodsmall (1988), Dilts, Epstein, & Dilts (1991).

Self-Analysis:
__ Procedure/**O**ption/**B**oth Option-Procedure

Contexts:
__ Work/Career	__ Intimates
__ Relationships	__ Hobbies/Recreation
__ Sports	__ Other: _____
__ High/**M**edium/**L**ow level	__ Driver MP: **Yes/No**

#22. Adaptation Sort:
Judging/Perceiving
Controlling/Floating

Concept: In adapting ourselves to life, and to the information that influences our personal worlds, we can adapt in one of two broad styles—we move through life seeking to understand life on its own terms and so just perceive it. Or, we can make plans to order, regulate, and control life's events. In the first case, we just *perceive* and float along with things. In the second we *judge* what we like or dislike, what we would like to improve, and the ideas we have to more effectively manage.

Elicitation: "Do you like to live life spontaneously as the spirit moves you or according to a plan?" "Do you find it easy or difficult to make up your mind?" "If we did a project together, would you prefer we first outline and plan it in an orderly fashion or would you prefer to just begin to move into it and flexibly adjust to things as we go?" "Do you have a daytimer-type of calendar? Do you use it? Do you enjoy using it?"

Identification: Do we seek to adapt to the environment we find or do we seek to get the environment to adapt to us? Those who *judge and control*, desire (and attempt) to make life adapt to them. They live their life according to their plans, ideas, beliefs, hopes, and desires and so seek to make things fit and to bring order to their world (#25). They like closure, definite boundaries (i.e. rules, laws, procedures, etc.), clear cut categories (#37).

Those who *perceive-float* adapt themselves to life and reality by perceiving, observing, noting, and accepting. They flow through life in an easy and gentle way with less judgments about right and wrong, and less of a sense of violation about their plans. Typically they will do what they feel like at the moment and take a more philosophical attitude toward difficulties. They tend to like their options to remain open and may even avoid closure. They may have more difficulty deciding, evaluating, and taking a stand on things.

Huxley (1954) described the shift of consciousness that he experienced in an experiment with mescalin in *The Doors of Perception*. For him, it moved him out of his normal everyday thinking and sorting style to one that he described as "a sacred mindset." He interpreted it as having connected with "Mind at Large" so that "the reducing valve of the brain and nervous system" shifted and he experienced a kind of out of body experience of just perceiving.

"As I looked, this purely aesthetic, Cubist's eye view gave place to what I can only describe as the sacramental vision of reality. I looked at those bamboo legs, and did not merely gaze at them, but actually *being* them—or rather being myself in them... The mescalin taker sees no reason for doing anything in particular and finds most of the causes for which, at ordinary times, he was prepared to act and suffer, profoundly uninteresting."

Languaging: Listen for lists and schedules in those who judge-act. They will frequently tend to also operate in a Through "Time" fashion—sequentially. They don't change their minds unless new data warrants it. Listen for ideas and terms indicating spontaneity, freedom, understanding, accepting, etc. in those who perceive-float.

Pacing: In pacing and communicating with someone judging-acting, relate to him or her with promptness, in an organized and decisive way, focused on an outcome, etc. Talk about order, about getting and staying organized, becoming definite, resolution, structure, and commitment. In pacing someone perceiving-floating, communicate and relate in a spontaneous way without insisting on time schedules. Frame decisions as "keeping one's options open," and avoid wrapping things up too quickly. Talk about the values of feeling free, open, flexible, waiting and seeing, keeping things open-ended and tentative.

Statistics: These patterns divide down the middle at 50%. Those who judge-and-control in their adaptation tend to operate in a decisive way, think sequentially, plan, use "to do" lists, function in a "left-brain" way, etc. Those who perceive-and-float along in their adaptation tend to value and act with spontaneity. They like change, act impulsively, need autonomy, tolerate complexity well, function in a "right-brain" way, and struggle with personal discipline.

Contexts of Origin: This corresponds with one's experience of "time" (#46, #47, #48). Beliefs and values about taking charge, controlling one's environment versus accepting, adapting to the environment greatly effects which way one chooses to primarily feel about these issues. Anthropologists have found entire societies that fall into one or the other extreme. Religion, political philosophy, etc. also effects this. Prolonged trauma that generates a sense of Seligman's (1975) "learned helplessness" can nudge one to adopt the perceiving sort.

Further Reading: James and Woodsmall (1988), Seligman (1975, 1991), Huxley (1954).

Self-Analysis:
__ Judging-controlling/**Perceiving**-floating

Contexts:
__ Work/Career	__ Intimates
__ Relationships	__ Hobbies/Recreation
__ Sports	__ Other: _____
__ High/**Medium**/Low level	__ Driver MP: **Yes**/**No**

#23. Reason Sort of Modal Operators
Necessity/Possibility (Desire); Stick/Carrot

Concept: How people language themselves makes all the difference in the world on their model of the world and the experiences they generate from that map. In linguistics, *Modal Operators* refer to those specific kinds of words that reflect the *mode* of relating and *operating* that a person does in the world. Such words describe the kind of conceptual world one lives in and has mapped out. They reflect the *reasons* (necessity or desire) that a person acts as he or she does (e.g. their mode of acting or operating). These terms also indicate the limitations incorporated within a person's map—what they map as required (must), impossible (can't), or not allowed.

In a person's motivation strategy, these linguistic terms show up in the auditory digital component. They comprise the words we use to get us moving. The general category of modal operators include necessity, desire, possibility, and impossibility. These words shed light on the more abstract conceptual states of choice, freedom, empowerment, victimhood, obligations, and possibilities.

Elicitation: Ask, "How did you motivate yourself to go to work today? What did you say to yourself that helped to get you moving?" Ask questions that presuppose motivation, then listen for Modal Operator words, and you will detect operational meta-programs at work. "Why did you choose your present job?" "Why have you chosen this school or that schedule?" Notice if the person responds by giving you *a reason*. If the person gives no reasons, he or she more typically comes from a mode of necessity—he or she *has to*! A "law" in their head demands it! If you get a reason, it will relate to possibilities, obligations, or desires.

Identification and Languaging: *Necessity words* include "must, have to, should," etc. These indicate that a person operates from a model of compulsion, control, law, etc. "I know I had to go to work." *Impossibility words* include "can't, shouldn't, must not," etc. "A person shouldn't miss work or show up late!" These indicate that we have mapped out a taboo law in our world against various proposed options. *Possibility words* include "can, will, may, would, could," etc. These reflect an optimistic model where we view various options and alternatives as possible. "Well another day, another dollar." "When I get to work today, I will work on..." *Desire words* include "want to, love to, get to," etc. These arise from a model of the world as including wants, desires, and passions. "I feel so lucky to get to go to work!" *Choice words* include "choose to, want to, I opt for," etc. These indicate a mental map that allows for human will, intention, and choice. "I choose to go to work."

These words arise from different models of the world. They also create differing emotional and behavioral responses. People who operate from the mode of *possibility* do what they want to do and so develop reasons. They look for new opportunities for expanding their options. Possibility people generally believe that they have some (or a lot of) control over life and so feel motivated to make choices and take action. *Necessity* people tend to look upon life as a routine or burden to which they have little or no choice. They often believe and therefore feel themselves stuck with their lot in life; and, given their model of limitation—so they act, so they perceive.

Those who use *both* necessity and possibility words and operate from both models will feel motivated by *both* options and obligations. Think of some task you will do in the near future. Now say to yourself, (1) "I must do...." and then, (2) "I can do...." and now, (3) "I get to..." Which works best for you in terms of enhancing your motivation?

Impossibility words (e.g. can't, shouldn't) usually create personal limitations and feed a passive style of coping which severely limits a person's responsiveness.

Such words typically indicate taboos, as in "I can't stand criticism." We can translate this as, "I don't give myself permission to stand or tolerate criticism." In these kinds of psychological *can'ts* we have a map that precludes certain concepts. They differ significantly from physiological *can'ts.* "I can't lift a car." "I can't fly."

Desire words lead to more motivation and drive—unless they map out wild and unrealistic dreams. In that case they lead to disappointment, disillusionment, and frustration.

Pacing: When packaging your communication, match the person's Modal Operators, which inevitably will operate as a powerful motivator for that person, or subtly provide reframes by suggesting other Modal Operators.

RET Cognitive Distortions: The person who operates predominately by *necessity*, when over-done, can get into *Should-ing and Must-ing* which Ellis has humorously designated as Musterbation Thinking. Such Should-ing and Must-ing puts lots of pressure on oneself and others and can evoke resentment and resistance. Too much Should-ing generates lots of unnecessary and inappropriate shame, guilt, self-contempt and other similar unresourceful states. In RET literature, people who live by these cognitive distortions can then move into a belief state of *Demandingness* on self, others, and the universe. This, in turn, then feeds an attitude of *Entitlement* which then deepens the disappointment, disillusionment, and depression. As a map-making style, it makes for poor adjustment to the constraints of reality.

Contexts of Origin: This valuational meta-program operates primarily as a languaged phenomenon. It probably arises first of all as a reflection of the kind of language used to motivate us by parents and teachers, "You have to listen to me." "Think about what you can get from this experience." Trauma and hurt can drive a person away from the world of possibility and desire as a maneuver to protect oneself from disappointment. Strict and overly disciplined homes and communities can evoke one to adopt the necessity mode and impossibility mode.

Further Reading: Bandler and Grinder (1975), Ellis (1976).

Self-Analysis:
__ **Possibility** (Desire)/**Necessity** (Impossibility)

Contexts:
__ Work/Career	__ Intimates
__ Relationships	__ Hobbies/Recreation
__ Sports	__ Other:_____
__ **High**/**Medium**/**Low** level	__ Driver MP: **Yes**/**No**

#24. Preference Sort:
Primary Interest—People/Place/Things/Activity/Information

Concept: People have preferences regarding their interests. When we ask about a person's *favorite way* to take a vacation, most favored kind of work, one of his or her top ten experiences in life—we will typically evoke the person's meta-program of preference. Primary interests fall into categories of *people* (who), *place* (where), *things* (what), *activity* (how) *information* (why, what information), and *time* (when).

Elicitation: "What would you find as really important in how you choose to spend your next two week vacation?" "What kinds of things, people, activities, etc. would you want present for you to evaluate it as really great?" "Tell me about your favorite restaurant." This value filter identifies those factors that we esteem and choose as most crucial. This provides information about a person's specific carrots.

Identification: Some people care most about *who* they experience something with (people), *where* they go for the experience (the location or place), the *things* that it involves (objects or things), the kinds of behaviors and *activities* that they do there (activity), or the kind of *data* that they obtain or experience (information). This sorting style leads to, and suggests, one's values and choices.

1. *People.* Those who prefer people as their primary value care most of all about *who*. So they talk (sometimes incessantly) about people: what others say, think, feel, do. They can fall into the habit of gossiping when they over-do this preference. They relate well socially, but hate to experience alone-ness, turning it into "loneliness."

2. *Place.* They have geography and location on the mind! *Where* really counts as of supreme importance. So they find lots of meaning in terms of the environment—what they see, hear and feel in that context. They generally take lots of pride in their "places" (home, office, garden, shop, etc.) in terms of locality, layout, furnishings, etc.

3. *Things.* These people focus on *what* lies in their environment: possessions, money, food, surroundings, etc. They tend to take pride over both tangible things (house, car, clothes, etc.) and intangible things (degrees, status, security, power, etc). They tend to seek to find meaning and happiness via these things. Positively, this means that they will take care of things. Negatively, this suggests that they will do so to the neglect of people. They will "love" people by giving and/or using things.

4. *Activity.* People with this preference focus on the *how* of a process or set of actions primarily. They like doing things, going places, feeling the rush of activities. They prefer liveliness and motion and strongly dislike "just sitting around" type of activities. Boredom really puts them off.

5. *Time.* James (1989) includes "time" as a part of the activity category. But we separate it here, as many others do. Those who value any of the many meanings and categories of "time" (see Bodenhamer and Hall, 1997), can endow this semantic-conceptual reality with lots of importance. It shows up in such beliefs as, "Time is money." "Time is a commodity." "Don't waste time." This person wants to know "how much time will it take?" "How long will we stay there?" "*When* will we return?"

6. *Information.* Those who prefer ideas (*the why and what* of information) sort for things in terms of what they will learn, from whom, the value of the information, how they can apply it, etc. Rather than where, with whom, and when these people care about the learning experience that they will experience.

Pacing and Languaging: Listen for and match back the specific kind of preferences that the person offers.

Contexts of Origin: Since we can give value to all of these experiences, and do, we undoubtedly develop our sorting style from our own experiences of pleasure and pain with them, as we also model those significant ones in our life.

Further Reading: Woodsmall (1988).

Self-Analysis:
__ People/Places/Things/Activity/Information
__ Combinations of such: _____

Contexts:
    __ Work/Career   __ Intimates
    __ Relationships   __ Hobbies/Recreation
    __ Sports   __ Other: _____
    __ High/Medium/Low level __ Driver MP: Yes/No

#25. Goal Striving Sort—Adapting to Expectations:
Perfectionism/Optimization/Skepticism

Concept: People differ in how they think-feel and then choose to go after their goals. Some process goal-setting and reaching in a *perfection style,* others do so in an *optimization style,* and yet others avoid the whole subject as they try to step aside from it and choose to *not* set goals (a goal itself!).

Elicitation: "Tell me about a goal that you have set and how did you go about making it come true?" "If you set a goal today to accomplish something of significance, how would you begin to work on it?"

Identification:
1. *Perfectionism Sorting.* Going for "perfection" (flawlessness) turns one into a perfectionist who tends to never feel satisfied with his or her performance. They can always see a flaw in their performance and the performance of others! Because they set their goals unrealistically high, they constantly stay frustrated. They view the *end-product* as their criteria for moving toward their goal and tend to discount the joy and challenge of getting there as part of the process. By setting extremely high goals and criteria, people who use this style tend to treat themselves and others with harsh judgment for anything that falls short. Often they fall into procrastination as a protective device.

Perfectionism frequently involves a future orientation that becomes excessive. I (BB) used to live that way. I lived so much oriented toward my future that I missed a lot of the present. And as I held a belief against ever attaining satisfaction (in order to leave room for improvement), I generally lived in a state of continual frustration and dissatisfaction! Eventually this led to burnout—a good burnout that got me to change my goal sort metaprogram.

2. *Optimizing Sorting.* Those who move forward toward their goals optimizing operate more pragmatically. They simply do the best with what they have, and let it go at that. They also set goals in small steps so that they can appreciate little stages of success along the way. For them, half the fun involves *the process of moving toward a goal.*

As I (BB) recovered from my burnout, I came across this: "When planning a vacation, enjoy the packing as much as the actual vacation!"

An extreme optimizer can adopt such unrealistic "positive" thinking-feeling that he or she will deny and/or ignore real problems and constraints.

3. *Defeatist Sorting.* Those who avoid goal-setting and achieving think-and-feel pessimistically and skeptically about the whole subject. So they choose to avoid directly thinking about the future or taking effective action to give it birth. Expecting only the worst to happen, they refuse to participate in managing themselves and their objectives through time.

4. *Realist Sorting.* Those who adopt this style aim primarily at relating to goals only in terms of "facts." They do little of the dreaming, desiring, and hoping of the optimizing style, they reduce it to the bare bone facts—the pure sensory-based world.

Languaging: This meta-program enables us to predict when a person will stop in his or her efforts (i.e. persevering), and the manner in which the person will set goals, strive for them, and recognize meeting them. This program shows up whenever we invite someone to talk about a goal, objective, dream, or possibility. "Tell me about a goal that you have recently set for yourself?" "Tell me about an instant when you motivated yourself by setting a goal." "If we did a project together, would you take more interest in getting started, maintaining during the middle or wrapping it up?"

Those who operate perfectionistically begin projects well. But then they often get bogged down in details and/or caught up in negative emotional states (e.g. frustration over flaws). They talk a lot about the end product, and yet block themselves from getting there. The end product never seems good enough for them. Optimizers seem to flow along a lot better, and ironically, produce higher levels of excellence because they do not aim at getting it "just right." The skeptical defeatists treat goal-setting talk as worthless and useless and will tell stories of how it has never worked or caused great disappointment.

A note about the term *"realistic."* People in each category assume themselves as the only "true realist!" What else could we expect when, after all, each uses his or her "reality strategy" (model of the world) to define the "real?"

Pacing: Once you know a person's style of moving toward a goal, match it in your communications about an objective you want to offer him or her.

Emoting: Expect to see and hear lots of excitement, passion, and motivation in the optimizers, wild-eyed expectations and/or total frustration in perfectionists, and skepticism and negativism in those who avoid goal-setting.

Contexts of Origin: How we actualize our valued goals and go about fulfilling them describes a learned phenomenon. We learn this via modeling, instruction, pain and pleasure that either rewards or punishes our first feeble efforts, and the language we use to articulate supporting beliefs. Trauma experiences can knock a person out of the running so that he or she becomes skeptical about the whole process. The more shoulds, musts, and have tos that a person uses in motivating themselves (#23), the more likely she or he will aim perfectionistically.

Further Reading: Woodsmall (1988).

Self-Analysis:
__ **Perfectionistic/Optimizing/Skepticism**

Contexts:
__ Work/Career	__ Intimates
__ Relationships	__ Hobbies/Recreation
__ Sports	__ Other: _____
__ High/Medium/Low level	__ Driver MP: **Yes/No**

#26. Value Buying Sort:
Cost/Convenience/Quality/Time

Concept: When it comes to purchasing and deciding to purchase, we typically sort for four primary values. These tend more often than not to the forefront of consciousness: *cost, convenience, quality, and time.*

Elicitation: "What do you primarily concern yourself with—the price, convenience, time, or quality, or some combination of these when you consider making a purchase?"

Ask the person to imagine two-triangles sitting on top of each other (Figure 5:1). Let each end stand for each of these factors of cost, time, quality, and convenience. This double-triangle diagram can help one sort out and decide about how to prioritize these things. "Now put a dot at the place that represents where you feel that you put most of your concern in the double-triangle." Doing this brings to the foreground of awareness the trade-offs between these values. It also assists a person to avoid feeling victimized if he or she whimsically changes their mind later and then expects another to have guessed it! "What do you primarily want?"

Figure 5.1

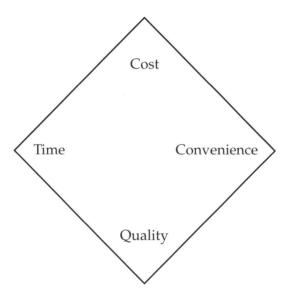

Identification: Some people mainly concern themselves with (and focus on) the price, others focus principally on the convenience factor, others on quality, and yet others on the time factor, or some combination of these. These *values*, applied to purchasing, often conflict with each other. While we often mention cost as the chief, or only, purchase decision factor, a person could process and sort for his or her values anywhere on a continuum involving these factors. A list of convenience and comfort features can quickly override the first-mentioned cost factors.

Pacing: Once you know the priority of values between cost, convenience, quality, and time, match the person in your communications.

Languaging: Listen for words indicating these values.

Contexts of Origin: How we learn to value one of these experiences over the other in our choosing to buy something undoubtedly arises from those from whom we learned, the value system encouraged by the contexts of religion, culture, social status, etc. Negative trauma experience with cost, quality, and time can make these "sore spots" that we may not carefully guard against.

Further Reading: Reese and Bagley (1988).

Self-Analysis:
__ Cost/Convenience/Quality/Time

Contexts:
__ Work/Career   __ Intimates
__ Relationships   __ Hobbies/Recreation
__ Sports   __ Other: _____
__ High/Medium/Low level   __ Driver MP: Yes/No

#27. Responsibility Sort:
Over-Responsible/Under-Responsible/Balanced

Concept: People think about, sort for, and emote about *the concept of "responsibility"* in different ways (For this reason, this operating system operates as a *meta* meta-program, and yet we have chosen to put it here because it also plays such a crucial role in this realm of choices. This also illustrates the arbitrary nature of these categories.) For those who love, desire, and want responsibility, they move toward it, and view actions, speech, emotions, etc. in terms of feeling responsible for things. Others dislike, do not want, and find the concept aversive. They may have much pain associated with the idea of "responsibility." So they move away from it, either by ignoring and not noticing it, or by thinking of the opposite— how others have responsibility for things—even their own thoughts, emotions, and behaviors.

Elicitation: "When you think about having and owning responsibility for something in a work situation or personal relationship, what thoughts and emotions occur to you?" "Has someone ever held you responsible for something that went wrong that felt very negative to you?" "What positive experiences can you remember about someone holding you responsible for something and/or validate you as 'response-able'?"

Identification: The *ability* to *respond* describes a basic human power. As a concept, this ability to respond divides into two areas: responsibility *for* self—for thinking, emoting, speaking and behaving, and responsibility *to* others. The first describes *"accountability,"* the second describes *"relation-ship."* In the first, we own and accept ourselves as accountable **for** our responses. This describes our "circle of response" or our "power zone" (the zone where we truly have "the ability to do" something). The second describes how we relate **to** others in terms of how we speak to them and treat them. This describes our "circle of influence" *with* others.

1. *Over-responsible sorting.* Those who assume too much responsibility take on caretaking roles. They excel at problem solving, sympathizing, caring, and wanting to make things better. Over-done they can play out co-dependent roles to someone who cops out on his or her responsibilities. Such persons, more frequently than not, fail to distinguish between response-ability *for* things in their arena of response and response-ability *to* other people.

In over-responsible sorting, people aggress beyond their circle of response into the "power zone" of others. When over-done, this comes across as intrusive and as sending the message, "I don't trust you to be responsible."

2. *Under-responsible sorting.* Those who fail to respond appropriately **for** their own thinking, emoting, speaking, and behaving tend to rely on others to take care of them. During the dependency of infancy and childhood, this operates effectively and appropriately. In adulthood, infantile dependency continues in some people who fail to accept their own response-ability **for** themselves.

In under-responsible sorting, people think of themselves as dependent and needy. This deepens their sense of victimhood and so easily turns into blaming and demanding. When over-done, they live from a state of entitlement and hold others, government, etc. as responsible *for* their happiness.

3. *Balanced.* Those who appropriately accept and assume the ability to respond *for* themselves and *to* others. They look to, and use, appropriate context markers to let them know when to give and when to receive.

Languaging, Emoting & Pacing: Over-responsible people tend to *care* too much and get into care-taking and co-dependency relations. They typically talk about the problems and hurts of others, and do so associatedly. When they feel the need, they then assume responsibility for others—which ironically weakens those in need. The under-responsible tend to want such care, define it as "being loved," accuse and blame if it doesn't come, and do not know the feeling of true independence or inter-dependency.

In my (BB) experience, I've noticed that the *intensity* of co-dependency directly correlates with how much an individual goes second position to others.

Contexts of Origin: Since we do not have the high level concept of "responsibility" at birth, it develops through the years as we mature. We all start out under-responsible, totally dependent upon caretakers. Here family, cultural, and racial style plays an important part, as do the values from these sources as well as religion, politics, school, etc.

Trauma can send a person either way in how one runs his or her brain about "responsibility." One can play the victim and refuse all responsibility or one can play the great rescuer, care-taker, and adopt a messianic complex to save the world.

One form of dysfunctional parenting involves training children to take care of and feel responsible for the emotions of the parents. If the child buys it, he or she will grow up and adopt two toxic beliefs: (1) My worth lies in my ability to perform for others and please them. (2) I will only get someone to love me if I take care of them and become responsible for them.

Further Reading: Hall (1989), Beattie (1987).

Self-Analysis:
__ Over-responsible/Under-responsible/Balanced

Contexts:
__ Work/Career	__ Intimates
__ Relationships	__ Hobbies/Recreation
__ Sports	__ Other: _____
__ High/Medium/Low level	__ Driver MP: **Yes/No**

#28. People Convincer Sort:
Distrusting/Trusting—Paranoid/Naive

Concept: Growing out of how "minds" process *evidence* and therefore experience a state of feeling convinced (#17), this meta-program addresses the same processes—only in terms of the way our Operating System applies this to *people* and in terms of *relating* to them. Some people use a thinking-feeling pattern of distrust, others of trust.

Elicitation: "When you think about meeting someone new, do you immediately have a sense of trust and openness to the person, or thoughts and feelings of distrust, doubt, questions, jealousy, insecurity, etc.?" "How do you typically choose to relate to a person, or a group of people, before you know them very well—with trust or with caution?"

Identification:
1. *Distrusting.* People who immediately question, wonder, feel a little (or a lot) defensive will hold back, explore, make sure about the person's motives, intentions, and style. They will typically adopt a jealous, guarded, defended position, and do not immediately trust. They will come across as unfriendly and not very approachable (which then becomes a self-fulfilling prophecy—proving their belief!).

2. *Trusting.* People who immediately trust, feel connected, and act trustingly quickly move out to people and will even embrace the stranger. Typically, they will come across as warm, friendly, interested, and outgoing. When over-done, they will naively trust anything people say—which then allows them to get manipulated and taken advantage of easily.

Languaging and Personality: The distrust orientation forms a person so that he or she will move out into social situations and new relationships very cautiously, never feeling convinced about the other's motives or intentions. When difficulties arise, they can quickly access a state of "abuse," feeling controlled and manipulated. This will then deepen and prove the importance of distrusting others. The trust orientation as an Operating System causes one quickly and immediately to reach out to others with warmth, charm, and sometimes naivety.

Contexts of Origin: Erickson's (1959, 1968) model of the psycho-social stages of development details the trust/distrust stage as occurring between two and five years of age and primarily concerning parents and early emotionally significant persons. Did they behave in a trustworthy way? Could the child trust the provider's words as accurate representations of the world and of the behaviors that they would then do? Later traumas of betrayal, violation of trusts, etc. can also generate the distrust program.

Further Reading: Erickson (1959, 1968).

Self-Analysis:
__ Distrust/Trust Orientation

    __ Work/Career
    __ Work/Career   __ Intimates
    __ Relationships   __ Hobbies/Recreation
    __ Sports   __ Other: _____
    __ High/Medium/Low level __ Driver MP: **Yes/No**

Conclusion

Everyday we all make hundreds of *choices and decisions* about how to think-and-feel and how to act as we move through life.

- Should I approach or avoid this or that?
- Do I want options or a clear and specific procedure for advancing?
- How can I make this event, thought, or person fit into my reality?
- Or, How can I enjoy this experience and observe it more fully?
- Do I have to go to work or do I get to?
- Must I act kind and thoughtful, or shall I so choose?
- What facets of life shall I give my primary interest to?
- Shall I set some goals for what I want today?
- How shall I set this or that goal and "make it happen?"
- What should I focus on when I buy this product?
- Shall I own and claim responsibility or would I prefer to reject such?
- Should I trust people or treat people with caution?

This conative dimension of consciousness obviously intimately involves our thoughts-and-feelings. Rollo May said that when we break down the old word "will" psychoanalytically, we find two processes—*intending and attending.* In *intending* we consider what we want, desire, like and value and so focus our consciousness on that object. In *attending* we do the directive work of noticing our consciousness and constantly nudge or swish it back to our intention

#20.	**Direction Sort:** *Toward/ Away From, Past Assurance/ Future Possibilities; Approach / Avoidance*
#21.	**Conation Choice in Adapting:** *Options/ Procedures*
#22.	**Adaptation Sort:** *Judging / Perceiving; Controlling/ Floating*
#23.	**Reason Sort of Modal Operators:** *Necessity/ Possibility (Desire); Stick / Carrot*
#24.	**Preference Sort:** *Primary Interest— People/ Place/ Things/ Activity/ Information*
#25.	**Goal Sort—Adapting to Expectations:** *Perfection/ Optimization/ Skepticism*
#26.	**Value Buying Sort:** *Cost/ Convenience/ Quality/ Time*
#27.	**Responsibility Sort:** *Over-Responsible/ Under-Responsible*
#28.	**People Convincer Sort:** *Distrusting / Trusting*

Chapter 6

The "Response" Meta-Programs

Meta-Programs in Outputting, Responding, Communicating
(#29-39)

We defined a "**state** of consciousness" as first involving the *attention* of consciousness involved in such components as "mind," "emotion," and "will." A **state** also involves a meta-level patterning and structuring that displays its *products*. Thus we not only "think" in terms of what we notice and input, what we process and internally structure, what we incorporate in our body (somatize), but also in terms of what we *output*. Don't you?

Don't you pay attention to things (your input)? Don't you take those thoughts-and-emotions and build an internal world with them? Don't you then emotionally experience (somatize) these things in your very body? And don't you pay attention to *how you come across* in your talk, gestures, and behaviors?

This last question suggests that we also sort for, and have awareness of, **our social context.** It suggests also that we pay attention to (use our recursive awareness of) the effect that our output has on others as we communicate and respond.

Thus our operating system, as any computer operating system, has an active and *recursive* interface. This word "recursive" means that the information that *results* from one stage in our processing then becomes *the input* for the next stage. Using this systems language implies that human consciousness in its sorting operates as **a system**.

Depending on what kind of operating system a computer uses (e.g. Dos, Windows 3.1, Windows 95, OS2, etc.) *how* that system outputs its structures and patterns radically governs how then, in turn, one works with it.

In the human meta-program operating system, we output in the way we talk and communicate, how we somatize, act, behave, gesture, how we interact socially, etc. Thus with these meta-programs, human consciousness reaches further and further out to take in more and more of its environment. This implies that "mind" and human processing and sorting does not just occur in the brain.

Should we think in this way about consciousness? Should we not, as philosophers and psychologists have for centuries, postulate "mind" as existing solely in the head, or at least inside the body? Modern philosophers in the field of systems, like Gregory Bateson, think otherwise.

Bateson (1972, 1976), Jerome Bruner (1990), and other theorists emphasize "mind" as located not only inside the skull of an individual person, but also systemically into the immediate physical and cultural environment of the person. To think of "mind" as transcending the brain may offer such a radically different perspective, the reader may have to suspend his or her judgments to give this facet of "mind" an open hearing.

Bateson (1972) asks about "mind" and "self" when he uses the illustration of a blind man with his walking stick,

> "...ask anybody about the localization and boundaries of the self... consider a blind man with a stick. Where does the blind man's self begin? At the tip of the stick? At the handle of the stick? Or at some point halfway up the stick? These questions are nonsense, because the stick is a pathway along which differences are transmitted under transformation, so that to draw a delimiting line *across* this pathway is to cut off a part of the systemic circuit which determines the blind man's locomotion.

> Similarly, his sense organs are transducers or pathways for information, as also are his axons, etc. From a systems-theoretic point of view, it is a misleading metaphor to say that what travels in an axon is an 'impulse.' It would be more correct to say that what travels is a difference, or a transform of a difference." (p. 318).

> "The total self-corrective unit which processes information, or, as I say, 'thinks' and 'acts' and 'decides,' is a *system* whose boundaries do not at all coincide with the boundaries either of the body or of what is popularly called the 'self' or 'consciousness'; and it is

important to notice that there are *multiple* differences between the thinking system and the 'self' as popularly conceived... The network is not bounded by the skin but includes all external pathways along which information can travel." (p. 319).

I (MH) mentioned this aspect of "mind" as a *cultural construct* in my dissertation (1996d) and suggested that it leads us to think about our "self" and our consciousness in a very different way. Normally, we think of the "self" and "mind" as inside our heads rather than as part of the walking stick or as part of our cultural constructs. Bruner (1990) wrote,

"It is man's participation *in* culture and the realization of his mental powers *through* culture that make it impossible to construct a human psychology on the basis of the individual alone. ...Clyde Kluckhohn used to insist, human beings do not terminate at their own skins; they are expressions of a culture. To treat the world as an indifferent flow of information to be processed by individuals each on his or her own terms is to lose sight of how individuals are formed and how they function. Or to quote Gertz again, 'there is no such thing as a human nature independent of culture.'" (p. 12).

#29.	**Rejuvenation of Battery Sort:** *Extrovert, Ambivert, Introvert*
#30.	**Affiliation & Management Sort:** *Independent/ Team Player/ Manager*
#31.	**Communication Stance Sort**: *Communication Modes*
#32.	**General Response:** *Congruent/ Incongruent/ Competitive/ Cooperative/ Polarity/ Meta*
#33.	**Somatic Response Style:** *Active / Reflective/ Both/ Inactive*
#34.	**Work Preference Sort:** *Things / Systems / People/ Information*
#35.	**Comparison Sort:** *Quantitative / Qualitative*
#36.	**Knowledge Sort:** *Modeling/ Conceptualizing/ Demonstrating/ Experiencing/ Authorizing*
#37.	**Completion/ Closure Sort:** *Closure / Non-Closure*
#38.	**Social Presentation:** *Shrewd & Artful/ Genuine & Artless*
#39.	**Hierarchical Dominance Sort:** *Power/ Affiliation/ Achievement*

#29. Rejuvenation of Battery Sort:
Extrovert, Ambivert, Introvert

Concept: How people process their thoughts-and-feelings about their social experience with others, especially in the context of needing to "renew one's battery," identifies this meta-program. In this regard, we tend to sort for experiencing lots of time with people (extrovert), lots of time away from people and with self (introvert), or a balanced mixture of the two (ambivert).

Jung described the *Introvert/Extrovert* category as an attitude preference. It begins with an awareness of whether we pay attention to ourself or others, whether our attention moves inward or outward. "What attitude do you take toward the external world of people as evidenced by your behavior?"

Elicitation: Extroversion and introversion refer to a person's desire, need, and enjoyment of experiencing other people and social environments or solitude when down, discouraged, negative, or stressed. We can discover this pattern by asking, "When you need your batteries recharged, do you want to get with others or get away by yourself, or can you equally recharge your batteries in either situation?"

Identification:
1. When it comes to the context of wanting to experience some mental-emotional rejuvenation, encouragement, support, and personal renewal, some people primarily turn their attention outward to others and so have an *extroverted style* of relating when stressed.

2. Others turn their attention inward, get off by themselves when they need to deal with their stresses, negative emotions, demotivations, etc. Thus they adopt a more *introverted style* under stress.

3. Those who can do either, equally, have an *ambiverted style*.

James and Woodsmall (1988) say by *introverting*, a person tends to have fewer friends but deeper relationships, reflects before acting, enjoys working alone, scores high on aptitude tests, loves concepts, values aesthetics, and looks to self for causes. By *extroverting*, a person has lots of friends and acquaintances, but usually not many deep relations. They look outside of themselves to others or the environment for causes, and may even fear aloneness.

Pacing and *Languaging:* Listen for their values of needing people for encouragement and validation, or if they value doing such themselves. Listen for self-referencing and other-referencing when it comes to the context of feeling down and needing a shot in the arm.

Emoting: The context of this meta-program occurs when a person feels down and wants to move to feeling better. Does the experience of interacting with others recharge their batteries or expend them?

Each feels most comfortable within the given realm. Those who *introvert* enjoy the peace in his or her own inner world of personal thoughts and ideas. They experience such as solitude. The extreme introverting style enjoys a reclusive style. 25% of the population adopt this style. Because they attend to ideas, concepts, thoughts, they often have a greater depth of concentration and introspection. They view extroverting as shallow and inauthentic.

Those who *extrovert* prefer the company of others and so love crowds, parties, events, etc. 75% of the population adopt this style. Because they love people, they tend toward a sociable, action-oriented, and impulsive style involving high social adjustment skills, talkative, gregarious, outgoing, etc. Typically, these people experience the aloneness of solitude as the distress and pain of loneliness.

Contexts of Origin: Some neurological studies suggest innate factors that predispose a person toward a more shy and retiring style versus a more engaging style. Yet that doesn't entirely explain this program. How significant persons modeled social interactions, skills, whether they make it a joy or a living hell, powerfully conditions one toward extroversion or introversion.

Further Reading: James and Woodsmall (1988).

Self-Analysis:
__ Extrovert/Introvert/Ambivert

Contexts:
- __ Work/Career
- __ Relationships
- __ Sports
- __ High/**Medium**/Low level

- __ Intimates
- __ Hobbies/Recreation
- __ Other: _____
- __ Driver MP: **Yes**/No

#30. Affiliation & Management Sort:
Independent/Team Player/Manager

Concept: This meta-program refers to how a person processes and handles the experiencing of working with other people in a task-oriented situation. How does he or she want to experience himself vis-a-vis the group? People generally process this question in terms of staying *independent, team playing,* or *managing.*

This meta-program relates primarily to any context that involves getting a task accomplished and so it has significant applications in the context of business. It provides valuable information for determining a person's suitability for self-management, working as a team player, and/or managing others. It also provides insight into a person's flexibility in inter-personal relations. Does their consciousness naturally go out with interest to the success of others, do they desire to assist them, etc.?

Elicitation: Ask the following three questions successively in the following order:

1. "Do you know what you need in order to feel and function more successfully at work (or at this task?)"
2. "Do you know what someone else needs in order to feel and function more successfully?"
3. "Do you find it easy or difficult to tell a person what he or she needs to do to succeed?"

When you ask these three questions in this order, various patterns may result: Self and others, Self only, Team Players, Others only, Self but not others.

Identification:
1. *Self and others* (managing) will answer "Yes" to all three. They do so because they process, value, and orient themselves by *managing* both self and others. They know what they need to do to increase their success, know what others need to do, and don't hesitate to say so (estimated at 60% to 80% of the U.S. population). Often these managing types, with their "take charge" attitude(!), will assume that others should have and use the same principles and values that they do (see judging #22).

2. *Self only* (independent workers) will answer "Yes, no, no." This describes those who process, value, and orient themselves *independently.* They have the capacity for management in the fact that they know the strategies for succeeding, but they do not want to manage (estimated very low, 1% to 2%).

3. *Others only* (dependent workers) will answer "No, yes, yes-or-no." They tend to wait on the boss, the system, a spouse, etc. to tell them what to do. They may intuitively lack awareness about what to do, or not trust their own judgments, or function by a passive and waiting operational style. Typically, once given instructions, they do not hesitate to take action. Bureaucrats also will answer "No, yes, and yes." (estimated at 6% to 7%).

4. *Self but not others* (potential managers) will answer "Yes, yes-or no, no." They know what it will take for others to succeed, but they feel hesitant and inhibited from intruding or getting involved in such communications. Various beliefs, values, experiences, lack of skills, etc. could hold them back. This means that they typically do not even desire to manage (estimated between 15% and 20%).

5. *Team players* will answer, "Sometimes, sometimes, sometimes." This describes those who process, value, and orient themselves via a *team playing* mode. Depending upon the circumstances and contexts, they may or may not want to play a manager role, but may want to co-facilitate the success of the group as a whole.

Languaging: By using the following open-ended question, we can discover a person's need for affiliation, team playing, or independence. "Tell me about a work situation where you felt the happiest. When and where did that occur? What factors contributed to your sense of fulfillment?"

Emoting: Independent persons like to do things on their own. They also like to assume and take responsibility for their own motivation and management. They score high on self-control and discipline (Self-Referencing, #14). Those who operate from a polarity response will sort for independence because "they can't be told anything." *Team players* like the camaraderie that comes with working as a team and doing something together. They like the terms and concepts of togetherness, "family," "just being around people," etc. *Management players* enjoy the supervisory role of directing and guiding people.

Pacing: Pace your communications according to the person's sort.

Contexts of Origin The debate continues about whether leaders come wired that way from birth or not. To date we have no evidence of "born" leaders. Here the style of social action in early life, the thoughts-and-emotions surrounding such, identifying or disidentifying from such models seems to primarily create this way of sorting. Obviously, trauma experiences can provide a strong stimulus to stay away from trying to work with or through people!

Experiences early in one's career may help to solidify this meta-program. The person who experiences a great deal of satisfaction through working on a team or in management will undoubtedly attach a lot of pleasure to such. The same may occur if one experiences a positive role model in this area.

Further Reading: James and Woodsmall (1988).

Self-Analysis:
__ Management/Independent/Dependent/Potential Manager/Team
   Player

Contexts:
__ Work/Career	__ Intimates
__ Relationships	__ Hobbies/Recreation
__ Sports	__ Other: _____
__ High/Medium/Low level	__ Driver MP: **Yes**/No

#31. Communication Stance Sort:
Blamer, Placator, Distracter, Computer, Leveler

Concept: Virginia Satir noted that communication involves both content and style. She distinguished five styles or modes of communicating that we now designate as the "Satir Communication Categories." The basic stylistic modes of communicating in her model involve four typically ineffective and non-productive stances, although on occasion we may put them to good use. These involve *placating, blaming, computing, and distracting.* She designated the generally healthy mode as *leveling.*

Elicitation: "How do you typically communicate in terms of placating, blaming, computing, and distracting, or leveling?"

Identification:

1. *Placating* refers to soothing, pleasing, pacifying, and making concessions. When a person "has" to please he shows an addiction to the approval of others. Emotionally, placators feel frightened that others will get angry, go away, or reject them. So they talk in an ingratiating way, trying always to please, forever apologizing, and never disagreeing. Verbally their words aim to agree and please. The placating posture seems to say, "I'm helpless and worthless." Placators wriggle, fidget, lean. Like cocker spaniel puppies, they desperately want to please.

To try *the placating stance* on—orient yourself to think-and-feel like a worthless nothing. Aim to act like a "Yes Man." Talk as though you can do nothing for yourself and as if you *must* always get approval. Tell yourself, "I'm lucky just to be allowed to eat." "I *owe* everybody gratitude." "I feel totally responsible for everything that goes wrong." "I could have stopped the rain if I only used my brains, but I don't have any." Agree with all criticism made about you. Act in the most syrupy, martyrish, bootlicking way that you can.

Imagine yourself down on one knee, wobbling a bit, putting out your hand in a begging fashion, with head up so your neck hurts and eyes begin to strain so in no time at all you'll get a headache. Talking from this position your voice will sound whiny and squeaky. You won't have enough air to keep a rich, full voice. Then say, "Oh, you know me, I don't care." "Whatever anybody else wants is fine with me." "What do I want to do? I don't know. What would you like to do?"

After Vince turned twelve, his fathered died. Vince then saw his "incompetent" mother flounder and so he came to take over the responsibilites of rearing his two younger siblings. Then at fifteen, he spent a couple days away from home with a friend.

Upon returning home, Vince discovered an empty house. His mother had moved without his knowledge so he returned to an empty house and no food. In that traumatic moment he decided, "If I ever get married, no matter what happens, I will not lose the relationship or closeness to my children."

Later when Vince married, he held true to that decision. After thirty-one years his wife died. At that time, his 29 year old daughter moved into the business and took over maintaining the office of his auto body shop. Recently, Vince discovered that she had embezzled $35000 from the business. In her long history of stealing and writing bad checks, Vince had always bailed her out—his belief and decision about "family" demanded it.

Vince sorted using the meta-program of placating with his daughter. Coming out of his limiting belief, he would do anything to please her to maintain the relationship.

Getting well for him meant learning how to shift to the Computer and Leveler modes when setting limits, problem solving, and discerning the boundaries of responsibility.

2. *Blaming* refers to finding fault, dictating, and bossing. The blamer acts superior and sends out the message, "If it weren't for you, everything would be all right." Blamers feel that nobody cares about them. Internally blamers feel tightness in muscles and organs which indicate rising blood pressure. A blamer's voice is usually hard, tight, shrill, and loud.

To try on *the blamer stance*—adopt a loud and tyrannical voice; cut every-thing and everyone down; point with your finger accusingly. Start sentences with "You never do this, you always do that, why don't you.." Don't bother about an answer. Treat any answer as unimportant. Take more interest in throwing your weight around rather than finding out about anything.

Blamers breathe in little tight spurts, holding their breath often. This makes the throat muscles tight. A first-rate blamer has eyes that bulge, neck muscles and nostrils that stand out; they get red in the face, and their voice gets hoarse. Stand with one hand on your hip, the other arm extended with index finger pointed straight out. Screw up your face, curl your lip, flare your nostrils, call names and criticize. Then say, "You never consider my feelings." "Nobody around here ever pays any attention to me." "Do you always have to put yourself first." "Why can't you think about anybody but yourself?" Blamers use lots of parental words: never, nothing, nobody, everything, none.

3. **Computing** refers to taking a detached attitude to your emotions. The computer focuses on responding in a very correct and reasonable way that shows no semblance of feelings. He responds calmly, coolly, and as collected as Mr. Spock of **Star Trek**, the ideal model of computing. In Computing, your body will feel dry and cool; your voice will sound monotone and you will use abstract words. Typically people get into this stance out of fear of their feelings.

To try on *the computer stance,* use the longest words possible (after one paragraph no one continues to listen anyway). Imagine your spine as a long heavy steel rod. Keep everything as motionless as possible. Let your voice go dead, have no feeling from the cranium down. "There's undoubt-edly a simple solution to the problem." "It's obvious that the situation is being exaggerated." "Clearly the advantages of this activity have been made manifest." "Preferences of this kind are rather common in this area."

The dissociation of the Computer Mode may offer a valuable stance for defusing someone when you don't need your emotions to get in the way. In this mode, "play anthropologist" or scientist and use a lot of big vague words. To the indirect criticism, "Some people really don't know when to stop talking," respond in full Computer Mode, "That is undoubtedly an interesting idea and certainly true of some people."

4. **Distracting** refers to responding in an unpredictable way that always alters and interrupts others and oneself. The Distracter will cycle rapidly among the other patterns and constantly shifts modes. Whatever the distracter does or says has no relevance to what anyone else says or does. His internal feeling will involve dizziness and panic. The voice often takes on a singsong style, one out of tune with the words and which goes up and down without reason. It focuses nowhere. The distracter will alternate between blaming, placating, and leveling and will then move into irrele-vance. This makes for the relational pattern of "crazymaking" (common to "borderline" cases).

To try on this *distracting stance,* think of yourself as a kind of lopsided top, constantly spinning, but going nowhere. Keep busy moving your mouth, body, arms, and legs. Ignore questions, or come back on a different subject. Start picking lint off the other's garment. Put your knees together in an exaggerated, knock-kneed fashion. This will bring your buttocks out and makes it easy for you to hunch your shoulders.

5. *Leveling* represents communicating and relating in an assertive way so that one's words and actions straightforwardly, directly, and forthrightly expresses one's true and honest state. A genuine leveling response communicates messages congruently so that one's words matches one's facial expressions, body posture, and voice tone. This makes relationships non-threatening, more caring, and capable of true intimacy.

Pacing: Except for leveling, these patterns reveal a mismatch between the way the person feels on the inside and the way he expresses it in language and behavior. As a guideline, two persons using the same Satir stance will go nowhere in their communications. So, except for the Leveling Mode, do *not* match the Satir Mode coming at you. When you match a Satir Mode it will intensify it. For an extensive use of these stances, see **The Structure of Magic—II** where Bandler and Grinder relate them to representational systems and the meta-model.

Contexts of Origin: These communicating stances develop from our social imprinting by significant persons and the pain and/or pleasure attached to them.

Further Reading: Satir (1972), Bandler and Grinder (1976).

Self-Analysis:
___ Blamer/**Placator**/Computer/**Distracter**/**Leveler**

Contexts:
___ Work/Career	___ Intimates
___ Relationships	___ Hobbies/Recreation
___ Sports	___ Other: _____
___ High/**Medium**/Low level	___ Driver MP: **Yes**/No

#32. General Response Style:
Congruent/Incongruent/Competitive/Cooperative/Polarity/Meta

Concept: When we respond to people, things, information, and events we can do so in various ways according to the style and the energy expended: *congruently, incongruently, competitively, cooperatively,* with *polarity,* or a *meta* response.

Elicitation: "When you come into a situation, how do you usually respond? Do you respond (1) with a sense of feeling and acting congruent and harmonious with your thoughts-and-feelings or, do you respond with a sense of not feeling or acting congruent and harmonious with your thoughts and feelings? (2) Do you respond with a sense of cooperation with the subject matter, or a feeling of disagreement? (3) Or, do you prefer to go above the immediate context and have thoughts about the situation?"

Identification:
1. To *congruently* respond means to feel in accordance with something. A congruent response to a serene nature scene, seen as a quiet place of green grass and bubbling brook, would consist of feeling relaxed and calm. The response fits the nature and quality of the internal state representations.

2. Conversely, to respond *incongruently* involves thinking-and-feeling one way while responding another. This *out of sync* response style means that our response does not fit our representations or state. So if we look at the calm scene and feel angry, our incongruous response indicates that we have another model of the world in our head vying for attention.

3. A *competitive* response involves processing an experience, thought, and emotion in terms of comparison and competition: "Who do I evaluate as the best, the first, ahead, etc.?" A competitive responder might get excited, "I bet I can relax faster or more completely than you can!"

4. A *cooperative* response involves thinking in terms of assisting and helping other people to share the experience. "How can I make this a more pleasant, enjoyable, resourceful experience for everyone?" The competitive response patterns thinks in Win/Lose terms, whereas the cooperative response pattern thinks in Win/Win terms.

5. A *polarity* response refers to flipping to the opposite pole of a choice or response. To a serene scene, one may respond with more stress and tension. The mind might entertain thoughts of danger, "The peace can't last; this isn't real!" It processes the opposite (it Mismatches, #2) and so the person reacts. Since the polarity meta-program describes a person automatically responding with an opposite response to the one you may seek to generate, *playing polarity* offers an option. Here use the Brer Rabbit approach. When Brer Fox threatened him, Brer Rabbit begged that above all things he would not throw him into the briar patch. Of course, he did.

6.   The *meta*-response refers to processing information at a higher logical level by going *above* the immediate content and having thoughts about it. "I find it interesting to realize that the images of that calm scene look fuzzy, and not quite clear. If we make the pictures with a sharper and more focused image, that would make for less serenity."

The more flexibility we have, the more we can produce all of these responses at our choice. People with less flexibility will often get stuck in one or two of these response styles. Strong-willed persons who tend to do polarity responding tend also to adopt a competitive and combative style so that they compete (#41).

Pacing: Match the person's style of responding before you attempt to lead to a different response.

Languaging: Listen for the language of congruity, cooperation, or competition, polarity ("yes, but..."), and meta ("above, about").

Contexts of Origin: Typically we learn how to respond given how we have been socially conditioned to do so. Further, pain and trauma experiences can contribute to us adopting the thinking pattern of incongruity, competition, and polarity as coping responses of protection.

Further Reading: Bandler and Grinder (1976).

Self-Analysis:
__ Congruity/Incongruity/Competitive/Cooperative/Polarity/Meta

Contexts:
__ Work/Career	__ Intimates
__ Relationships	__ Hobbies/Recreation
__ Sports	__ Other: _____
__ High/Medium/Low level	__ Driver MP: **Yes/No**

#33. Somatic Response Style:
Active (reactive)/Reflective (inactive)/Both

Concept: We saw this meta-program before as applied to our feeling responses to the world (#16). Here we apply it to *the social context* as we respond to people and events. As such, we can do so in various ways according to the style and the energy expended: *actively (proactively and reactively), reflectively (inactively), or both.*

Elicitation: "When you come into a social situation (a group, class, team, family reunion, etc.), do you usually act quickly after sizing it up or do you engage in a detailed study of all of the consequences, and then act? How do you typically respond?"

Identification:

1. The *socially active* person immediately takes action. He or she will aggress toward the person or event, either out of a sense of threat (aggression) or desire (toward values). If too active, this person can respond impulsively and unthinkingly. Action oriented people tend to make lots of mistakes. They also tend to score lots of successes. They talk fast, they think fast, and they act fast. They like to get things done and they like to "take the bull by the horns." When well-balanced, they operate as proactive persons. More typically they operate in a self-referencing way. Pace them by "Just get up and do it." "Go for it." Overdone and the impulsive energy can lead to *reactivity*. Well-balanced and modulated, it can lead to the resourceful state of proactivity. (Estimated between 15% and 20% of the U.S. population.)

2. The *socially reflective* type of person likes to study and think prior to taking action in reference to groups. They can even let things go for a long time without taking any action at all. They feel more inhibited about taking action out of fear of making a mistake. They usually feel less confident and more insecure. When overdone, they may procrastinate to their own detriment and turn into an *inactive.* We rarely find the inactive in the forefront of the business world. These typically operate in an other- or external-referencing style (#14). They work best in contexts that demand more thought and reflection. (Estimated between 15% and 20% of the U.S. population.)

3. *Socially balanced.* People who *utilize both styles* in a balanced way eagerly pursue their goals in group contexts with sufficient reflection about them. They take time for analyzing feedback before they move forward. (Estimated between 50% and 65% of the U.S. population.).

Contexts of Origin: Very similar to the emotional response pattern (#16). That meta-program described the way one has somatized his or her responses while meta-program one focuses on responses to the social and work environment.

Further Reading: Woodsmall (1988).

Self-Analysis:
__ Active/**R**eflective/**B**oth

Contexts:
__ Work/Career   __ Intimates
__ Relationships   __ Hobbies/Recreation
__ Sports   __ Other: _____
__ High/Medium/Low level   __ Driver MP: **Yes**/**No**

#34. Work Preference Sort:
Things/Systems/People/Information

Concept: When we engage in "the significant activity" of work, career, vocation, etc. we operate with preferences about what to work with: *things, systems, people, information* (this meta-program relates closely to the affiliation filter, #30).

Elicitation: Use the same set of questions as in the affiliation sort (#30) or by inviting a person to share some work situation wherein they felt the happiest or most pleased.

Identification:
1. *Things.* Those who primarily orient themselves toward working with *things* will talk about such rather than people, ideas, or systems. They will seldom focus on people or their feelings, but on the task—on getting a job done, accomplishing goals, and the end result of a task completed.

2. *Systems.* Those who orient themselves toward working with *systems* think and care primarily about processes, inter-relationships, cause-effect relations, plans, and procedures. They too don't care so much about people or their feelings as the functioning of the system, how things work, etc.

3. *People.* Those who primarily orient themselves toward working with *people* focus on the thoughts, feelings, and well-being of persons. They like people, interact well socially, have well-developed social skills, love to talk, want to help, etc.

Contexts of Origin: This meta-program arises as does the emotional sort for preferences (#24), and applies specifically to work and task oriented situations.

Further Reading: Woodsmall (1988).

Self-Analysis:
__ Things/**S**ystems/**P**eople/Information

Contexts:
__ Work/Career	__ Intimates
__ Relationships	__ Hobbies/Recreation
__ Sports	__ Other: _____
__ High/**M**edium/Low level	__ Driver MP: **Yes**/No

#35. Comparison Sort:
Quantitative/Qualitative

Concept: This meta-program informs us about the nature of the comparisons that we and others use in comparing things. It arises whenever a person's consciousness moves into the process of deciding between two or more options. We then make comparisons and we do so in two broad ways: quantitatively and qualitatively.

Elicitation: "How would you evaluate your work?" "How would you evaluate things in your relationship?" "How do you know the quality of your work? "Upon what basis do you say that?"

Identification: Listen for whether the person speaks about *quantity* (numbers, times, amounts, etc.) or *quality*. Does the person prefer quantification research and validation or qualification?

1. *Quantification Sorting.* People with this style will reply to questions by giving numbers, ranks, order, measurements, standards, etc. "I came in first in production this week." "I brought up my standing 4% this month." Here the person's consciousness goes to external standards, empirical see, hear, and feel indicators (sensors #5), and because they start with concrete details, they will think and reason inductively (#1).

2. *Qualification Sorting.* People with this style of processing will reply with words indicating and referring to the *quality* of the experience: good, better, poor, bad, excellent, etc. "I am doing very well, thank you." "We have never felt closer or move loving." Here their consciousness goes to internal factors, meanings, principles, etc. (intuitors, #5). And because they start at the global level, they will think and reason deductively or abductively (#1).

Languaging: When a person makes a comparison, the Meta-model suggests that we can challenge vagueness by asking, "compared to what, to whom, to what standard or criteria, etc.?" In response, people will present *their favorite kind of comparing* (qualitative or quantitative) and the standard that they use. "I'm doing just as good as two years ago" provides a quality ("good") and a quantity measurement (two years ago) up against the criteria of one's past self. "I'm doing as good as one can expect given the circumstances" presents only qualitative comparisons ("good," "expect"). "Next week I will feel much better" compares a quantity (next week) with a future self using a qualitative standard ("better"). "I'm doing better than most people my age" uses the standard of others.

Contexts of Origin: Here right and left brain physiology patterns may contribute to whether we like working with and measuring effectiveness in terms of external numbers (Quantative) or internal meanings and emotions (the Quality of the experience). Obviously contexts that validate, approve, confirm, reward and/or punish one or the other will greatly effect the sorting pattern we prefer.

Self-Analysis:
__ Quantitative Sorting/**Qualitative Sorting**

Contexts:
   __ Work/Career   __ Intimates
   __ Relationships   __ Hobbies/Recreation
   __ Sports   __ Other: _____
   __ **High/Medium/Low level**   __ Driver MP: **Yes/No**

#36. Knowledge Source Sort:
Modeling/Conceptualizing/Demonstrating/Experiencing/Authorizing

Concept: This meta-program provides information about how a person decides that (s)he can do something and where (s)he gathers the data for that decision. Similar to the Convincer meta-program (#17), this one does not address *how* a person knows and feels something as true, but the *source* of that information.

Elicitation: "What source of knowledge do you consider authoritative and most reliable?" "From where would you gather reliable information that you can trust?" "When you decide that you will do something, where do you get the information to do it from?"

Identification: People differ in that they gain life knowledge via modeling, conceptualizing, seeing it demonstrated, experiencing it, having it authorized by an authority.

1. Those who gather information via *modeling* look externally to those who have both a knowledge base (beliefs, ideas, understandings) and the ability to produce.

2. Those who use *conceptualizing* as their program for gathering information do so by studying, researching, thinking, talking, etc. Such individuals tend to have a strong internal dialogue and self-referencing style.

3. Those who use *demonstrations* as the source of information feel most impressed by what they see or experience. While the modeling filter copies and reproduces a model, demonstration involves a less personal and more distant style of learning—as in a classroom demonstration rather than a personal model.

4. Those who use *experiencing* as their style tend to gather information self-referentially using their kinesthetic system. Information seems real when it comes from "having done it."

5. Those who use an authority figure (study, school, scholar, etc.) to *authorize* information believe that if an authority source says so, that confirms it. They obviously use an other-referencing mode (#14) to see, hear or feel valid external originating information.

Languaging: Listen for words and terms designating models, concepts, demonstrations, experiences, or authorities.

Contexts of Origin: We can, and do, obtain information and knowledge from each of these sources, positive conditioning within each of these realms strengthens and reinforces it as a sorting pattern just as negative conditioning through pain and deprivation can make any one a taboo area.

Further Reading: Woodsmall (1988).

Self-Analysis:
__ Modeling/Conceptualizing/Demonstrating/
    Experiencing/Authorizing

Contexts:
__ Work/Career	__ Intimates
__ Relationships	__ Hobbies/Recreation
__ Sports	__ Other: _____
__ High/Medium/Low level	__ Driver MP: **Yes/No**

#37. Completion/Closure Sort:
Closure/Non-Closure

Concept: Whenever we process information, we sometimes complete it and sometimes we do not complete the information processing. Sometimes we run out of time, sometimes we don't have enough information, sometimes the information doesn't even exist. Whatever the reason, this meta-program addresses the subject of how we handle *closure* and/or the lack of closure. Do we have a high drive for closure or a low drive? Does our operating system allow our mind-emotions to live comfortably with an unfinished gestalt?

You may also want to look for comparisons and relationships with closure and non-closure with "In "Time"" and "Through "Time"" (#47). Typically, those who sort "time" via the "In "Time"" mode will tolerate non-closure better than those who do so by the "Through "Time"" mode.

Elicitation: "If, in the process of studying something, you had to break off your study and leave it, would you feel okay about this or would you feel it as disconcerting?" "When someone begins a story but doesn't complete it, how do you feel about that?" "When you get involved in a project, do you find yourself more interested in the beginning, middle, or end of the project?" "What part of a project do you enjoy most?" *Identification.* The experience and concept of *closure* relates to our *adaptation sort* (#22) in how we move through the world—making life adapt to us or ourselves to it. This meta-program focuses on the internal experience of living with something unfinished, whereas the adaptive meta-program focused more on one's style of adaptation.

1. *Non-closure style.* People who enjoy and perform better in the beginning and middle of a task, project, relationship, etc. do not seem to need closure as much as those who enjoy and feel more completion in bringing a project to completion. Listen for how a person talks about completing or not completing something. Listen for levels of anxiety in both.

Richard Bandler often utilizes open loops in the way he puts together workshops and presentations. This refers to sharing a story or metaphor at the beginning and not completing it until the end of the presentation. In the middle he will offer the central data he wants to communicate. We describe this structure as opening a loop. Some people find themselves more highly influenced by suspended open loops than others. It will have less effect upon those with the non-closure style.

2. *Closure style.* Those who live in compartmentalized worlds tend to want everything neatly wrapped up at the end of the day (high closure feelings). They will think in more definitive, black-and-white ways (#6). Opening and suspending a loop will most powerfully impact such persons.

Contexts of Origin: Which value did our family, cultural, religious, political, and racial context value and reinforce—closure or non-closure? Significant pain and confusion in early life can elicit either program in a person. Then everything can seem as "unfinished business" without closure. This can result in a person staying constantly and perpetually over-involved with "the past," "old hurts," resentments, and the like. Or a person builds the opposite program, he or she may bring premature closure when no need exists to do so.

Further Reading: Hall (1996c)

Self-Analysis:
__ Closure/Non-Closure

Contexts:
__ Work/Career	__ Intimates
__ Relationships	__ Hobbies/Recreation
__ Sports	__ Other: _____
__ High/Medium/Low level	__ Driver MP: Yes/No

#38. Social Presentation:
Shrewd & Artful/Genuine & Artless

Concept: Cattell (1989) describes those who move through life with an operational system, in relation to other people and social groups, as artless, warm, spontaneous, and naive, and those who move in a shrewd, artful, and socially "correct" way.

Elicitation: "When you think about going out into a social group or out in public, how do you generally handle yourself? Do you really care about your social image and want to avoid any negative impact on others so that they recognize your tact, politeness, social graces, etc.? Or do you not really care about any of that and just want "to be yourself," natural, forthright, direct, transparent, etc.?"

Identification:
1. *Shrewd and artful.* People, who in their social presentation really care about the impressions they make on others, and want to insure that they create no negative impressions, value the image they create in the minds of others (other-referencing #14). This motivates them to value politeness, tact, etiquette, protocol, etc. and to strongly disvalue too much self-disclosure, expression of thoughts and feelings, spontaneity, etc. Such people usually have lots of social ambition. When over-done, such persons can act very manipulative, "political," selfish, etc.

2. *Genuine and artless.* People who disvalue the whole social presentation think of it as play acting, "not being real," "being a fake," or hypocrital, prefer to "just let things hang out," have little or no social ambitions, more resilient to disappointments with others, can come across as artless and crude in their social manners (or lack of them) (self-referencing, #14). When over-done, a person may behave rudely and inappropriately in public, he or she may even develop an anti-social style.

Languaging and Personality: Which set of values does the person highlight and talk about the most? These operational system processes leads to the social butterfly, the politician, and the socially adept or to the socially crude and rude, the artlessly forthright person who always speaks his or her mind.

Contexts of Origin: These styles typically arise from modeling and identification with early role models, parents, teachers, etc. who showed a positive portrait of the importance of social adeptness, or dis-identification from hypocrites and manipulators, and/or modeling within an anti-social group of rebels.

Further Reading: Cattell (1989).

Self-Analysis:
__ **Shrewd & Artful**/Genuine & Artless

Contexts:
    __ Work/Career   __ Intimates
    __ Relationships   __ Hobbies/Recreation
    __ Sports   __ Other: _____
    __ **High/Medium/Low level**   __ Driver MP: **Yes/No**

#39. Hierarchical Dominance Sort:
Power/Affiliation/Achievement

Concept: When David McClelland of Harvard developed the McClelland Model, he looked at three central aspects of human interacting: power, affiliation, and achievement. This model describes how people handle experiences of dominance. Joseph Yeager (1985) used it to construct the "Yeager Power Grid."

This meta-program relates to how a person adapts to the power moves of others (one-upmanship, put-downs, bossiness, etc.). It describes the style a person uses in handling power (or not handling it). Yeager connects this to the passive-aggressive program (#13) using a 1-to-10 scale, 1 for passive (like Charlie Brown), 5 for assertive (like Snoopy) and 10 for aggressive (like Lucy or Attila the Hun).

Elicitation: "Evaluate your motives in interacting with others in terms of your motivational preferences between Power (dominance, competition, politics), Affiliation (relationship, courtesy, cooperation) and Achievement (results, goals, objectives) and using 100 points as your scale, distribute those hundred points among these three styles of handling "power.""

 __ Power (dominance, competition, politics)
 __ Affiliation (relationship, courtesy, cooperation)
 __ Achievement (results, goals, objectives)

Total: 100

Identification:

1. People who *sort for power* operate fully as "a hierarchical animal" (Yeager, 1985, p. 110), and value the experience of dominating, competing, playing politics. When they feel satisfied in this pursuit, they feel combinations of superiority and satisfaction. They think Win/Lose. When overdone, they think, "It's not enough that I win... others must lose." (Attila the Hun).

2. People who *sort for affiliation* operate by managing relationships by turning on courtesy and cooperation. They value and care more about creating and maintaining good relationship with others via thoughtfulness. They think in Win/Win terms.

3. People who *sort for achievement* care most of all for getting things done, practical results, etc.

Languaging and Personality: Listen for the words indicating one of these three arenas in the context of social groups and organizations.

Contexts of Origin: The value and style that predominated in the way one's parents and teachers operated in the family and school may predispose one to likewise sort. Did one identify and model this style or did one dis-identify from that style of orientation?

Further Reading: Yeager (1985). McClelland (1953).

Self-Analysis:
__ **Power/Affiliation/Achievement/Balanced**

Contexts:
 __ Work/Career   __ Intimates
 __ Relationships   __ Hobbies/Recreation
 __ Sports   __ Other: _____
 __ High/**Medium**/Low level   __ Driver MP: **Yes**/**No**

Conclusion

Our operating systems do not occur in a vacuum, but in a socio-political, spiritual, and personal *context*. Given our self-reflexive consciousness which always, and inevitably, reflects back onto its own thoughts-and-emotions, and actions—our interactive responses in the world comprises a large element of "mind." The more expansive model for understanding "mind" and these meta-programs invites us to consider our "mental-emotional" processing and sorting in terms of *people, tasks, communicating,* etc.

What have you learned about your own sorting style for perceiving with regard to these facets of consciousness? Which ones operate so strongly in you that they *drive* your everyday experiences? How well do your meta-programs in the social arena serve you?

#29. Rejuvenation of Battery Sort: *Extrovert, Ambivert, Introvert*
#30. Affiliation & Management Sort: *Independent/ Team Player/ Manager*
#31. Communication Stance Sort: *Communication Modes*
#32. General Response: *Congruent/ Incongruent/ Competitive/ Cooperative/ Polarity/ Meta*
#33. Somatic Response Style: *Active / Reflective/ Both/ Inactive*
#34. Work Preference Sort: *Things / Systems / People/ Information*
#35. Comparison Sort: *Quantitative / Qualitative*
#36. Knowledge Sort: *Modeling/ Conceptualizing/ Demonstrating/ Experiencing/ Authorizing*
#37. Completion/ Closure Sort: *Closure / Non-Closure*
#38. Social Presentation: *Shrewd & Artful/ Genuine & Artless*
#39. Hierarchical Dominance Sort: *Power/ Affiliation/ Achievement*

Chapter 7

The *Meta* Meta-Programs

Meta-Programs About Conceptual/Semantic Realities
Identity/Self/"Time" etc.
(#40-51)

Not all meta-programs occur on the same meta-level. Some occur at a level *meta* to the meta-programs themselves. We here offer this **new distinction in NLP** to distinguish between those meta-programs that occur just one logical level up with regard to our thinking, information processing, sorting, attending, etc. and those that occur at two levels up.

We detailed this model and distinction in chapter one. Here we now describe it more fully. With this further extension of the meta-programs model, we can answer such questions as:

- How do "values" (a nominalization) relate to the meta-programs?
- How do "beliefs" fit into this model?
- Where do we put the Kantian categories (time, space, causation, etc.) with regard to human perception?

In this chapter we look at the meta-programs that lie *meta* to all of the other meta-programs (MMP). These exist *above and beyond* all of the specific meta-programs.

#40.	**Value Sort**: *Emotional "Needs," Beliefs*
#41.	**Temper to Instruction Sort**: *Strong-Will / Compliant*
#42.	**Self-Esteem Sort**: *Conditional/ Unconditional*
#43.	**Self-Confidence Sort:** *High / Low*
#44.	**Self-Experience Sort:** *Mind/Emotion/Body/Role*
#45.	**Self-Integrity**: *Conflicted Incongruity / Harmonious Integration*
#46.	**"Time" Tenses Sort**: *Past/ Present/ Future*
#47.	**"Time" Experience**: *In "Time"/ Through "Time";* *Sequential Versus Random Sorting*
#48.	**"Time" Access Sort**: *Random / Sequential*
#49.	**Ego Strength Sort**: *Unstable/ Stable*
#50.	**Morality Sort**: *Weak/ Strong Super-ego*
#51.	**Causational Sort**: *Causeless, Linear CE, Multi-CE,* *Personal CS, External CE, Magical, Correlational*

Meta-programs Meta to the Meta-Programs

In Chapter One we began this work suggesting the computer metaphor of information processing as one analogous in some ways to *the neurological information processing* that occurs in humans. The output of our human "software" (on the "screen of our consciousness") results from neurological inputting of billions of stimuli in the environment as processed by the human nervous system and brain.

This metaphor suggests the existence of, at least, two separate dimensions of consciousness and perception, namely, how consciousness-perception *forms* and how it finally *expresses* itself.

First, consider **the end result** of meta-program distinctions in the form that our "thoughts" take. This refers to how our *processing* manifests itself by its focusing of "attention" and "perception" on the "screen of consciousness" (Figure 7:1, column 4 p.159). It does this by **formatting** our perception according to the meta-programs (big/small; matching/ mismatching/ VAK/etc.). Thus every thought and every perception has *a meta-program code*. We have already sorted for whether something matches or mismatches, globally or specifically, etc.

Thought always comes out in some meta-program configuration. It can do no other. That we usually lack consciousness of it merely speaks about it operating at a level *meta* to the content of our thought.

Second, consider *the source* from which the meta-program distinctions arise. As the meta-program focuses, shapes, forms, and formats *perception*— the ongoing dynamic process of neurological information processing—it does so according to various conditions, constraints, and categories.

In other words, our operating system (the meta-programs) arises and comes from previously formatted categories. Think of the meta-programs themselves as an expression of a dynamic mental-emotional process wherein we engage in "focusing, attending, thinking, and information processing." Think of this *stream of cognizing the world* and "attending" as having both a style, format, and form (as articulated in the meta-programs) *and* prior conditions and constraints from which it arises.

This separates the meta-programs into those *prior* to the dynamism of "mind" that attends and perceives. It, secondly, separates those that format the attending *afterward* as it shows up on "the screen of consciousness."

Those that attend afterward comprise the majority of the meta-programs as detailed in the previous chapters (Chapters 3-6). Those that describe the *prior formatting* of perception consist of those conceptual, semantic categories that constrain consciousness. It does this before it begins to operate—constrains it to operate according to its conditions. This consists of those meta-programs that concern such categories as "time," "self," "values" etc.

Figure 7:1

Prior To...	Attending/Perceiving	Format	Result
Conditions out of which attending comes: Categories Constraints	Work of consciousness in focussing, noticing, sorting, processing...	Form of thought MP of Match/Mismatch etc.	"Thought"
Meta MP	Consciousness	Sorting the MP	The end product of Thinking

First, we turn this model upright so that it takes a vertical position. Then we have two meta-levels to the primary level of consciousness *about* things in the world "out there" beyond our skin.

To recognize the recursiveness of consciousness, we have built into this model the recognition that thought-and-emotion always and inevitably *reflects back onto itself* (the arrows going up and back down, see Figure 7:2 p.160). Thus as the meta-programs governing our thoughts habituates, this solidifies as a mental-emotional **"form."** This format then develops into a meta-program and later on a *meta* meta-program. The place of "values" arises because by "giving a **form** (format) of thought" (global, matching, visual, whatever) repeated occurrence—values it as useful, significant, real, etc. and then this "valuating" and "valuational" process results in the nominalization "values."

Figure 7:2

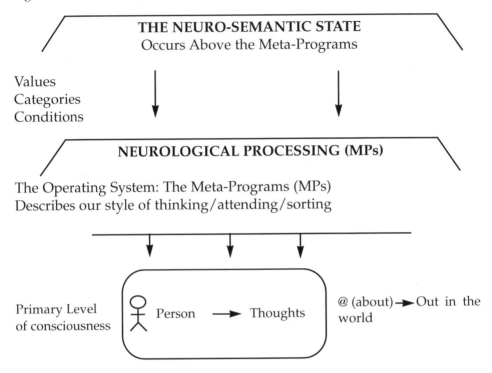

The Significance of Distinguishing Meta-Programs (MP) and Meta Meta-Programs (MMP)

By distinguishing meta-programs from **meta** meta-programs (MMP) we articulate a distinction that exists between the levels at which a "sorting program" can operate. What significance does this have?

1. The MMP will have impact more pervasively on the entire perceptual system than the MP. Higher logical levels always drive, modulate, organize, and form the lower levels (Hall, 1997a). So, the place for us to go in order to do more pervasive change, consists of the higher logical levels, to the **meta** meta-programs involving a person's values, "time" codings, "self" codings, etc.

2. The MP, via habituation, creates/generates the MMP. This provides another insight into why a person values/believes what they believe, namely, it has habituated to a higher logical level. It also warns that we should run "ecology checks" and both time-and-space index the meta-programs least we empower them (through habituation) to turn into values, beliefs, and identity structures.

[To time-space index we check the coordinates of *when and where* an event occurred. Since Einstein, the elementalism of "time" and "space" as separate elements has given way to the modern recognition that every event occurs at some place in some time and that we do not and cannot have "time" apart from "space" or "space" apart from "time." Hence, Einstein's formulation of the time-space continuum within which all events occur.]

3.   This further distinguishes between the realm of neuro-linguistics (at the MP level) and the realm that we have chosen to call *neuro-semantics* (at the MMP level). The meta-programs that we have so far explored (Chapters 3-6) have primarily concerned how we code, pattern, and format consciousness. The *meta* meta-programs involve another layer or level of conception that brings to bear upon the fabric of consciousness itself.

#40. Value Sort:
Emotional Needs/Belief Systems

Concept: Our values (a nominalization for *valuing*) arise from, and take form, from our thoughts, ideas, and understandings about what we deem as *important* (e.g. significant and meaningful). Via our valuation thoughts we appraise various things, people, experiences, qualities, ideas, etc. as of importance in living life according to our map about life as we should live it.

Our "values" as *abstractions of importance* arise (at a meta-level) when we think thoughts of "value, importance, and significance," *about* certain thoughts. In other words, we **bring a state of "value"** to our representations of a person, place, thing, event, idea, etc. and this energizes and intensifies those representations. We then experience meta-states of appreciation, joy, concern, love, desire, etc. *about* these nominalized abstractions (i.e. our values).

What we appraise as a "value," we also believe in (another meta-level structure). We believe in *the importance and significance* of the "value," and so we give ourselves to the value, trust in it, and act on it. Consequently, our beliefs-about-values organizes us in how it structures our life and endows life with meaning.

Structurally, a "value" contains a two-level phenomenon. To the primary level thought we first have it in some meta-program format (global/specific, VAK, match/mismatch, etc.). Then to the meta-program format we have a thought of *importance and significance* **about** it.

Conversely, every meta-program we use regularly and habitually, *we value.* Does a person think globally? Then expect that person to perceive global thinking as valuable. Does a person mismatch? Bet on that person valuing the ability to sort for differences. Does a person move away from values? Anticipate discovering that they actually have many reasons and motivations for engaging in such thinking! Our *values* arise, in part, from our meta-programs themselves, especially our **driver** meta-programs.

Figure 7:3

Meta Meta-Level

Meta-Level

Primary Level

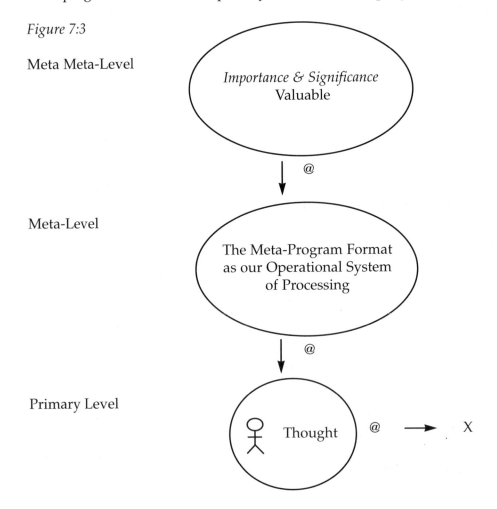

Elicitation: As you inquire about anything, ask what the person thinks valuable, important, or significant about that thing whether a job, relationship, idea, etc.

Identification: Maslow (1950) created a hierarchical list of emotional values that included: survival, security, love and affection, belonging, self-esteem and self-actualization. These do not exhaust the possible list of motivating values that we may adopt in life. Many other nominalized abstractions serve as "values" for humans: power, control, achievement, affiliation, transcendence, ease, pleasure, romance, sex, knowledge, religion, harmony, challenge, etc. Whatever we believe holds significance—we transform into a value: politics, physical fitness, confrontation, non-confrontation, children, volunteering, reading, etc.

Languaging: To listen carefully to the nominalizations of abstract values that people believe and value alerts us to their "values." To do this, plant the question in your mind, "What motivating value does this person reveal within or behind his or her words?" Then listen for *the value words* and those that imply values. Ask yourself, "What do I sense from these words and expressions, that holds value for this person?" "What values seem most central?" "What values does this person seem to go toward?" "What values does he or she move away from?" Note how the person's values match with their style of Passivity and/or Aggression.

Pacing: To pace and communicate with a person in an influential and persuasional way, *appeal* to the person's values. People cannot but respond to their own values! Laborde (1989) describes a person's value words as "the correct passwords to [the other's] reality."

Emoting: Values inherently carry a lot of emotional impact. The nominalizations that summarize the valuing process function as anchors for inducing one into his or her valuation state. Look for the person to emotionally associate when speaking about his or her values.

Contexts of Origin: Generally we learn to value whatever brings us pleasure and protects us from harm and pain. We also learn to value anything that fits with and supports any meta-program that we have already installed. Every meta-program, as our operational system, provides a value. Global thinkers value the big picture, detail thinkers value specifics, etc. We adopt many values also due to the family, cultural, religious, political, and racial contexts within which we live—unless we disidentify with it.

Further Reading: James and Woodsmall (1988). Andreas and Andreas (1987).

Self-Analysis:
__ Toward Values/Away From Values

Contexts:
__ Work/Career	__ Intimates
__ Relationships	__ Hobbies/Recreation
__ Sports	__ Other: _____
__ High/Medium/Low level	__ Driver MP: Yes/No

Make a list of one's hierarchy of values:

Value List
Power	Control	Affiliation	Safety
Dignity	Love	Peace	Understanding
Control	Actualization	Sex	Romance
Feeling good	Achieving	Status	Optimism
Independence	Competence	Equality	Intelligence
Connection			

The "Self" Semantic Constructions (#41-45)

Central to our processing and sorting of information lie several *semantic concepts* that foundationally define and determine our experienced "reality." Among these we have our sense of *"self"* as a person, our sense of "self" in terms of our efficacy, confidence, skill, our self-definition that we create via our experiences, etc.

None of us ever leave home without our "self" filters. We take these meta-constructions with us everywhere we go and use them as perceptual filters. This enables us to use almost every experience, conversation, and interaction to both express our "self" and be influenced as a "self."

#41. Temper to "Instruction" Sort:
Strong-Will/Compliant

Concept: This meta-level meta-program relates to how we experience ourselves when face-to-face with someone *"telling"* us something. How do we relate and respond when another person provides us information? How do we relate and respond when another person mandates, orders, and instructs? Do we have a natural tendency to comply, to question, or to resist such information? If we imagine a continuum between the extremes of complying and resisting, then we have this meta-program that relates to our style of "being told" something. Imagine a continuum between highly compliant and highly strong-willed.

Elicitation: "Can someone 'tell' you something?" "How do you think and feel when you receive 'instructions?'" "How well can you 'tell' yourself to do something and carry it out without a lot of internal resistance?"

Identification: A person who comes from the sorting style of strong-will has a very difficult time "being told anything." When someone begins to use any kind of communication that "tells" (orders, instructs, informs, etc.), he or she will have an almost immediate and automatic response within to resist. They do not like "being told" at all. By contrast, a compliant person responds just as immediately and automatically by complying in a pliable, receptive, open, and sensitive way.

We can identify these patterns by simply noticing whether, and to what extent, a person bristles in a context where someone tells, orders, demands, forces, etc. In this "temperamental" factor, people fall along a continuum between extremely compliant to extremely strong-will. Most people will lie somewhere in the middle.

For the strong-willed, various belief filters can arise and get in their way thereby interfering with the reception of information. A strong-willed person will tend to read "telling" as "control," "manipulation," "memory of a trauma of some intrusive person," "insult," etc.

Pacing: To pace and communicate with a strong-will person, avoid all direct frontal "telling" styles. In fact, set it in mind to *not* tell that person anything. Instead, replace telling with suggesting, hinting, prodding, planting idea seeds, playfully teasing, etc. Move to using the indirect communication skills. To pace and communicate a compliant person, on the other hand, just express your thoughts directly and straight-forwardly.

Languaging: Linguistic markers for the strong-willed by temperament: "Why do I have to?" "I hate it when people tell me what to do." "I have a problem with authority figures." "I'm not going to jump through your hoops." Linguistic markers for the compliant: "Sure." "Whatever you say." "How high do you want me to jump?"

Emoting: The strong-willed will experience lots of emotions of "resistance"—dislike and aversion. They will "feel" put-upon, forced, "controlled," manipulated, etc. The compliant person will experience much kinder/gentler emotions even in contexts where someone truly imposes their will upon them.

Contexts of Origin: Those strong-will *"by temperament"* tend to have an innate disposition toward not "being told." They probably also experience and define their "Self" in terms of choice and will (see #44). To therefore preclude their choice feels like a basic violation of their Self. Those strong-will *by trauma*, experience boundary intrusions once too much, reach a threshold, and make a decision to "not be told." Those strong-will *by belief* have simply made up their mind about this or that subject and have "closed the store."

Further Reading: Dobson (1970), Hall (1987, 1990).

Self-Analysis:
__ Strong-willed/Compliant

Contexts:
 __ Work/Career   __ Intimates
 __ Relationships   __ Hobbies/Recreation
 __ Sports   __ Other: _____
 __ High/Medium/Low level   __ Driver MP: **Yes/No**

 __ Strong-willed by
 __ Temper   __ Trauma   __ Belief

#42. Self-Esteem Sort:
High Self-Esteem/Low Self-Esteem

Concept: One of our most basic modalities of awareness involves that which deals with *our "sense of our self."* Our images, concepts, ideas, verbalizations, and definitions of our self pinpoints a core area from which we do our thinking, processing, sorting, and valuing. Because these more abstract understandings of our conceptual "self" usually occur "below" (or "above") the level of awareness, they therefore operate "outside" of consciousness. This makes them more difficult to access, but not impossible.

For the sake of distinction, we here use these terms in the following way. *Self-esteem* refers to the valuation of worth, dignity, and being-ness to our ontological self. *Self-confidence* concerns our sense of competency regarding our skills, abilities, and doings. *Self-efficacy* refers to our sense of effectiveness or empowerment in using our consciousness to effectively deal with the world. *Self-conscience* refers to our sense of self as a moral or ethical being regarding right and wrong, etc. When we confuse, mix and fail to distinguish between these conceptual facets of "self," we create identity confusions that unnecessarily complicate our sense of self.

Here we use *self-esteem* to refer to our sense of worth (esteem, appraisal of value) in terms of how we "rate" ourselves. This may fall along a continuum between extremely worthless (rotten) to extremely valuable (low to high self-esteem). One may make this evaluation (mental appraise of value) based on temporal and conditional factors or upon unconditional factors (conditional self-esteem or unconditional self-esteem). In either case, one's esteeming or not-esteeming of one's being-self (personhood) arises from one's *belief* and value about human being-ness as a person.

By contrast, our *self-confidence* refers to our sense of competence regarding our *feelings* of capacity, ability, experience, and pride that we can *do* certain things with skill and ability. We have *faith* (fidence) *with* (con) ourselves. Self-confidence then obviously operates conditionally and arises from our experiences (positive and negative), training, beliefs, relationships, etc.

When a person suffers from low self-esteem *and* tries to build that mental appraisal of self as a person upon the foundation of one's competencies—he or she links their right to self-esteeming upon temporal conditions. This puts them on a treadmill of achievement and establishes the belief, "I will become okay as a person or human being *if* I achieve enough, accomplish enough, etc. or *when* I do." This then establishes that person's "self-esteem project." Yet because it posits human "worth" and "dignity" conditionally upon external things, it leaves one unable to ever feel sure or confident. And with that construction, one may lose the right to esteem oneself of value and dignity.

Further, this process tends to promote states of self-contempt and/or egotism as well as the idea that *people* as human beings must "earn" the right to treat oneself as valuable and inherently worthwhile as a person. This confuses person with behavior. By contrast, to posit our self-value as *a given* enables us to think-and-feel in a self-forgetful and unpretentious way. It creates *a healthy center of value and dignity* from which to live and act.

Elicitation: "Do you think of your value as a person as conditional or unconditional?" "When you esteem yourself as valuable, worthwhile, having dignity, etc. do you base it upon something you do, have, or possess, or do you base it upon a given i.e. your inherent humanity, made in God's image and likeness, etc. ?"

Identification: Listen for how a person thinks-feels about their self as *a person* and as *a doing* (human being/human doing). Do you hear conditional factors? Does their ability to esteem their self go up and down according to their fate or experiences?

Pacing: Appeal to someone's inherent and innate self value and dignity to reinforce the person who operates from unconditional self-esteem. Appeal to the factor/s that will expand and provide a richer and more resourceful experience.

Languaging: Listen for statements of conditionality or unconditionality.

RET Cognitive Distortions: Cognitive problems can arise when a person get his or her "fill" of conditional self-esteeming. It can also occur when environmental circumstances prevent a person from reaching and fulfilling all of the conditions for esteeming the self of value. When such occurs, one can fall into thinking patterns of emotionalizing and personalizing. Also, a weak sense of personal values and boundaries can lead to personalizing. Here a person interprets the words, behaviors and events of others as having something to do with their worthwhileness, value, lovability, etc. as a human being. This results in negative self-rating that Ellis has warned against.

Contexts of Origin: As a meta meta-level conceptualization this program, as most of these in this arena, arises from the belief and value systems we experience from the various groups in our life. The languaging that we receive from our caretakers especially play a crucial role in whether we have heard (and therefore formulated, structured, and patterned our consciousness) conditional or unconditional self-valuing. Almost every-body receives an unmeasurable amount of conditional self-worthing via their experiences in school, sports, life with peers, etc. Almost any hurt or trauma experience can undermine our ability to esteem our self of unconditional value, worth, dignity, lovability, etc.

Further Reading: Hall (1991, 1995, 1996), Nathaniel Branden (1969).

Self-Analysis:
__ Conditional Self-Esteem/Unconditional Self-Esteem

Contexts:
__ Work/Career	__ Intimates
__ Relationships	__ Hobbies/Recreation
__ Sports	__ Other: _____
__ **High/Medium/Low level** (if conditional)	__ Driver MP: **Yes/No**

#43. Self-Confidence Sort:
Low Self-Confidence/High Self-Confidence

Concept: One's *faith* ("fidence") in (or with, "con") our *abilities* or *skills* to do things lies at the heart of the phenomenon that we call *self-confidence*. This differs from self-esteem. It refers to more of an emotional/experiential factor of self, whereas self-esteem refers more to our mental appraisal or rating of our self as a person. Self-confidence addresses what we can **do**. Thus it focuses on human doing-ness rather than human being-ness.

Elicitation: "As you think about some of the things that you can do well, and that you know, without a doubt, you can do well and may even take pride in your ability to do them skillfully, make a list of those items." "How confident do you feel about your skills in doing these things?" "How have you generalized from these specific self-confidences to your overall sense of self-confidence?"

Identification: Everybody who lives a fairly normal life has lots of things that he or she can do with confidence, from the simple things like making one's bed, cooking a meal, going to work, dressing, to the more complex, like playing an instrument, doing complicated math, fixing an automobile, typing, programming a computer, etc.

Those who may filter things *pessimistically* (#7) may not "count" many, if not most of their confidences, and focus only on the things that they cannot do well and so develop low self-confidence about almost everything. Those who seek to achieve their goals via a perfectionistic style (#25) may also create an overall sense of low self-confidence.

Languaging and Emoting: Those lacking the feeling of self-confidence will feel unsure, indecisive, confused, etc. They will talk about their doubts, questions, "not knowing," etc. Those with a healthy dose of self-confidence believe that they can learn, and so feel confident, sure, definite and will talk in that manner. Those who over-do the confidencing may exaggerate it to the point of foolishness so that they egotistically present themselves as a know-it-all!

Contexts of Origin: One's feelings of faith and trust in one's skills obviously arise from the experiences of life. Taking on too much too quickly can undermine both the developmental process of learning and feeling good about learning to develop skills. Too much criticism and too harsh criticism too early, can also knock the spirit and motivation out of a person. Modeling by significant persons about how to self-validate one's skills also critically affects this meta-program.

Further Reading: Hall (1985, 1989).

Self-Analysis:
__ Low Self-Confidence/High Self-Confidence

Contexts:
__ Work/Career	__ Intimates
__ Relationships	__ Hobbies/Recreation
__ Sports	__ Other: _____
__ High/Medium/Low level	__ Driver MP: Yes/No
__ Self-Confidences in what:	

#44. Self-Experience Sort:
Mind/Emotion/Will/Body/Role or Position/Spirit

Concept: People differ in their concept of "self" and the factors that they use and factor into their self-definition. What and how a person defines him or herself, plays a central role in the self out of which they come—and the self that they use at the meta-meta level.

Elicitation: "As you think about your thoughts, emotions, will, body, roles, and positions that you experience in life—which facet or facets of yourself seems the most important, real, or valid?" "Do you think of yourself primarily as a thinker, emotional person, chooser, in terms of your physical looks or body, in terms of your roles and positions, or what?"

Identification: We can take any one of these facets of self, or a combination of them, or none of them, and conceptually define ourselves in terms of them. Korzybski (1941/1994) constantly argued against *identification* with anything as if that thing or process existed as "the same as" our neuro-semantic and neuro-linguistic label. The more Associated a person (#15), the more likely the person might use feelings to define themselves as a feeler. The more Dissociated (#15), the more likely they might over-identify with their thoughts. The more they sort for choice (#40) in the strong-will continuum, the more likely to identify with their will. Other's define themselves primarily via their jobs, roles, experiences, degrees, etc.

Languaging and Emoting: Listen for the facet that may play more of a role in a person's self-definition. Does the person seem to identify him or herself with any of these facets?

Contexts of Origin: Again, as a high-level conceptual construction about one's self-definition, this sorting program grows and develops from the lower level meta-programs. Where a person finds pleasure and/or pain, one tends to create their constructs. The languaging one receives from significant others also plays a critical role. What did others say that entered into the formulation? How well did the person screen it out or suck it in without any screening (#9)? With whom did a person identify or dis-identify?

Self-Analysis:
__ Mind/Emotion/Will/Body/Role/Position/Spirit

Contexts:
__ Work/Career	__ Intimates
__ Relationships	__ Hobbies/Recreation
__ Sports	__ Other: _____
__ High/Medium/Low level	__ Driver MP: **Yes/No**

#45. Self-Integrity
Conflicted Incongruity/Harmonious Integration

Concept: How do you sort regarding living up to your values? How do you think about your ideals, and especially your ideal self, and then evaluate how well, or how poorly, you live up to those ideals? This awareness generates a sense of self-integration, or its lack. This involves feeling conflicted and incongruous with one's highest self.

Elicitation: "When you think about how well or how poorly you live up to your ideals and in actualizing your ideal self, do you feel integrated, congruous, doing a good job in living true to your values and visions, or do you feel torn, conflicted, un-integrated, incongruous?"

Identification: Cattell (1989) says that this factor in "personality" works "co-extensively with Erickson's sense of identity" and that it

> "grows out of the recognition that one's attachment, values, and beliefs tend to endure over time. It observes how well one is living up to personal ideals. Failing to live up to personal ideals results in self-degradation, shame, or anxiety." (p. 278).

1.   Those who experience the comparison between their ideals and ideal self with their actual experiences as congruous and fitting feel that they have "self-integrity." This provides a strong sense of self-acceptance and centering. It enables one to even more effectively devote mental and emotional energies for actualizing one's values and visions.

2.   Those who lack that sense of congruence feel inwardly torn and at odds with themselves. This frequently leads to the expenditure of lots of internal energy conflicting and fighting with oneself, negative emotions, negative judgments of insult toward one's self.

Languaging and Personality: Congruity shows up in personality and language when all of a person's talk and behavior fits his or her values. The person speaks, sounds like, looks like, and behaves like they have a good solid grasp on themselves, their values, their ability to handle the problems of reality (#49), etc. The conflicted and incongruous shows up in all kinds of forms of incongruity—they say one thing but live another.

Contexts of Origin: This meta-program derives less of its presence to the past and more to ongoing and current experiences. The more "dysfunctional" the early life experiences, the more difficulty one may have in even recognizing and knowing the meaning of self-integrity and self-actualization.

Further Reading: Erickson (1959, 1968), Maslow (1954).

Self-Analysis:
__ Incongruency /Congruency

Contexts:
__ Work/Career   __ Intimates
__ Relationships   __ Hobbies/Recreation
__ Sports   __ Other: _____
__ High/Medium/Low level   __ Driver MP: Yes/No

The "Time" Semantic Constructions (#46-47)

Immanuel Kant (1787) identified "time" as one of the *a priori* categories that all humans experience. It exists innately within our species. How we process "time" determines how we understand "time" as a concept at various meta-levels, how we experience it at the primary level as events and rhythms, and how we respond to it. The characteristics that we represent about our understandings of this concept include such qualities as direction, duration, orientation, continuity, etc.

#46. "Time"-Tense Sort:
Past/Present/Future

Concept: Inasmuch as we can sort and distinguish between *events* that have already occurred, those that now occur, and those that will occur, most humans in most cultures sort for three central *"time" zones*. These show up in the linguistic tenses as well as the temporal tenses of the past, present, and future. Conceptually, a fourth kind of "time" occurs—the atemporal. How does the person have his or her "time-line" coded in terms of past, present, and future? To what extent do they have one of the "time" zones coded and represented as right in front of them?

Elicitation: "Where do you put most of your attention—on the past, present, or future? Or, have you developed an atemporal attitude so that you don't attend to 'time' at all?"

Identification and Languaging:
1. *Minding the "Past."* People who live a lot of time in the "past" "time" zone think about what they have experienced and what those experiences or events meant to them. They use a lot of past references and past tenses in their language. History seems to carry a lot of weight for them, as does tradition. This person corresponds to the "feeler" in the Myers-Briggs® instrument.

2. *Minding the Present.* Those who live in "today," in the "now," have a more present-tense orientation in the way they talk and reference things. When overdone, the person may live "in the now" to such an extent that he or she fails to think consequentially of future results or goals. This person corresponds to the Myers-Briggs® category of "sensor." Jung labeled them "sensors" because they prefer to use their senses in the present moment.

3. *Minding the "Future."* Those who live in the "future," conceptually, focus primarily in the use of future tenses and references. When overdone they project themselves and their consciousness so much into the future that they fail to make plans today for that desired future. These people correspond to the Myers-Briggs® "intuitors" inasmuch as they forever attempt to intuit about tomorrow and the future.

4. *Not minding "time."* The atemporal category describes those who live outside of a "time" consciousness. Sometimes they correspond to the Myers-Briggs® "thinkers."

Pacing: Speak to the "time" tense that predominates in the person's language patterns.

Emoting: This depends entirely upon whether the person has his or her "time" representations coded associatedly or dissociatedly and to the specific meanings (positive or negative) that they give to "time."

RET Cognitive Distortion: If a person gets stuck in the future "time" zone, or overly worries about future events, this can encourage one to "Prophesy the Future." This cognitive distortion, like mind-reading, involves jumping to conclusions about life, others, fate, the universe, God, etc. The person speaks about what "will" happen in the future—without any qualification, without tempering it in any way, in an all-or-nothing way.

Contexts of Origin: "Time" represents another high level construct that grows according to how one thinks and feels about past events, current happenings, and possible future events. Cultural, racial, religious, and family definitions about "time," about which "time" zone one "should" live in, has permission to live in, etc. also critically affects this operating system. Trauma tends to keep most people locked into the "past" trying to finish an event that they didn't like the way it finished.

Further Reading: James and Woodsmall (1988). Bodenhamer & Hall (1997a).

Self-Analysis:
__ Past/Present/Future/Atemporal

Contexts:
__ Work/Career	__ Intimates
__ Relationships	__ Hobbies/Recreation
__ Sports	__ Other: _____
__ High/Medium/Low level	__ Driver MP: Yes/No

#47. "Time" Experience Sort:
In "Time"/Through "Time"
Sequential vs Random Sorting

Concept: How we code our sense of historical "time" and its duration from event to event over a period of "time" creates our representational image or icon of it. This typically takes the form of a "time-line" of some sort (Other configurations do exist: circles, photo albums, boomerangs, etc. Yet the "line" seems more typical than not for people of most cultures as noted by Bandler, James, Woodsmall, and others.)

This *line metaphor* leads us to either perceive our "time-line" as moving through us so that we feel caught up *in* it. This describes the *"In "Time""* *processing style* and leads to experiencing "time" in an associated way. This means experiencing "time" as an eternal now, ever-present, all around us, and ourselves as forever participating in it.

If the "time-line" does not go through us, but stays apart from us, so that we live *out* of "time", then we have a *"through time" processing* style. If we sort it as outside of us, and at some distance, then we have a more objective, clear, meta-position to "time." I (MH) would have called this an *"out of time"* processing style. These facets of our processing refer to the way that we store our memories.

Elicitation: Use the traditional NLP time-line elicitation question to identify a person's style of processing this concept of "time."

> "As you take a moment to relax, and feel inwardly calm, allow yourself to recall a memory of something that occurred sometime in your past... And something else from long ago... Now think of some event that occurred today... and another... Now think of an event that will occur, one of these days... and another future event... As you now stand back or above those 'time' places in your mind, point to the direction of your future, and point to the direction of your past..."

Identification:
This meta-program concerns how we "measure" our sense of "time" past, present, and future in our brain. How do we code this concept? How do you tell the difference between events that have already occurred, those now occurring, and those that will occur?

1. *Through "Time."* People who use a *through "time"* way of storing their memories do so from left to right, or up to down so that, for them, "time" has a continuous coding along a continuum. This line may extend in a "long" or "short" way, but it operates as sequential and continuous so that the person has an awareness of "time's" duration. They typically have their memories dissociated. "Time," for them, seems linear in that it has length. This corresponds to the Myers-Briggs® "judger" inasmuch as we judge or evaluate "time" as we organize and sequence it.

Those with the *Through "Time"* style tend also to sort things sequentially. They will typically go by-the-book, like structures in life, hence rules, protocols, and procedures ("clocks" that keep "time"). They also approach thinking, deciding, buying, etc. in a basic systematic manner. They will appreciate a well-established presentation sequence. Again, this corresponds to Myers-Briggs® "Judger."

2. *In "Time."* People who use an *in "time"* style store their pasts behind them and their future in front of them. Whether their time-line extends from front to back, or up to down, it will go through their body so that they will end up *in* the line. They will typically code their memories as associated and will not have much awareness of the duration of events. Such persons will tend to more easily get caught up in "the eternal now," so that they will not know the "time" (chronological "time"). This style corresponds to the Myers-Briggs® "perceiver."

Those with the *In "Time"* style tend to sort things out more randomly. They often go off on their own tangents and seemingly have less regard for "time" constraints. As they more randomly sort, they enjoy bouncing creative ideas around, making new connections and insights, brainstorming, etc. They will frequently seem tangential, all over the place, interrupting and asking off-the-wall, and out-of-sequence questions.

Pacing **and** *Languaging:* Listen for sequential kind of words, terms, and phrases in those who use the *Through "Time"* coding. Listen for randomness, chaos, and tangential terms in the *In "Time"* processors.

Emoting: The *Through "Time"* processors will express themselves more objectively and dissociatedly or with emotions appropriate to the event. *In "Time"* processors will come across with more associated and primary emotions as well as inappropriate emoting.

Contexts of Origin: These programs arise to a great extent from our cultural experiences in community. Generally, we think of *In "Time"* as an expression of Eastern consciousness and *Through "Time"* as an expression of Western consciousness. In more recent history, the West has been characterized more and more by assembly lines, schedules, day-timers, etc. The meta-program of options/procedures (#21) significantly contributes to this, so does right and left hemisphere dominance, and associated/dissociated (#13).

Further Reading: Bodenhamer & Hall (1997)

Self-Analysis:
__ **In "Time"/Through "Time"** (Random/Sequential)

Contexts:
__ Work/Career   __ Intimates
__ Relationships   __ Hobbies/Recreation
__ Sports   __ Other: _____
__ **High/Medium/Low level**   __ Driver MP: **Yes/No**

#48. "Time" Access Sort:
Random/Sequential

Concept: This meta-program relates to how we *access* our memories of the past and functions as a sub-category of how we store or code "time" itself. Two overall patterns prevail: those who use a random accessing style and those who use a sequential accessing style.

Elicitation & Identification: Use the "time" accessing questions as in the previous pattern (#47).

1. *Random Access.* Notice if a person randomly accesses his or her memories. Do they easily jump from one memory to another? Do they have their memories stored in an unconnected way so that they can quickly and directly jump across boundaries of time, subject matter, and people? This describes *the random access style*. In this style, a person organizes memories by comparing different events that occurred at different times. They move to a meta-level position and hold two memories simultaneously.

2. *Sequential Access.* This style results from having coded one's memories in a linear and connected way. Accordingly, the person does not move from one memory to another in a random way, but in a highly sequenced way. They may view the events on their time-line as the cross-ties on a railroad track. Such sequential storage tends to make it more difficult to access memories—the person has to start somewhere else and then move linearly until they get to a memory.

Languaging/Pacing: We can assist the person with accessing by saying, "Imagine your past as a photo album and that you can now flip back through the pages of your history and just allow your unconscious mind to surprise you as your past history unfolds one memory at a time."

Contexts of Origin: Same as #46

Further Reading: Bodenhamer & Hall (1997).

Self-Analysis:
__ **R**andom Accessing/**S**equential Accessing

Contexts:
__ Work/Career	__ Intimates
__ Relationships	__ Hobbies/Recreation
__ Sports	__ Other: _____
__ **H**igh/**M**edium/**L**ow level	__ Driver MP: **Yes/No**

The Concept of "Reality"

Consider a word like "reality." The problem we have with it involves how it operates multi-ordinally, i.e. at so many different levels of abstraction. *Multi-ordinality* refers to a linguistic distinction that Korzybski (1941/1994) developed that Bandler and Grinder did not bring over into the meta-model (see Hall, 1997a, 1997b). It refers to a nominalization that has only a very general meaning, but which specific meaning changes given the level and context of abstraction. Here we use the term to designate the world that exists apart from us, beyond our nervous system, "out there," and not directly subject to our wants and wishes.

#49. Ego Strength Sort:
Unstable/Stable—Reactive/Proactive

Concept: Freud originally defined the "ego" as a set of cognitive and perceptual functions that serve adaptive purposes as we learn to cope with our environments. The ego moves out into voluntary movement at its command for the task of preservation and effectiveness. Cattell (1989) writes,

> "The ego is a problem-solving structure that mediates between needs and the environment... it recognizes tension that signifies existence and the strength of an inner need..." (p.40).

Inasmuch as we generally define "intelligence" as the ability to make accurate discriminations, this also lies partially at the heart of "ego strength."

Elicitation: "When you think about some difficulty arising in everyday life, a disappointment, problem, frustration that will block your progress, etc., what usually comes to your mind? How do you feel about such events? How do you typically respond to internal needs or external hardships? Where do your mind-and-emotions go when you face a problem?"

Identification: Along a continuum of the strength or energy of one's "ego" to rise up, identify reality for whatever one finds, address it, etc. we find people ranging along a continuum. On one end we find those who have almost no ability to look reality in the face, accept it on its own terms, and expend the energy to deal with it. On the other end we find those who have lots of ability to face and address reality. Those on this end can "face the facts" of life as they find them and do so instantaneously. They can do so without wasting time in feeling angry, upset, frustrated, depressed, or whining.

1. *The Unstability Sort.* Those who easily and quickly feel frustrated by the tiniest little annoyance become unstable in the face of difficulties. They can perceive almost anything as a "difficulty," worry and fret about it, feel insecure, unstable, emotionally distressed, etc. This generally describes how we all responded during infancy and childhood and the childish coping style of throwing tantrums, raging whenever frustrated, not tolerating delays, etc.

2. *The Stability Sort.* Those who take a more philosophical attitude toward life and progress toward any worthwhile goal know that this will involve expecting and accepting problems, road-blocks, problems to solve, etc. In the face of such undesired occurences, they stay calm, cool, unruffled, and objective. They immediately go into problem-solving in a matter-of-fact way without wasting a lot of time fuming and fretting. Ellis (1975) writes,

> "The world has great difficulties and injustices, but you don't have to whine or make yourself furious about them."

Languaging and Emoting: Expect to find lots of associated negative emotions in those who operate from low ego-strength. They will delay and procrastinate, hate and guilt, and contempt themselves, others, life, etc. They will feel panicky, act impulsively and reactively, and quickly alternate moods. Expect to hear and see more objectivity, flexibility, and a problem-solving orientation in those who operate from a highly developed ego-strength. They work patiently, with endurance, and avoid all of the melodramatic drama characteristic of the other side of the continuum. They acknowledge the problem without undue delay and confront it even with a sense of mastery and pleasure.

Contexts of Origin: Physiological determinants concern neurological well-being and normal brain developing so that a person can move through the Piagetian cognitive development stages. Those who suffer from developmental delay or retardation comprise individuals who cannot move beyond the concrete thinking stage. This limits their ability to go into formal operational thinking, and higher levels of cognitive development. They live their lives at the concrete thinking stage, or earlier, and so experience very little "ego strength." Brain lesions, cancers, and damage can put any of us back into that place. Trauma, especially chronic or acute trauma situations (e.g. war, rape, molestation, sexual abuse, etc.) can so overwhelm a person's coping skills, and reality testing abilities, that one can experience much instability in terms of ego strength. Lack of good role models or deficiencies in education, good support group, etc. can also make for instability. Good ego strength arises through learning, discipline, skill development, support persons, etc.

Further Reading: Cattell (1989).

Self-Analysis:
__ **U**nstable/**S**table
Contexts:

__ Work/Career	__ Intimates
__ Relationships	__ Hobbies/Recreation
__ Sports	__ Other: _____
__ **H**igh/**M**edium/**L**ow level	__ Driver MP: **Yes**/**No**

The Concept of Morality or Right-and-Wrong

Another seemingly innate, and therefore *a priori,* category in the "mind" seems to comprise our inescapable ability to evaluate behavior in terms of ethics and morality. This kind of "knowing" related to knowing about the *quality* of our actions and their effects and consequences on others. Do we behave in a "good" or "bad" way in terms of the societal rules and spiritual beliefs that govern our culture. These meta-programs concern the "spiritual" in humans, "conscience," morality, etc.

#50. Morality Sort:
Weak/Strong Super-ego

Concept: How people sort for issues and concerns that fall into the category of right-and-wrong, morals, ethics, etc. differ. Some see, hear, and sort for moral issues everywhere and all the time; others seem to operate as if such categories do not exist. Freud defined the "super-ego" as an internalized set of rules that enables us to process for "rightness" or "wrongness" of a behavior.

Elicitation: "When you think about some misbehavior that you engaged in, what thoughts-and-feelings arise when you realized that you had acted in an inappropriate way that violated legitimate values?" "When you think about messing up, doing something embarrassing, stupid, socially inept, etc., what thoughts-and-feelings flood your consciousness along with that realization?"

Identification: The proneness toward guilt, innocence, righteousness, worthiness, etc. describes this *meta* meta-program. Some people sort for guilt, wrongness, badness, shame, and worthlessness in every action; others seem to never sort for such things. Along a continuum we can plot an anti-social lack of conscience to guilt-proneness or conscientiousness.

1. *The Unconscientious Sort.* Those who have a weakly developed super-ego tend to not recognize or sort for true guilt—the violation of a true moral standard. So they disregard obligations, rules, ethics, morals, etc. They live self-indulgently, narcissistically, disrespectful of morals, choosing whatever they find expedient for their immediate goals. Others can't depend on their moral consciousness to do "the right thing." Over-done, this leads to the criminal mind lacking any "conscience," hence sociopathic.

2. *The Conscientious Sort.* Those who have a well-developed super-ego sort for the rightness or wrongness of events, especially those that truly fulfill or violate genuine moral standards. This internalized moral consciousness results in creating individuals who have a high level sense of responsibility (#27), personally disciplined, having a strong sense of duty, staid to immediate pleasures to do wrong, moralistic, etc. When over-done, the conscientiousness can create a guilt-proneness so that any mistake or expression of fallibility evokes within them feelings of badness, wretchedness, condemnation, etc.

Languaging and Emoting: The unconscientious can lie, cheat, misbehave, undermine moral standards, etc. and do so without any "pangs of conscience." They seem to have little to no internal guidance system about morals. They develop a "personality" that we label amoral or antisocial. Once they have constructed a way of thinking-feeling and acting ("personality") designated as the "antisocial personality" (DSM IV), they seem callous to hurting others, lack any sense of empathy for the distresses of others, seem almost unable to learn from their own mistakes, lack appropriate fear, and may develop beliefs that validate their right to take advantage of, or hurt, others. The conscientious will talk about doing "the right thing," the "responsible" act of doing what they say, etc. They will tend to have a strong sense of spirituality or religion and believe that right actions play an important role in the universe. Those who over-do this adapt a "self-righteous" style, sometimes in a fanatical and rigid way, develop a distorted view of self, and fail to see their own fallibilities. Others who over-do it develop obsessive-compulsiveness in their focus on orderliness, cleanliness, etc.

Contexts of Origin: This represents another high level construct that arises almost entirely dependent upon the contexts of culture, politics, religion, family, etc. Some neurological studies suggest genetic deficiency in those who later develop sociopathic ways of thinking-feeling and living, indicating a predisposition to such. Pain and pleasure conditioning factors in early childhood surrounding the moral training of recognition of the rights of others, respect for human life and property, development of empathy, etc. obviously play a crucial role. The stereotype of the Obsessive-Compulsive cleaner that arose from the field of psychoanalysis suggests someone who may have felt "dirty" via some form of sexual abuse.

Further Reading: Kohlberg (1980).

Self-Analysis:
__ Unconscientious/Conscientious—Weak/Strong Super-ego
Contexts:

__ Work/Career   __ Intimates
__ Relationships   __ Hobbies/Recreation
__ Sports   __ Other: _____
__ High/Medium/Low level   __ Driver MP: Yes/No

#51 Causational Sort:
Causeless, Linear Cause Effect (CE), Multi-CE, Personal CE,
External CE, Magical, Correlational

Concept: How does a person think about the "cause" of an event or experience? What brings something into existence? Does inexplicable magic direct linear cause-effect as in mathematics and physics, does a whole range of contributing factors, or does nothing actually cause other things, at best, effects only exist in a correlational relationship to other events?

Elicitation: Ask any question that involves some kind of causational presupposition. "When you think about what caused you to work at the job that you work at, how do you explain that?" "What brought the current situation of your life to exist as it does?" "What makes people behave as they do?" "How did their relationship get into that state?" "Why did you get divorced?"

Identification: This meta-program addresses the possible ways of how we relate to the conceptual category of "causation" and existence. As a higher level *meta* meta-program, it grows out of *Frame of Reference sort* (#14) where people *referentially* think-feel in terms of self or other (external). It also grows out of the *Responsibility sort* (#27) program. Now moving up into this "reality" *meta* meta-program, this one focuses on how we relate to the concept of causation itself and the conceptual explanations that we invent to orient ourselves in the world.

Andreas and Andreas (1989) refer to the concept of this meta-program (without identifying it as such) in their presentation of "The Naturally Slender Eating Strategy." Someone said, "You're *lucky* to be so slim. I'm just not that kind of person. I just don't have that body type." Here the client viewed slenderness or overweight as the result of genetic accidents over which she had no control. So as she operated from the meta-program of *external causation*, she shifted to Other-referent (#14), at least in the context of eating. This had a dramatic effect on her strategies. When she "saw food," she felt compelled to eat (V K). "She did not consider whether she was hungry or full, whether the food tasted good, how it would affect her if she ate it, or anything else." (p. 122).

1. *No causation.* This describes those who think that no causation exists, and so no explanation of processes. These people live in a world that does not make sense in terms of cause-effect, consequences, etc. Things just happen. No intelligence drives the world, only total randomness and chance.

2. *Total and absolute Linear CE.* Those who live at the other end of the continuum of "cause" believe in a closed-system world where everything results from direct and immediate causation. Their style of thinking works really well in the "hard" sciences of mathematics, physics, chemistry, mechanics, etc. It works very poorly in the "soft" sciences of human behaving, politics, economics, communication, etc. This fits more with the Aristotelian sort (#11).

3. *Multi-CE.* Those who think of "causes" operating in an open-system think systemically about "cause" recognizing that almost always a multiple of contributing factors come together to cause various effects. They can think above the linear level and move into higher logical levels where gestalt of configurations arise. This fits the thinking processes of the Non-Aristotelian sort (#11).

4. *Personal CE.* People who think in terms of their role in causing, effecting, and influencing things. Generally this entails the Self-referent (#14) feeling sort and the Balanced Responsibility Choosing sort (#27), although when over-done, moves towards over-responsibility.

5. *External CE.* People who think that they play no role in causing, effecting, or influencing things come from the Other-Referent position of feeling (#14), the under-responsibility conation sort (#27) and therefore unduly empower circumstances, events, environment, genetics, etc. as the controlling factors in life as in the Andreas' story.

6. *Magical.* Those who live in a magical world believe that *everything* arises as "caused" by something, namely by forces and/or entities beyond this world or this dimension. Therefore they think superstitiously about how to adjust and/or appease these powers of the heavens (the stars and constellations), angels, demons, gods, ancient persons, saints, etc. For them, ritual repetition of various secret knowledge holds the key to causation.

7. *Correlation.* In addition to the causation continuum, some also assume that many so-called "causes" actually exist only as correlations. That children typically gain weight during their time in elementary school as they grow mentally does not mean that weight causes greater intelligence. We can correlate the relationship of these diverse factors of experience without reading "cause" into them.

Source of Origin: Arises to a great extent from the philosophies about cause and "why" presented and believed among parents and teachers, also in the larger cultural environment.

Further Reading: Munshaw & Zink (1997).

Self-Analysis:
__ Causeless/Linear CE/Multi-CE/Personal CE/External CE/
    Magical/Correlational

Contexts:
__ Work/Career	__ Intimates
__ Relationships	__ Hobbies/Recreation
__ Sports	__ Other: _____
__ High/Medium/Low level	__ Driver MP: Yes/No

Conclusion

Not only do we have meta-programs by which we sort for things, but we also have programs *meta* to those programs. Of the number we have addressed here, only values and "time" had previously appeared in lists of meta-programs. Yet as analysis shows, these appear at a higher logical level than the other meta-programs, though they frequently grow out of the other meta-programs.

#40. **Value Sort:** *Emotional "Needs," Beliefs*
#41. **Temper to Instruction Sort:** *Strong-Will / Compliant*
#42. **Self-Esteem Sort:** *Conditional/ Unconditional*
#43. **Self-Confidence Sort:** *High / Low*
#44. **Self-Experience Sort:** *Mind/Emotion/Body/Role*
#45. **Self-Integrity:** *Conflicted Incongruity / Harmonious Integration*
#46. **"Time" Tenses Sort:** *Past/ Present/ Future*
#47. **"Time" Experience:** *In "Time"/ Through "Time";*
Sequential Versus Random Sorting
#48. **"Time" Access Sort:** *Random / Sequential*
#49. **Ego Strength Sort:** *Unstable/ Stable*
#50. **Morality Sort:** *Weak/ Strong Super-ego*
#51. **Causational Sort:** *Causeless, Linear Cause Effect (CE), Multi-CE,*
Personal CS, External CE, Magical, Correlational

Part III

Utilization

Design Engineering
With Meta-Programs

"By Human Engineering I mean the science and art of directing
the energies and capacities of human beings
to the advancement of human weal." (p. 1)

"Production is essentially a task for engineers;
it essentially depends upon the discovery and the application of natural laws,
including the laws of human nature.
Human Engineering will embody the theory and practice—
the science and art—of all engineering branches united by a common aim—
the understanding and welfare of mankind." (pp.6-7)

The task of engineering science is not only to know, but to know how. (p. 11)
(Korzybski, 1921)

Chapter 8

Context
And Meta-Programs

The Context Determines the Reality

Throughout this work we have emphasized the critical importance of *context.* In fact, in Part II, after every single meta-program, we provided a checklist for noting various contexts. We did that purposely and yet without any explanations. In this chapter we now want to explore the concept of context a little further and offer some theoretical understandings about *how it plays such a crucial role* in the experience and structuring of our meta-programs.

The Critical Role of **Context**

In the field of Cognitive Psychology **no "thinking"** occurs without a context. Remember, we use the term "thinking" holistically to designate all forms and expressions of human consciousness: perceiving, emoting, somatizing, valuing, believing, etc.

Consider this idea for a moment and let its obviousness register. To say that thinking *always* occurs in a context may at first glance seem so obvious that it may seem unnecessary to mention it. But try to imagine a **thought without a thinker**. What would that consist of? Try to imagine *thinking* occurring—apart from any and all contexts of "time," space, culture, environment, people, physiological state, etc.

Okay, now that we have put the idea of contextless thinking out of its misery, we can direct our consciousness to ask a set of more sane questions.

- *How* does context affect "thinking?"
- *What* contexts tend to initiate *what kinds of "thinking?"*
- *How* do contexts of contexts affect thinking?

Context and Contexts in NLP

In the field of Neuro-Linguistics, we especially highlight the role of context. We do so usually by describing it in terms of *frame* (as in frame-of-reference). Yeager (1985) puts it most succinctly,

> "Thinking occurs within a context, purpose or frame of reference that is unique to the individual. If you don't know the context of another's thinking, many things can seem illogical.... When you think of what you want for dinner you think in terms of the context of where (location), with whom or when (time) or even in terms of good nutrition (biochemistry). These are all contextual factors. Yet the definition of a context is typically subjective...
>
> Some people think of time mostly in the past tense. Others think in the present tense... This characteristic is *a learned preference and it 'frames'* the range of behaviors...possible within that subjective context. In this sense, a context is a set of limits that defines what is and, reciprocally, defines what is not at issue.
>
> Context is a stabilizing reference point that locates where you are or are not in your subjective world. If an individual habitually thinks in terms of precedent (the past tense), it will be difficult for the person to imagine 'possibilities' (future tense) if history isn't 'imagined' into the 'changed future.'" (pp. 23-24).

Yeager's description leads us to realize that *our meta-programs function as our thinking contexts*. Consider the significance of this. When we speak about these "programs" ("thinking" sorting styles, our operating system for how we use our nervous system) that lie *meta to* our primary level thinking—we essentially identify the **contexts** for thinking, our "thinking contexts."

This leads to a set of most important questions to ask ourselves or any person with whom we communicate:

- *Within what context do you do your thinking?*
- Within *what* frame-of-reference does your thinking occur?
- As you think about things right now—do you use a global or specific frame?
- Do you use a match or mismatch frame?
- Do you use a past, present, or future frame?
  etc.

Why do we describe these as *most important questions?* Because if we do not know a person's frame-of-reference for their "thinking"—we will not understand their meanings, emotions, or responses! We will not know or understand the person's *stabilizing reference point.* Human thinking always, inevitably, and *inescapably* occurs within some frame. And, in that frame, the "thinking" (emoting, perceiving, behaving) makes perfect sense! It functions *"logically"* to that internal frame.

It only seems *illogical* **to other frames**. Do you think-and-feel that someone's way of thinking seems really illogical? Then you do so *from* a different frame of reference, from a different model of the world.

Korzybski, for this reason always hyphenated the word "psycho-logical" (psycho-logics, psycho-logist, psycho-logicians, etc.). Most people find this a very strange use of the word. He did so to underscore that *the "logics"* that occur within any given psyche (neuro-psychic organism) operate logically within that context. Yeager (1985), again, describes this by saying that in NLP "subjectivity is unavoidable which makes it reality." (p. 17).

So, our meta-programs not only comprise our context thinking, but also our **psycho-logics**. Do you now know your *psycho-logics?* Do you know, or do you know how to recognize the psycho-logics of those with whom you do business, relate, have fun, etc.? When you find and identify their meta-programs, you have a very solid clue to their context thinking and psycho-logics. The next step? To pace and work with those psycho-logics.

Meta-Programs as Role Inductions into Various Contexts

Personality "role" theory has long assumed and described these same processes. How we experience ourselves, others, our thoughts and emotions, how we express ourselves, the skills and resources available to us, or not available to us, depends on *the roles* that we have learned to play (or not learned to play). In social psychology (including sociology, anthropology), the function of various *role inductions* in culture serve as those "context markers" that cue a person (or anchor one) to shift meta-programs. Such role inductions occur as rituals and ceremonies, special places and events, belief systems, social institutions, etc.

So the context thinking we do via our meta-programs simply describes *how* we think, attend, and sort information *in relation to our environment* in terms of **the roles that it invites us to play**. This means that as we identify more fully the *internal* contexts that we bring with us, and bring to bear upon our experiences, we gain greater awareness of how our meta-programs induces us into various roles.

Use the context of global thinking and you play more of a philosopher or artist's role. Use the context of detail thinking and you play the role of the inductive scientist. Whatever thinking context you bring to bear on things creates the ability and induces you into certain roles.

Examine your *driver* meta-programs in terms of this. Do you use the judging adaptation operating system (#22) more than the perceiving sort? What role does that induce you to play in life? The critic! How well does this serve you? Do you move through life using the extrovert battery rejuvenation sort (#29)? What roles does that get you to play? Do you like playing these roles?

What roles can you *not* play? What roles do you not play very well? What roles would you like to use in order to experience more effectiveness in this or that facet of life? What meta-programs would assist you to do precisely that? And conversely...

The Roles and Experiences We Have Played—Create Our Meta-Programs

If we think in either-or terms, we generate the unanswerable chicken and egg question about which came first. But if we think in terms of recursive loops in an interconnected system of thought-and-experience-and-thought then we can easily recognize that *the contexts of life* can and do invite us to "think-emote" in certain ways. Then, out of those contexts we develop our operating systems for running our brains (our meta-programs). Then, consequently, we take our thinking-contexts (our meta-level concepts and semantic psycho-logics) everywhere we go. We never leave home without them!

Given this, no wonder our *Significant Emotional Experiences of Pain (SEEPs)* inevitably play a powerful role in the development of our meta-programs. *In what context* did you first learn to "run your brain?" In what inter-personal contexts did you first learn to use your nervous system to abstract information from the stimuli of the world? How healthy or unhealthy, how respectful or disrespectful, how validating or how toxic, how empowering or limiting, etc. did you find those first contexts?

Bateson and associates (1972) noted that if a person grows up in a schizo-phrenic environment where they receive double messages constantly on the order of "I love you, you stupid, worthless bastard!" And within that context, the person receives disconfirming messages about their own perspectives, *and* they feel that they cannot step outside of the frame (go meta) to meta-comment about the "crazymaking." Then, that person has a powerful context within which to learn to run their brain schizophrenically. It makes sense. The person does not have "bad," "corrupted," "weird," or "flawed" psycho-logics. His or her psycho-logics work perfectly fine.

Every day they wake up and run their brain according to those same thinking-contexts. They use the same operating system for making sense of things. Their thinking-emoting and behaving operates systematically and regularly in an orderly way. It may not work well when they leave that original environment. It may sabotage their sense of well-being, their ability to function in the world outside that environment. It may make their internal thoughts-and-feelings a living hell, but it works logically *according to their psycho-logics.*

This highlights how we all inevitably **internalize contexts** as we move through life. Not only does the schizophrenic *internalize* his or her early family contexts so that such contexts then operate as the structuring formats of consciousness, but so do we all. We make our *mental maps* about life, others, the world, self, etc. via the contexts that we have internalized. To a great extent these create and influence our meta-programs.

A Context for Burn-Out

Now, for a personal story. I (BB) grew up as a middle child in the family and we lived in a financial state of poverty up in the mountains of North Carolina. My father had to work constantly to keep us alive, so from my perception I got very little attention. In that context I learned early that if I excelled in performance, dad would give me a dollar for an "A," which really impressed me, "That's a lot of money for a poor mountain boy!"

As the years passed I also learned that as I hired myself out to local farmers, that hard work brought lots of reward, financial, as well as the reward of compliments and verbal validation. Though younger than the other boys in the community, I soon made as much money as they did simply because I worked as much and even more than they.

Now that I look back on those experiences I can see clearly the meta-programs that I created and that developed. First, I moved through time with a judger orientation (#22 "personality") always evaluating myself and others in terms of "how much I work produced" (#13 aggressive, #20 toward). I moved through life trying to make the world adapt to me than adapting to it. This developed the value of receiving attention (and love) through work, productivity, effectiveness, etc.

Later when I moved into the pastorate, this mountain boy preached grace, but he lived a life of work. He continued to work extremely hard to get "attention" (and love), and could not say "no" to requests, even ridiculous ones, because at some unconscious level he believed that people would not love him if he did. Apparently, I took my "hard driving Type-A judging style" with me everywhere I went! So, at the age of 46 I found myself suffering from "the burned out" syndrome.

Since that time my own meta-programs have changed tremendously as a recent retesting score on the Myers-Briggs Type Indicator® has confirmed. I have moved from a high level "Judger" (49 points in 1990) to a low level score (15 points in 1997).

How to Explore Your Own History for the Origins of Your Meta-Programs

What *contexts* of learning have you grown up with? How has your contextual thinking played a role in creating the psycho-logics of your current meta-programs? What inter-personal *contexts* have you experienced, endured, grown up inside, coped with, etc.? To what extent have you internalized a "toxic" context? Have you "left home" physically and externally, but have that early home context so internalized that you now take it with you everywhere you go?

To discover such **contexts,** use your own biography. In NLP we talk about the fact that we all, inevitably and inescapably, to make sense of language, experiences, events, etc. do a TDS (transderivational search) to our referential index. In other words, we "go inside" and use our "library of references"—our memories, experiences, and references. These internal contexts then provide us with "meaning," "significance," association, etc. No wonder they play such a formative role in generating our meta-program!

Elicit your own *library of references* by telling your story to a trusted friend, tape recorder, therapist, or journal. We highly recommend that you get the story in written form in some way or another so that you can then return to it repeatedly. Then you can examine it from second position (as an observer watching yourself) rather than from first position. You can examine it as a "text" or narrative. Then, as you step-back from it you can more objectively examine the meta-programs that it presupposes.

Imagining New Contexts

What context have you never experienced...yet? What context have you not yet experienced, but if you had—and had fully experienced—it would have created a whole new way of thinking-and-feeling within you? Suppose you had grown up in another century, in another culture, in another social class, in another race... Suppose you had received all of the loving and nurturing you wanted? Suppose you had received unconditional self-esteeming from parents, teachers, and others? Just suppose...

If we inescapably *internalize contexts*—then we do not stop doing that at the age of eighteen or whenever you left home. We continue to do such. So, given this human tendency, nurture your mind-and-emotions, your very soul, on some delightful, wonderful, and resource-laden contexts in your imagination.

In doing so, you can *design engineer* the kind of contexts that will empower you to internalize new contexts for new meta-programs. Design engineer this positive and enhancing thinking context by modeling one that you have read about (perhaps the biography of some creative genius who you highly admire) or fully imagine it.

Another powerful transformational tool for redesigning your thinking contexts (i.e. meta-programs) involves *storytelling.* When we tell our personal, family, cultural, and racial stories—we in essence tell about the formative contexts that have molded and formed us. The stories of human community formulate both *what* and *how* to perceive. They provide both primary and meta-level values and sorting patterns.

Given this role of stories, (shared stories, real, and mythical stories), how have you been *storied?* Who storied you? What stories did they tell you? How empowering have you found those stories? What story could you enter into, tell yourself and others, and use as a thinking context that would give you a whole new lease on life?

Conclusion

Meaning always occurs and arises from contexts—personal and internal or offered by a culture or environment. Without knowing contexts—we cannot understand the meaning of anything. To understanding and figure out another human being, we have to develop an understanding of the contexts out of which that person came, the contexts that he or she has built inside their consciousness, and the contexts that they live in.

To work with a person (even ourselves) once we take context into consideration, then we can develop a working understanding of which contexts we need to address and transform in order to transform ourselves.

Chapter 9

Changing Meta-Programs

*Learning to Become a Different **Kind** of Person*

The NLP model pre-eminently highlights the plasticity of human nature and consciousness. We have "programs," but we do not have programs so written in stone that prevents us from altering them. We can alter them. In fact, in the normal process of growing up—we do.

What the NLP model offers, and what we have attempted to make explicit here, concerns *the processes* whereby we can consciously, intentionally, and effectively **transform** the way we think-and-feel and therefore the very structures of what we call "personality."

In other words, we always have options about what operating system to run in our heads as software for how to think-feel and respond. We always have options *if* **we know** *how to think* **about those options.** Of course, without knowing how to even think about options, alternative meta-programs, different thinking patterns and thinking context, different psycho-logics—without them we have no sense of choice.

Using Meta-Level Processes for Making the Shift

Robert Dilts (1990) suggested using of the meta-position to demonstrate that we can take a person to a meta-level on their time-line to alter a meta-program. From the meta-position we can access resources and transfer resources back into memories to alter the thinking context we have incorporated. The meta-position provides *a space* different from "the problem space," and offers one from which to shift submodalities, build enhancing identity beliefs, reimprint, change history, etc. And doing these things enables us to alter our meta-programs. Dilts wrote,

> "In a way, the reimprinting context provides you with a means to change meta-program patterns and sorting styles. For instance, you can easily influence a person to be *in time* or *through time, away from* or *toward* or sort by *the present to the past* or *the past to the future,* or *the present to the future.* You can have the person sort by *self,* by *others,* or *context.*" (p. 137)

How to Determine what Meta-Programs to Alter

Why would a person want to change a meta-program in a given context anyway? The primary reason—*doesn't work very well*. In the *Meta-States Journal* (March, 1997), I (MH) wrote the following about creativity and the meta-programs. This illustrates that for the skill or strategy of *creativity*, some meta-programs work exceptionally well while others prevent it,

> "Several styles of sorting for things or processing information (called 'meta-programs' in NLP) significantly impact the state and strategy of *creativity*. Those people who we most quickly deem as creative have the meta-program of operating in the world by sorting for *'options'* (rather than 'procedures'). They also sort for *'differences'* when they think, perceive, notice, etc. (rather for "sameness").
>
> To run one's brain by asking for, looking for, and valuing **alternatives** or options obviously tunes one for generating even more new and different things. To run one's brain by sorting for 'the different,'for what doesn't fit, for the out-of-the-ordinary, etc., puts one into an orientation that has a greater probability of creating something new and different.
>
> Another meta-program that enhances creativity involves operating from an authority sort of *'self-reference'* (rather than other-reference). This one enables a person to operate from *an inner locus of control/authority* rather than 'other-reference' (and external locus of control). By doing so, this contributes and supports a 'creative' way of living, thinking-emoting, and responding since the person 'knows within' what he or she likes, values, appreciates, dreams, etc.
>
> The other-referent way of sorting tends to put us into an orientation where we care too much for pleasing others, getting their approval, conforming to their values, not-conflicting by presenting something too different or weird, and fulfilling their criteria. By way of contrast, if you sort self-referently, this enables you to bring forth the new and wild and different ideas and imaginations that occur within *without* worrying about what others think or whether others will like or approve. Your vision and excitement carries you forward rather than the accolades from the approval of others." (pp. 5-6).

A Meta-Programs Change Pattern

Robbins (1986) says that one way to change a meta-program involves "consciously deciding to do so." Yet because most of us never give a thought to the mental software, we simply don't. This means that we must first recognize our operational system, and use that awareness as an opportunity for new choices. Since a meta-program informs our brain about *what to delete*—if we move toward values, then we delete awareness about what we move away from. If we sort for the details, we delete the big picture. By directing our awareness to what we normally delete describes how we can shift focus and change our operating systems.

The Pattern:
1. *Identify the meta-program* that currently governs your sorting, processing, and attending. Specifically identify when, where, and how you use this meta-program that does not serve you well and how it undermines your effectiveness in some way.

2. *Describe fully the meta-program you would prefer to have.* What meta-level processing would you prefer to "run your perceiving and valuing?" Specify when, where, and how you would like this meta-program to govern your consciousness.

3. *Try it out.* Imaginatively adopt the new meta-program and then pretend to use it in sorting, perceiving, attending, etc. Notice how it seems, feels, works, etc. in some contexts where you think it would serve you better. Even if it seems a little "weird" and strange due to your unfamiliarity with looking at the world with that particular perceptual filter, notice what other feelings, beside discomfort, may arise with it.

If you know someone who uses this meta-program, explore with them their experience until you can take second position to it. When you can, then step into that position fully so that you can see the world out of that person's meta-program eyes, hearing what he or she hears, self-talking as he or she engages in self-dialogue, and feeling what that person feels.

4. *Ecology check it.* Go meta to an even higher level and consider what this meta-program will do to you and for you in terms of perception, valuing, believing, behaving, etc. What kind of a person would it begin to make you? What effect would it have on various aspects of your life?

5. Give yourself permission to install it for a period of time. Frequently, a person can "install" a meta-program filter by granting oneself permission to use it. After you grant yourself such permission, go inside and see if any part or facet of you objects. If no, then future pace. If yes, then use the objection to reframe the so that it incorporates the objection in its meanings.

For example, suppose you have typically operated using the Other-Referencing meta-program (#14) and you give yourself permission to shift to Self-Referencing. Yet when you do, you hear an internal voice that sounds like your mother's voice in tone and tempo, "It's selfish to think about yourself. Don't be so selfish, you will lose all of your friends."

This voice objects on two accounts: selfishness and disapproval that leads to loneliness. So rephrase your permission to take these objections into account. "I give myself permission to see the world referencing centrally from myself—my values, beliefs, wants, etc., knowing that my values including loving, caring, and respecting others and that this will keep me balanced by considering the effect of my choices on others."

6. Future pace the meta-program. Practice, in your imagination, using the meta-program and do so until it begins to feel comfortable and familiar.

Troubleshooting. If you have difficulty, then do this same procedure on your time-line by floating first *above* yourself and your line (to your meta time-line) and then *float back* along the line into your past until you come to one or several of the key experiences wherein you began using the old meta-program..

Then ask yourself, "If you knew when you originally made the choice to *operate from the Other Referent (name the meta-program you want to change)*, would that have been, before, after, or during birth?

Use one of the time-line processes to neutralize the old emotions, thoughts, beliefs, decisions, etc.: the visual-kinesthetic dissociation technique, decision destroyer pattern, etc. Once you have cleared out the old pattern, you can install the new meta-program.

Changing Meta-Programs In and With "Time"

If meta-programs refer to our strategies for filtering the information that we input via our senses, then we should update any strategy that seems sluggish, inappropriate, maladjusted, etc., should we not?

Sometimes this occurs naturally and inevitably anyway. Bodenhamer (1996) noted this,

> "Over the last seven years I have been quite amazed at how my client's meta-programs have changed through the therapy that I have done with them. I use various NLP techniques and language patterns in NLP therapy. These include: reframing, anchoring, the Techniques of Time Line Therapy™, advance language patterns like Cartesian logic, hypnotic patterns, and time-lining patterns. I still find it amazing at how meta-programs change directly and indirectly through these processes."

Why does "time" have such affect on our meta-programs? As *events* come and go over a period of months or years, these ever-changing events create new *learning contexts*—contexts within which we learn to pay attention to, sort for, and perceive in different ways.

So when we do pseudo-time orientation using various time-line patterns, we use a meta-level structure that alters our thinking contexts. Additionally, we use an inherently hypnotic process when we "go inside" and access our time-line and then float above it back to our "past." This enables us to access a highly receptive and suggestible state which, in turn, amplifies our responsiveness to the change patterns. That explains *why. (For lots of time-lining patterns, see Bodenhamer and Hall, 1997).*

Pace Before You Lead to a Change

We meet someone at his or her model of the world by matching the language, gestures, movements, breathing, etc. that they produce. By so pacing, they experience a sense of similarity and likeness, and so they relax. By contrast, people usually resist interactions and messages that do not match their image of the world. So we first pace, then we lead.

Whether a person operates by Introverting or Extroverting (#22), they usually do so based upon some decision they made during a Significant Emotional Experience(s) of Pain (SEEP) which they made at an earlier time in life. This usually involves an identity issue and frequently occurred during the imprint period (from birth to age 7). If a person uses one of several time-line processes, you can eliminate the painful emotions and disconnect the person from such limiting decisions.

Whether a person operates by Intuiting or Sensing (#5) usually arises from the person's preference in "chunking" their language. An Intuitor processes information globally while a Sensor does it more specifically (in details). The language patterns of the Meta-Model and the Milton Model provide us a wide range of choices about how to move up and down the scale of specificity and abstraction. Learning this gives us more flexibility in choosing which level (global/specifics) to use in any given context. (See the diagram, "Hierarchy of Language" in Appendix D. p. 245).

Does a person operate rigidly in his/her emotional state as Associated or Dissociated (#11)? This frequently arises from, and depends upon, unresolved traumatic experiences. When a person goes through an extremely painful experience, he or she can get "stuck" in either the Association or Dissociation mode. Again, using time-line processes, the visual-kinesthetic dissociation process, the decision destroyer, etc. can facilitate a person reclaiming flexibility of consciousness about how to code and think about the trauma. This then leads to having choice about when to experience and feel from first person and when to dissociate from feeling.

We mentioned earlier the unique relationship between *Judging* (#17) and *Through "Time"* (#35) and *Perceiving* and *In "Time"*. Changing these meta-programs simply involves changing one from processing "time" from the *Through "Time"* style to the *In "Time"* format, or vice versa. When you do this, take care. This can have very powerful change effects and you may have to get use to it. If you change your formatting of this distinction, and some time passes, and you still do not like it, change it back! Since you always have choice, you can always change it back.

In changing your *Direction Sort (#15)*, you will recall that with this meta-program we structure ourselves *toward* our positive values and beliefs and *away from* our negative values. Since we move Away From and/or Toward our high level values which make up a major part of our "personality," transforming this software will inevitably create major re-orientations in life. We can change this meta-program by most of the NLP "technologies" because toward and away from values have their own unique submodalities structures.

By contrast, expect to invest more time and trouble into transforming the meta-program of one's *Frame of Reference Sort* (#10). James and Woodsmall (1988) suggests that a person use the context of deep trance when attempting to change this filter.

With regard to the *Convincer Demonstration Sort* (#14), this generally arises from a gestalting of life's experiences and decisions. From repeated experiences we generate our Convincer Demonstration Sort. Change this one by using some of the techniques of time-lining to eliminate the negative emotions from these experiences. Then reimprint the new gestalts.

To transform the *Relationship Sort* (#2) from matching to mismatching or vice versa, James and Woodsmall (1988) suggest that the person who totally sorts for sameness (or totally sorts for differences) probably does so from an associated position and this prevents bringing in some of the other pattern. To test it for yourself, try the following thought experiment. Make an associated picture of something (anything will do). Now try to bring up another picture for comparison... Most people find this impossible. As long as we stay in an absolute position of association, we will find it impossible to bring in other pictures. So shifting from Sameness to Sameness with Exception involves first facilitating the ability to create dissociated representations.

Changing Meta-Programs by Anchoring New Responses

Yeager (1985) described a process for transforming "the mindless use of the polarity response." He does so in the context of "installing a compulsion" and learning to utilize the essential NLP presupposition that the more choices a person has, the better,

> "All individuals are polarity responders in some contexts. That is, polarity responders will notice what is wrong (according to personal experience and ideals) before noticing what is right in their perceptions of reality. Problems will occur with inflexible polarity responses in anyone if the response is compulsive instead of appropriate." (p. 33).

1. First, he suggests, regress back to childhood and recover your natural curiosity and positive expectations...by thinking about some of your many exciting firsts: your first rollercoaster ride, your first ride on an airplane, visit to a zoo, etc. Float back on your time-line and recapture, associatedly,

some of these kinds of positive and fun experiences. Anchor this fully and completely. Then future pace to all of the things that you could look out at with eyes of excitement, fun, interest, curiosity, etc. as you move out into tomorrow, and next week.

2. Recontextualize the polarity response by explaining its real usefulness as a protective behavior for contexts of true danger. If a school bully pushes other kids around, then polarizing to that behavior may serve one well. A meta-level awareness, "Oh, so I have come to learn to typically respond in sorting for differences so much that I always look for the opposite pole of things..." can sometimes turn on enough light and awareness that one reclaims choice, and therefore control. Now where would I find this response useful? Where would I not?

3. Access a state of choice. Perhaps look around the room and begin to notice all the things that you can notice. You can direct your consciousness to the colors, the lines and forms, the textures, light, furniture, sounds, smells, etc. As the growing awareness that you have so many choices about what to attend, anchor this "sense of choice." Repeat with several other references and keep stacking the anchor.

4. Next, using the person's driving submodalities, turn their "sense of choice" up until it gets bigger, brighter, more intense—until they develop a *compulsion to choose*. Then future pace this choosiness.

Conclusion

The stabilizing reference points that reflect our learning history, psycho-logics, values, and frames-of-reference arose as we learned to so pattern our consciousness. This created our first meta-programs. Given this nature of meta-programs, we can unlearn them and learn much better ways to pattern our consciousness. Since the choice lies in knowing our meta-programs, we first need to develop a comprehensive understanding of our patterns. To design engineer your own style of attending and sorting infor-mation, *choose* which meta-programs you want to use in specific contexts. Then, as you give yourself permission to shift focus, consciously pay atten-tion to what you usually delete. Do this faithfully for a few days or weeks and it will drop out of conscious awareness as your newly designed meta-programs.

Chapter 10

Design Engineering In Profiling People

*"Shifting from 'the way we **are**' to 'the way we function'*
installs the ability to think more flexibly about human nature."
(Michael Hall)

"Increasingly states have outlawed the use of paper and pencil instruments in hiring and classifying employees. My wife works for Aetna Life and Casualty in personnel. Her company has not, for years, permitted the use of such instruments in interviewing potential employees. What can a manager or personnel director do? With such rules, the use of meta-programs becomes even more valuable. A person competent in understanding and using these meta-programs can elicit in ten to fifteen minutes the primary meta-programs that drives a person's way of functioning."
(Bob Bodenhamer)

Robbins (1986) has asserted that "Putting the right person in the right job remains one of the biggest problems in American business" (p. 229). We can now deal with this problem via the meta-programs. Once we know how to evaluate the ways that a job applicant processes information, *we can create a conceptual profile about how they function* (mentally, emotionally, behaviorally, etc.). Such profiling will then provide us with a more profound and accurate understanding of a given person's highest skills and where he or she will best fit in.

Profiling People Without Pencil and Paper Instruments

Because meta-programs function as human "software" behind the brain's everyday operations, they determine what we pay attention to and what we delete. Further, because they operate at a level *above* the content level, they have little to do with content and much to do with process or structure. They also give and create our sense of *the quality* of one's experiences inasmuch as they consist of the very patterns that determine a person's interests and *how* one attends those interests. These operational systems (as the formatting that operates at a meta-level) give experience a sense of continuity as they comprise some of the most basic building blocks in "personality."

As categories that describe internal patterns (and patterning), *meta-programs change over time and from context to context*. We use these meta-processing patterns according to our emotional state at any given time. In this, they frequently operate in a state-dependent way. Even how we use the same meta-program will differ according to our emotional state and the amount of stress present. The big picture of gestalt thinking will have a very different effect (emotionally and behaviorally) when in an unresourceful state compared to a resourceful one.

Now that we have developed and/or expanded our understanding of the programs themselves (Part II), our next step involves developing the skills and efficiency in working with them and using them to figure out ourselves and others. We have reproduced *Figure 1.3* (from Chapter 1) in Appendix E pp.246-247 in order that you can use this format to familiarize yourself with this model. You can use it essentially as a *sorting grid* for cuing yourself about what operational system any given person will tend to use in any given context.

As you learn the programs in Part II, you can do a quick "self analysis" as you study each meta-program. We have collected and reproduced that format to create the model in *Figure 10:2* p.212. We have also put it in Appendix F anticipating that you will want to copy and use that as you work with this model. Feel free to copy and replicate to your heart's content.

By using these charts and sorting grids with yourself, then with those that you know well, eventually you will use these meta-programs as a part of your thinking—then you won't have to use them at all. You will begin to recognize these meta-level sorting patterns conversationally as you talk with people. When you have mastered them at that level—you will have become a master practitioner of meta-programs. Congratulations!

Predicting Human Predictability (Within Limits)

As a meta-map about people and "human nature," meta-programs can help us to increasingly develop more accuracy in predicting how people will respond. *Figuring out people* to that extent will increase our "people literacy" so we will get unpleasantly surprised less frequently. The following process, based upon the meta-programs and models in this book, provide a way to increase your own **predictability skills in anticipating responses**.

1. Identify all of the **driver** *meta-programs in a person.* After you list the *drivers*, then identify all of the other meta-programs that play a significant part in the functioning of that person even though you might not call them "driver" meta-programs.

2. Specify the contexts of both the driver meta-programs and the others. We always and inevitably live in some context, and those contexts frequently determine which meta-programs we access and use. Frequently, recognizing the meta-programs we (or someone else) use in a given context provides insight into both our proficiencies and our limitations.

3. List the person's hierarchy of values. This provides further understanding about the model of the world from which he or she operates. What does this person value? What does he or she consider important and significant?

4. Summarize your analysis using the linguistic stem, "I can expect X to..." Now identify those ways and styles of responding, functioning, "being," etc. that *typically characterize* the person.

Figure 10:1

Driver *Meta-Programs*	**Contexts**	**Values**
_____	_____	_____
_____	_____	_____
_____	_____	_____
_____	_____	_____
_____	_____	_____
_____	_____	_____
_____	_____	_____
_____	_____	_____
_____	_____	_____
_____	_____	_____
_____	_____	_____
_____	_____	_____
_____	_____	_____
_____	_____	_____
_____	_____	_____

"I can expect .... **to** ....**"**
              name of person

_____

_____

_____

_____

_____

_____

_____

_____

Figuring Out the Person to Hire/Commission for a Task

Consider the context of work or of engaging in some task. What meta-programs do you need, or does someone else need, in order to complete the task or to do it with a high level proficiency? As a practical way to *figure out* who to hire, who to assign a particular task, who to manage, etc., we have designed the following schema based upon the meta-programs.

1. First identify the context. What factors play an important part in the context that you have under consideration? As specifically as possible, describe precisely the context within which a person will work.

2. Identify the distinctions of success. What qualities do you consider essential to the success of that task or job? What ways of thinking, feeling, speaking, behaving, relating, etc. function as one of the "absolute" distinctions or qualities of the situation? Which ones play a strong supporting role—although not essential?

3. Check against the person's meta-programs. Especially note the person's *driving* meta-programs to determine what kind of a "fit" you have. Which meta-programs will contribute to sabotaging the fit or make for a poor fit?

Figure 10:2

The Context Required	Success Distinctions	Person's Meta-Programs
Processing: Ideas (Data) (#1- 12)	Global/Details Matching/Mismatching VAK—A$_d$ Uptime/Downtime Sensor/Intuitor Black-White/Continuum Optimist/Pessimist Permeable/Impermeable Screening/Non-screening Origins/Solution Focus Static/Process Verbal/Non-verbal	_____ _____ _____ _____ _____ _____ _____ _____ _____ _____ _____ _____
Emoting: Emotional State (#13-19)	Passive/Aggressive Self-Referent/Other-Referent Feeling/Thinking (Assoc./Dissoc.) Active/Reflective/Inactive Looks Right/Sounds R/Feels R., Makes Sense Uni-directional/Multi-directional Desurgency/Surgency	_____ _____ _____ _____ _____ _____ _____
Choosing: Style of Deciding (#20-28)	Toward/Away From Options/Procedures Necessity/Possibility People/Place/Things/Activity/Information Perfection/Optimizing/Skepticism Cost/Convenience/Quality/Time Over-Responsible/Under-Responsible Distrusting/Trusting	_____ _____ _____ _____ _____ _____ _____ _____
Acting: Style of Responding Style of Relating to People (#29-39, 14, 28)	Extrovert/Ambivert/Introvert Independent/Team Player/Manager Blamer/Placator/Distracter/Computer/Leveler Congruent-Incon/Compet-Cooper/Polarity- Meta Active/Reflective/Both/Inactive Things/Sys./People/Information Quantitative/Qualitative Modeling/Conceptual./Experience./Authorizing Closure/Non-Closure Shrewd-Artful/Genuine-Artless	_____ _____ _____ _____ _____ _____ _____ _____ _____ _____
Conceptual—Values Style of Valuing -Treating as Important (#40, 26, 34)	List of Hierarchy of Values	_____ _____ _____ _____

Conceptual—Self Style of "Being" as a Person (#41-45)	Strong-will/Compliant High Self-esteem/Low Self-Esteem High/Low Self-confidence in given area Identify with Mind, Body, Emot. Roles, Conflicted-Incongru./Integrated Harmony	_____ _____ _____ _____ _____
Style of Timeliness (#46-48)	In "Time"/Through "Time" Sequential/Random	_____ _____
Conceptual— *Problem Solving* Style of handling Difficulties, Challenges (#49, 14, 15, 27)	Stable/Unstable Self-Reference/External or Other-Reference Associated/Dissociated Over-Respon./Under-Resp./Balanced	_____ _____ _____ _____
Conceptual—Moral Style of Conscientiousness (#50)	Highly Conscientious/Low Conscient.	_____
Conceptual—Authority Style of handling Hierarchy Dominance, etc. (#14, 41, 30)	Self-Reference/Other-Reference Strong-Will/Compliant Independent/Team Player/Manager	_____ _____ _____

Job Description—Design Engineering

Suppose you operate a business that involves "counter people" who meet the public either in person or via the phone. Given this, you would probably need someone who can first of all meet deadlines (#47 & #48 Through "Time" and Sequential), who also has the ability to work as a team member with others (#30), match what people say to create rapport (#2) and to create a positive and optimistic work environment (#7, #34 People), and who trusts people inherently (#28), and who can dissociate in that context (#15).

Or, suppose you run a business and need someone in accounting. Then you probably need a detail person·(#1), who sorts for differences (#2), externally or other-referent in that context (#14), dissociated in that context (#15), highly procedural (#21), prefers information (#24), perhaps distrusts in that context (#28), with a strong superego (#50).

The design engineering suggested here involves *figuring out* what traits, qualities, and skills you want or need in any employee in the first place. Then, secondly, it involves looking for people who have those natural meta-programs. Specifying the meta-programs of success for a given task further gives one an additional language of precision when writing a job description or advertisement.

Profiling and Leveraging

After we have *figured out* a person's meta-programs, then comes the task of using that information about their processes for more effective communication and relationship. This brings up the strategic thinking skill of inquiring and discovering *leverage points*. We did that in the previous exercises as we have sought to understand the natural leverage places in a person's functioning. In so doing, we looked at how the person has developed their own leverage points and incorporated them into their personality,

> "What style of thinking, emoting, choosing, acting, conceptualizing leverages this person's characteristic way of functioning in the world?"

Do "details" (#1) primarily leverage this person's way of being in the world? Can you inevitably count on Other-Referencing (#14) as having the most pervasive influence in a person's thinking-and-feeling? Once you identify the person's driver meta-programs—you generally have a powerful leverage point.

We can now go further in strategic thinking. "What meta-program primarily drives this behavior, response, or experience which, if we shifted it, would cause everything else to shift as well?" Or, "What meta-program shift will have the most pervasive impact for this person?" Yeager (1985) describes this way of thinking as *profiling a person's adaptability*,

> "To make a dent in day-to-day life events, a practitioner needs to profile the person's changeability or adaptability in terms of the change-causing tools at hand." (p. 108).

Then what? Invite the person to try on the other end of that meta-program continuum. A therapist or close and trusted friend might do this directly and overtly. After pacing the driving meta-program, the therapist might use the "as if" frame to invite the person to imagine fully and completely what life would look, sound, and feel like if the person used the other end of the meta-program. Doing this in trance will further amplify and strengthen the process.

To do it conversationally or covertly, we might use a story, relate a dramatic account from a movie, or tell about the opposite meta-program using a narrative about ourselves.

Figuring Out how to Confront Someone

As we all know, people greatly differ in their ability and skill at receiving *unpleasant information*. Yet in the everyday experiences of work, relationship, recreation, family, etc., situations inevitably arise wherein we need to *bring something up* to someone that they may not like or find "positive" or validating. Communicating such unpleasantries usually fall under such rubrics as "confrontation," rebuke, reproof, "setting someone straight," etc. Thus even the idea of encountering and communicating with someone "face to face" (the literal meaning of "confrontation") has gotten a lot of bad press. For most people the very idea of bringing up something unpleasant has gotten anchored to some very strong unpleasant thoughts-and-emotions.

Suppose then that an employee regularly turns in sub-standard work. Suppose a co-worker doesn't carry his or her load as part of a team. Suppose a spouse, friend, or child continually fails to come through with a responsibility. How can we *figure out* the best way to bring this up *so that* the person can hear the information? How can we design engineer a communication that will fit with the person's meta-programs?

Overall we will want to *pace his or her meta-programs* so that the person can process and at least understand **the content of what we say**. Yet before we *so pace* their operational system and thinking patterns, we will need to make sure that they can hear the *information* **without personalizing.** This highlights the importance of meta-programs #41-45, and #49.

1. Self-Esteeming Check. Does the person operate from conditional or unconditional self-esteem? If unconditional, you will have no problem in going ahead and talking about some behavior or problem. The person will probably not personalize and make it a statement about the inner self. Speak directly, in a kind and gentle way, about the area of difficulty.

If the person operates from *conditional* self-esteem, identify what *condition* they base their Personhood and Okayness upon. Does it have to do with the area that you want to address? If no, then begin your communications by clearly letting the person know that *what* you have to say has nothing to do with them as a person, just some behavior that you would like to see improve or change.

If the subject that you want to broach with them involves *one of the very conditions* that they use to esteem themselves or not, then you must proceed with extreme care. Here you will need to do lots of validation and affirmation of them as persons. Why? Because if they use this area to validate and affirm their very sense of themselves as a person, then to call it into question, calls *them* into question. And to do that will more than likely (odds stand for this one!), send them into a state of fight/flight (#13).

Do you want to avoid dealing with a passive or aggressive person? Then don't give them any reason for sending a message of "danger" or "threat" to their brain. Do the esteeming of their *self* that they won't. Use lots of affirmations and validations. Then check with them to see if they want to hear your concern. "I have something that I would like to talk to you about— and I want to do this to offer what I think. And of course I may have this wrong. I offer it in hope that it will improve your effectiveness. Could we talk about that?"

As you think strategically about *"where* do I stand with this person and *where* does this person stand with me," you can access the resources that you will need to bring to bear upon the situation so that the person can access a state of safety and security in order to listen. Avoid the assumption that if you have something to spit out—they should have the fortitude to hear it! Not a productive assumption!

Aim to facilitate *the kind of resourceful inter-personal state* that allows the person to feel safe, not attacked, validated, not insulted or put-down, etc. Otherwise, you will probably get a response that you don't want to get. If that happens, you then have two problems on your hands!

2. Invite dissociation. Strategically, if you know that most people do not take any form of *unpleasant* information very well, but will tend to label it as "criticism," "insult," "bitching," "complaining," "put-down," "confrontation," etc., then plan before you engage that person to assist them to code and represent **what** you have to say *dissociatedly*. Use your words in the past tense. Gesture to a place away from the person—where he or she stores past images and sounds. Or better yet, gesture to where they put dissociated images and sounds. Avoid using the word "you." "You" invites personalizing and typically feels like an attack to most people. Also avoid any form of exaggeration, "You *always* mess things up..." "You *never* get here on time..."

Use more impersonal forms. You may start out personal, then shift to the more impersonal, "When I think about you, Carl, as a worker... I usually run a video-tape up on the screen of my mind and I see that worker... (gesture as if up on a screen)... and sometimes things do go well for him... and, of course, as a supervisor, I just wonder what I can do to assist him in becoming more effective..."

3. Access the person's values for improving. Sometimes you will hear people say something to the effect that a person "has to earn the right to criticize us." For most of us, if we truly and profoundly know that a person really loves us, and cares about us, and has our best interests at heart—we can take a critique from that person in a way that we will not receive one from another. This underscores the importance of aligning with the positive intentions and values of the one we wish to reprimand. To do that we need to strategically consider, *What positive value could this reprimand have for this person?* How could my rebuke or unpleasant information serve any positive value for him or her? And conversely, what away from value will this person strongly avoid?

As we begin to ask ourselves this question, it enables us to use the NLP principle that what people do arises from a positive intention and that if they see a positive value in a piece of communication, they will more likely develop "ears to hear" and receive it. Thus appealing to their values offers a way to pace their reality, enter into their world, and assist them in becoming more effective, productive, happier, etc.

Case Study for Using Meta-Programs in Therapy

The following illustrates a therapeutic use of meta-program distinctions. Using meta-programs provides a therapist with a way to understand **the processes** at work in a person's life without needing to label him or her as "being" the label. Identifying the driver(s) meta-programs provides the therapist with an understanding of how to pace and lead, how to avoid evoking a resistant state, and how to view the processes as usually *over-done or under-done virtues*.

I (BB) saw Richard and Sara in therapy intermittently for a couple of years. Their problems centered around the marital conflict in their now fourteen year marriage. Recently, after not seeing them for several months, Sara brought in her daughter Beth, 17 years of age, highly distraught and full of anger.

She felt much consternation over her relationship with her father. She greatly feared her father due to his jealousy and roughness. She said that he never praised her and that if they played a game and she won, he would become extremely angry.

Richard admitted the problem and his anger. Through some questioning and interventions, I discovered that Richard had felt jealousy towards Beth since the beginning of his marriage to Beth's mother. Though Sara gave birth to Beth outside of marriage, she married Richard when Beth had turned three.

Prior to that Sara and Beth had an extremely tight bond and that continued after the marriage. And from that beginning, Richard felt jealous of Sara due to the attention her mother gave her. Yet for ten years Richard never expressed this. So as I worked with Beth, I began to suspect Richard's jealousy toward her. Then, upon checking with Richard, he acknowledge that he did feel slighted when Sara spent time with Beth.

This shifted my attention to Richard. Thereafter I asked Richard to associate into his jealousy and anger towards Beth. As he did he exclaimed, "She is not God's gift to all mankind!" With this attitude, no wonder Sara struggled to maintain a loving relationship with him while trying to nurture her daughter. I thereafter defined the problem as Beth not receiving the nurture she wanted from dad, Sara over-compensating by giving her even more attention, and that intensifying Richard's sense of jealousy and anger (a true systemic mess!).

What meta-programs drove these people? *Richard* operated primarily as an associated aggressor seeking conditional worth based on getting "respect."

#2. Comparison Sort. *Mismatcher.* Richard displayed intense emotion from not only this experience, but also from growing up with a younger brother whom he perceived as receiving all the love and attention in the family. "My younger brother got all the dates and phone calls from the girls." This issue now replayed in his anger toward Beth about the amount of time she spent on the phone with her boyfriend.

#13. Emotional State: *Associated.* Richard had a heavy kinesthetic response to the phone calls and other experiences. It re-anchored the jealousy and anger that he previously felt towards his little "perfect" brother. He also recalled painful memories in a very associated way.

#10. Emotional Coping Style: *Aggressive.* "I was passive with my brother but as an adult I determined to be aggressive." When he felt stress in the marriage, he would "go at" things hot and heavy, which, in turn, creates hurt feelings and a destructive pattern.

#18 Direction Sort: *Toward.* He strongly moved toward his values, especially the value of respect. Yet behind these feelings he had associated (dated) emotions of anger and jealousy of his younger brother. He also had stacked memories of more jealousy and anger towards both Beth and Sara. All of this gave him a strong *Away From* style—away from disrespect.

#29. General Response Style: *Incongruent.* His unconscious SEEPs of pain internally put him in conflict with himself. He said he loved Beth and Sara, yet his tonality and physiology displayed rage. This communication confused them.

#36 Temper To Instruction: *Strong Will.* Because Richard read lots of communications through his filter of disrespect, almost any information given him would trigger his gestalts of anger/jealousy/rage. To such he would respond with a strong willedness. And, as he "cannot be told" anything, wife and daughter stopped even trying!

#39. Self-Esteem: *Highly Conditional and Low.* Emotional starvation in child-hood has lead him to value himself conditionally, based on getting lots of respect every day.

Sara operated primarily as an associated passive in an over-responsible way who moves away from conflict. *Beth* operated primarily as an associated passive, with little ego-strength, moving away from anger and conflict.

Stop now for a minute and think about how you would *design engineer a therapeutic response* to Richard given this information.

What did Bob do? Bob considered Richard's three drivers: strong-willed to "being told," associated, mismatching, and away from disrespect while toward respect. Therefore, given the strength of his disrespect state, Bob began and continued throughout to provide Richard with lots of validations of his strengths, his dignity, etc. He listened thoroughly, reflected what he understood and asked for feedback, looked at him while he talked, etc.

Next Bob helped Richard to access a meta-position to his difficulties in the relationship so as to assist him from collapsing into negative feelings. Doing this, he also avoided direct "telling," and merely made suggestions and sometimes even elicited Richard's mismatching by telling him that he had an idea, but that it probably would not work in his case.

The Old Manipulation Question

"Will learning about processing styles and meta-programs make me more manipulative?" We sure hope so!

By "manipulative," of course, we mean that it will *enable your ability to "handle" yourself and others more effectively and respectfully.* Of course, whether you will take these skills and treat people with less respect as you try to "wrap them around your little finger" so that you can get something from them without giving something in return—will ultimately depend on your own ethics and morality.

Yet generally speaking, psychological understanding tends to help most people to respond in a more real and authentic way. Since it takes us beyond our own masks and roles it enables us to identify what lies behind, and below, the cover-ups. Rollo May (1989), in writing on this subject, noted,

> "The more penetrating your insights into the workings of the human personality, the more you will be convinced of the useless-ness of trying to fool others."

Conclusion

One of the central keys to effective and professional *communicating* involves developing the ability to make the crucial and needed distinctions about information processing. How do I process information? How does this or that person process this information? What do I or they sort for? Meta-programs provide these distinctions.

Now we no longer need feel angry *at* another's meta-programs. We can just notice them and work with that sorting style. We can now gauge and calibrate to the people around us and with whom we communicate. We can note their patterns for perceiving the world and pace their operational system and then, if valuable, lead to a new and different sorting program.

Chapter 11

Reading Meta-Programs On The Outside
And Pacing Them

"Excuse me,
but your Meta-programs are showing!"

After Eric Robbie (1987) worked on developing eye accessing cues for reading submodalities *from the outside*, he began to work on doing the same with meta-programs (1988). In the following we took our cue from his original work with the first fifteen or so meta-programs, and then expanded it to include the others in our list. This represents virgin territory where little attention and research has occurred. We offer the following only as suggestive of the possibilities that lie in this direction.

As you read the following "External Indications" of the meta-programs, do so by imagining yourself taking first position of someone communicating to you. As you do, the descriptions in the second column will specify the behaviors as if given TO YOU. Thus, for example, in #1 Chunk Size, you will see "hands gesturing big or small, close or far" in the first person speaking. Also remember that the following figure (11.1) represents lots of short-hand descriptions. If you find something that doesn't seem to make sense, refer back to the specific program (i.e. #1 or #31) for a fuller description in one of the previous chapters.

Figure 11.1

Meta-Programs: External Indications

Cognitive Processing—perception, thinking, valuing, believing, etc.	
#1 Chunk Size *General/Specific; Detail/Global*	Hands gesturing big or small, close or far Head/upper body moving close for detail, back for global
#2 Relationship *Matching/Mismatching;* *Same/Difference*	Hands gesturing together and coming close for same Hands gesturing apart, distance, at odd angles for difference
#3 Representational Systems *VAK A$_d$*	Eyes Accessing Patterns: up for Visual, level for Auditory, down for Kinesthetic. Visual, Auditory & Kinesthetic predicates
#4 Information Gathering *Uptime/Downtime*	Eyes scanning immediate environment for Uptime Eyes defocused, glazed look for Downtime
#5 Perceiving Process *Sensors/Intuitors*	Intuitor: Downtime (#4) Sensor: Uptime (#4)
#6 Perceptual Categories *Black-White/Continuum*	Hands gesturing either "this or that," digital-like chopping of air. Hands gesturing lots of in between choices, steps, stages
#7 Scenario Thinking *Best/Worst; Optimists/Pessimists*	Pessimist: Head shaking no, eyes in K position, down to right. Optimist: Head shaking yes, face smiling, body moving forward. Eyes up in visual access a lot
#8 Durability *Permeable/Impermeable*	Focusing of eye and stillness of body for Durable and Impermeable. Back and forth, moving, for Permeable
#9 Focus Quality *Screeners/Non-Screeners*	Focus for Screeners, warmer hands Easily startled for Non-screeners, colder hands
#10 Philosophical Direction *Why/How; Origins/Solutions*	Why: highly A$_d$ accessing. Body more quiet, contemplative. How: Involving more VAK accessing, moving more in body, hands, etc.
#11 Reality Structure Sort *Aristotelian/Non Aristotelian*	Listen for logical explanations, nominalizations black-and-white terminology, more rigidness in body / Listen for process language, "continuum" terms, looking for more smoothness in gesturing.
#12 Communication Channel *Verbal (digital)/* *Non Verbal (analogue)*	The A$_d$ channel: language, words, stories. More in Downtime-trance like state. All the non-verbal analogues: breathing, posture, muscle tone, eye movement, gesturing, etc. / More in Uptime. Look for which a person seems to favor in terms of "carrying" the communications and which a person seems to depend on for reception

Choosing: Conative, Willing, Deciding, etc.	
#13 Emotional Coping *Passivity/Aggression/Dissociated*	Passivity: Moving of body away and back, placating gestures (Satir Category). Aggression: Moving of body forward, movements more quick and definite. Assertive (balanced/dissociated): Fewer signs of external arousal (i.e emotional), more in access of thinking and speaking skills
#14 Frame of Reference *Internal/External;* *Self-Referent/Other-Referent*	Internals first look down or within, then out Externals stay in uptime mode, looking without
#15 Emotional State *Associated/Dissociated;* *Feeling/Thinking*	Associated: body more activated, moving, agitated, "emotional". Eyes in K access. Dissociated: body more still, calm. Eyes in A_d access
#16 Somatic Response *Active/Reflective/Inactive*	Similar to #13
#17 Convincer/Believability *Looks, Sounds, Feels Right Makes Sense*	Representational System eye accessing cues
#18 Emotional Direction *Uni-directional/Multi-directional*	Uni-directional: Body more relaxed, calm, gesturing definitely about the object of the emotion. Multi-directional: Body more agitated, more movement, gestures more fluid and global as if signaling that the emotion spreads around
#19 Emotional Exuberance *Desurgency/Surgency*	Similar to #13
#20 Motivation Direction *Toward/Away From;* *Approach/Avoidance*	Toward: Head and body moving toward, eyes in V^c (seeing goal) Away From: head and body moving back, facial expressions of tension as if "avoidance"
#21 Conation Adaptation *Options/Procedures*	Options: hands gesturing as if numbering off numerous choices. Procedures: hands gesturing as if sequencing things in space
#22 Adaptation *Judging/Perceiving*	Judging: hands, body gesturing "comparing" motion, "this or that." Perceiving: hands gesturing with smooth movements just "floating" through
#23 Modal Operators *Necessity/Possibility/Desire*	Necessity: tightness in voice, raised volume more rigidity in body. Possibility: hands gesturing as if numbering off numerous choices, body more fluid and relaxed. Desire: voice tone lifts and sounds more "up" and "excited"

#24 Preference *People/Place/Things/Activity/* *Information*	Place: hands gesturing as to point to a place Information: hands gesturing to head or brain. People: kinesthetic predicates. Information: A_d eye patterns. Activity: lot of gesturing, kinesthetic predicates
#25 Adapting to Expectations *Perfection/Optimizing/Skepticism*	Perfectionists: in Uptime access (#4) Skeptic: in Downtime access (#4) Optimist: alternates between Uptime & Down, feels comfortable doing so
#26 Value Buying *Cost/Convenience/Quality Time*	Cost: A_d, In "Time". Quality: A_d, In "Time" Convenience: both K and V eye patterns. Time: Judger (see #22)
#27 Responsibility *Over-Responsibility/Under-* *Responsibility*	Over-Responsibility: sometimes bent down at shoulders as if carrying a load. Under-Responsibility: accusing & blaming, using index finger to point
#28 People Convincer Sort *Distrusting/Trusting*	Distrusting: gestures to indicate distance, boundaries tension. Trusting: relaxed in face and muscles, hands reaching out, touching
Communicating/Responding	
#29 Battery Rejuvenation *Extrovert/Ambivert/Introvert*	This meta-program operative in "contexts of stress" or "down" feelings. Extrovert: Similar to #11. In Uptime access as if looking around and out. Introvert: In a more Downtime state as if looking in. Ambivert: Flexibly alternates between the two styles
#30 Affiliation/Management *Independent/Team Player/Manager*	Independent: A_d eye pattern In "Time". Team: V and K eye patterns, Uptime Manager: uses a combination of all eye accessing patterns, also looks relaxed
#31 Communication Stance *Blamer/Placator/Distracter/Computer/* *Leveler*	Satir's physiological description of each of these stances. Use of hands and fingers while talking!
#32 General Response *Congruent/Incongruent* *Competitive/Cooperative; Polarity/Meta*	Congruent: fits together. Incongruent: these non-verbal behaviors not fitting, out of sync. Polarity: more movement, agitation. Meta: more calm, less body movement
#33. Somatic Response Sort *Active/Reflective/Both/Inactive*	Similar to #13
#34 Work Preference *Things/Systems/People/Information*	People: uses personal pronouns, proper nouns. Systems: use plural personal pronouns. Information: A_d eye patterns, non-specific predicates. Things: Towards (#18), head and body moving forward

Semantic/Conceptual: Relating to Categories of Self, Time, Morality

#35 Comparison Sort *Quantitative/Qualitative*	Quantitative: listen for numbers, statistics, etc. Qualitative: listen for comparative deletions as "good, better" which indicate a quality or property
#36 Knowledge Sort *Modeling/Conceptualizing;* *Experiencing/Authorizing*	Modeling: in uptime access, focusing outward. Conceptualizing: in downtime, using more abstract and unspecified predicates, listen for nominalizations -over use of library cards! Experiencing: look for the activation of a person's "motor" programs, in Kinesthetic access. Authorizing: uses uptime to run external checks in reference to authority figure
#37 Completion/Closure *Closure/Non-Closure*	Hands gesture as the closing of a box, door, etc. for closure or lack thereof
#38 Social Presentation *Shrewd-Artful/Genuine-Artless*	Shrewd: more in Uptime mode, looking, checking out people, scanning. Artless: more in Downtime mode
#39. Hierarchical Dominance Sort *Power/Affiliation/Achievement*	Power: in Blamer mode. Affiliation: Leveler, Placator, Computer mode. Achievement: Proactive, eyes in V^c
#40 Values *List of Values* *Approach/Avoidance*	Stored "down right" as in "important" or up as "high value." Voice tone: matter of fact or high as in "important"
#41 Temper to Instruction *Strong-Will/Compliant*	Strong-will: body tense, rigid, "holding" self. Jaw set. Compliant: body more relaxed, calm. Placator's mode. High SE
#42 Self-Esteem *High SE/Low SE*	Holds head up. Low SE: lowers head, bows head, talks in less audible voice
#43 Self-Confidence *Specific Skills*	Context of self-confidence skill. Specific: list specific skills and aptitudes of the person; skilled in what?
#44 Self-Experience *Body/Mind/Emotions Roles*	Body: K eye patterns. Mind: A_d eye patterns. Emotion: K eye patterns. Roles: What roles has the person identified for him or herself?
#45 Self-Integrity *Conflicted/Incongruous/Congruous*	Conflicted: facets of output (words, tone, gestures) not fitting. Congruous: body relaxed and calm, movements and gestures all seem "together" and co-ordinated. Incongruous: facets of the person's output do not seem to fit together
#46 "Time" Tenses *Past/Present/Future*	Gesturing to where code "past", "present", & "future", typically: "past" to the left of a right-handed person, with "future" to the right. Listen for predicates of time

#47 "Time" Experience *In "Time"/Through "Time"*	Less movement, agitation, etc. for Through "Time" More movement, agitation for In "Time"
#48 "Time" Access *Sequential/Random*	Sequential: gesturing with hands in chopping way as if sequencing space. Random: gesturing more wildly, as if "all over", without a pattern
#49 Ego Strength *Stable/Unstable*	Similar to #13
#50 Morality *Strong/Weak Superego*	Weak Superego: listen for language indicating "not caring" about things, people, rules etc. Also exclusive self-referencing (see #14). Strong super-ego: listen for nominalizations of justice, fairness, right/wrong, spirituality, etc.
#51 Causation *Causeless/Linear CE/Multi-CE/* *Personal CE/Magical/Correlational*	Causeless: hands gesturing as if "throwing up hands" to indicate effects result from nothing. Linear Linear CE: hands gesturing in a sequential way. Multi-CE: hands gesturing in circles and spirals indicating various actions feeding back into a system of responses. Personal CE: hands gesturing to Self moving to chest. Magical CE: hands gesturing in a parallel fashion as if identifying two phenomena occurring but not intermingling.

Reading Meta-Programs by Detecting Meta-States

A close, though not identical, relationship exists between meta-programs and meta-states. Consequently, sometimes we can detect one by means of the other.

Though both of these terms (meta-programs and meta-states) begins with *"meta,"* they refer to very different phenomena. To avoid confusion between **meta-programs** and **meta-states**, remember the meta-program as a structuring or patterning process *about* perception and *thinking patterns.* A meta-state, by contrast, refers to a *state*-about-a-*state.* A meta-program refers to those sorting facets that determines *how we process information.* A meta-state refers to a state of thought-emotion or physiology (e.g. anger, fear, joy, comfort, etc.) that we now *bring to bear on another state.* This then generates a complex and layered form of subjectivity—as in fear-about-fear, anger-about-fear, guilt-about-anger, joy-about-depression, depression-about-joy.

We here use the term "state" to refer to **a mind-body state** that consists of thoughts-and-feelings. This makes it a holistic "neuro-linguistic" state *about* something. Perhaps we think-and-feel angry *about* the way John treats us. A state then represents a form of **human reactivity** (or responsiveness) to something.

A meta-state speaks about our reactions-to-our-reactions. I feel glad about my ability to feel afraid because it gives me important messages. I fear my anger lest it gets out of control. I guilt about experiencing too strong of an emotion. I joy in my learning and appreciate my joy about my learning.

In meta-states we no longer reference our thoughts-and-feelings *to* the world or *to* something outside our skin. We reference our thoughts-and-feelings *to* and *about* some of our other thoughts-and-feelings (states). In primary states, consciousness goes *out* to represent, filter, and give meaning to the world. In meta-states, consciousness *reflects back* to itself and some of its products (thoughts-feelings). By stepping back from our primary states, concepts, ideas, mental categories, internal experiences, etc. and "going meta" to them—we access a **meta-state** *about* them.

While meta-programs do *not* necessarily refer to, or comprise, **states** of mind-body consciousness, they certainly can. A meta-program can become a meta-state.

Suppose for instance, that a person uses a particular style of thinking-emoting nearly all the time, and with almost all kinds of contexts. That meta-program then begins to function as **a "driver** *meta-program."* (Hall, 1990). If global or gestalt sorting operates as the *driving* force and influences dominate nearly all of that person's processing of information (#1), then more than likely it will induce that person into *a kind of global state*—a state of mind-and-body wherein he or she thinks-and-feelings and sorts for larger level things.

If procedure (#2) **drives** another person, that meta-program may also correspond to, and induce, him or her into *a procedure state.* Driver meta-programs (and those we over-use) frequently describe and create mind-body states. In this way, meta-programs can become meta-states.

What mechanism would explain this? It arises because the **style** of processing and sorting (the meta-program) frequently involves the **kind of information** processed. As such, the meta-program carries some internal representations (including beliefs, values, understandings, etc.) that keeps inducing (and re-inducing) the person into corresponding states.

You have probably already noticed this in working with meta-programs, have you not? When we find a global person, that person not only processes information globally and deductively, but also *values* global thinking, *believes* in it and would argue against "watching the pennies in order to take care of the dollars." Similarly, the procedure person not only sorts for "step-by-step processes," but also *values* such and *believes* in the importance of such, etc. To get him or her to shift to "options" might, in fact, violate some of the person's beliefs and values. It would interrupt and contradict some of their most frequently experienced "states."

Thus to the extent that we have over-valued and/or over-used a particular meta-program, we will develop a tendency to view everything through that particular filter. Suppose it consists of the meta-program of "specifics/details" in sorting information. Suppose that filter drives a person. Suppose further that the person has no flexibility of consciousness to shift up to the global perspective. Or what if (s)he has used this mindset as part of his or her self-definition, "I *am* a detail person!" Or, we might suppose a person who has over-valued and over-used another meta-program, say procedures. This would then temper and affect most of that person's primary states making the person and those states fairly rigid and structured. When the person reflexively applies his or her thinking-feeling **about** a prior state—(s)he will tend to use this meta-program. *In this way, a meta-program can turn into, and induce us into, a meta-state.* Hence, we might find self-procedure, procedure-joy, procedure-love, procedure-anxiety.

Inasmuch then as **thoughts** (as internal representations) operate neuro-linguistically to induce us into states of mind-body, frequently used meta-programs will *habituate* and that habituation can *then induce a corresponding mind-body state.* Any habituated meta-program that generates a neuro-linguistic state, once we apply it to another state, generates a meta-state.

Using this Understanding in Profiling People

The value of meta-programs generally lie in the importance of recognizing *how* a person pays attention to things so that we can then match that style. In this way we can make our communication maximally impactful. If it matches (paces) a person's thinking, sorting, perceiving style—then it will have an inherent sense of familiarity, commonality, and feel of "making sense."

Similarly, if we recognize that a particular thinking-emoting pattern also operates as a meta-state in a person, then this can assist us in pacing that meta-state so that the person feels understood and validated.

Applying this to Corporate "Persons"

As individuals develop *perceptual styles,* so do corporate organizations and businesses. They develop their own patterns and styles of perceiving "reality" and processing information. These sorting devices or patterns of perception describe, to speak more metaphorically, "the channel" through which the person or the company communicates. To *not* know such leaves one to making communicational attempts in the dark as to what style will work with this person or company. To have the ability to "read" their meta-program (to pick it up from their languaging, their gesturing, their eye accessing cues, etc.) enables us to more quickly get to the same channel and speak their language.

Companies, like individuals, develop their own "personality," mood, and response style. In NLP we call the place from which one comes a **"state of consciousness."** When we recognize that a person operates from some state—we can take that into account in our communicating. This plays an especially important role whenever they have a strong state inasmuch as all of our learning, memory, behavior, perception and communication operates in a state-dependent way.

This also has great significance in terms of self-management, the management of our thoughts, emotions, moods, and behaviors. Without taking "state" into account without awareness, understanding, and skill in state-management, we tend to fall victim to our states, rather than operate as their director. The same applies to businesses.

Conclusion

For those who have eyes to see—we can learn to detect many of the meta-programs *from the outside*. This demands sensory awareness (uptime), understanding of the meta-programs, practice at calibrating, and a commitment. To do so we have to calibrate to the cues that each person uniquely produces in his or her patterns. To learn this, begin with yourself. Once you have made yourself fully acquainted with your own meta-programs, begin to notice the non-verbal cues that you give off as you show people everyday your meta-programs.

Appendices

Appendix A

A Comment On The Formatting Of The Meta-Programs

NLP literature contains several different structural formats for meta-programs. James and Woodsmall (1988) structured them from Simple to Complex. Others merely provide a list of the meta-programs. Others have structured them as a Personality Profile. As we have offered the meta-level analysis with a meta meta-level and sorted them according to five categories that make up a "state of consciousness," we have done so to offer yet another format. In doing so, we do *not* negate or discount in the least the value or usefulness of other methodologies or formats. Each has strengths and weaknesses. We developed this particular methodology because it offers another perspective about these meta-processes and out of this format another set of technologies.

From Simple to Complex Meta-Programs

I (BB) wrote my manual on meta-programs based on the model as presented by James and Woodsmall in their book *Time Line Therapy and the Basis of Personality*. Wyatt brought these meta-programs into NLP from the work of Jung (1923). Jung had sought to *type cast* people in such a manner so as to predict an individual's personality and, hence, behavior. Between 1942 and 1944 Isabel Briggs Myers and her mother Katherine C. Briggs, developed the Myers-Briggs Type Indicator®—an instrument also based on Jung's work and now widely used today in psychological profiling in government and business.

Wyatt and Tad (1988) hypothesize that the meta-programs, coming from Jung through Myers-Briggs® and into NLP, begin with simple forms and from those the more complex programs arise (p. 95). The three elements of human experience internal states (IS), internal processing of information (IP) and external behavior (EB)) correspond remarkably to Jung's Introvert/Extrovert, Sensor/Intuitor, and Thinker/Feeler categories. Isabel Briggs Myers and Katherine C. Briggs added the fourth category Judger/Perceiver (p. 91).

Assuming that these four psychological distinctions form four *Simple Meta-Programs* then Wyatt and Tad identified four basic meta-programs and the other *Complex Meta-Programs* that arise from them. To date, no experimental or research evidence exists for this. But it remains a viable construction that you may want to play around with as you learn and use this model. James and Woodsmall (1988) believe that the relationship, direction, attention direction, and frame of reference meta-programs function as "the most important meta-programs in predicting how a person will act and react." (Bodenhamer, 1995 p. 16).

Three Classifications

Sid Jacobson (1996) in a work on moving from problem states to solution states, organized 15 meta-programs into three categories: Convincers, Motivators, and Thinking Style. Developed entirely apart from our model, this classification does fit with ours that begins with Thinking Style, goes to Emoting Style or Motivators and then on to Conation Style or Convincers (p. 51-55).

Meta-Programs Elicitation	
1. When you pick up a book or think about attending a workshop, what do you pay attention to first—the big picture, book cover, or specific details about its value? If we decided to work together on a project, would you first want to know what we generally will do or would you prefer to hear about a lot of the specifics?	*Chunk Size* __ Global __ Specific
2. How do you 'run your brain' when you first attempt to understand something new to you? Do you look first for similarities and match up the new with what you already know? Or do you first check out the differences?	*Relationship Sort* __ Matching/Same __ Mismatching/ Differences
3. When you think about something or learn something new which sensory channel do you prefer?	*Representation Style* __ Visual __ Auditory __ Kinesthetic __ Language A_d
4 & 5. When you listen to a speech or conversation, do you tend to hear the specific data given or do you intuit what the speaker must mean and/or intend? Do you want to hear proof and evidence since you take more interest in your Intuitions about it? Which do you find more important—the actual or the possible? Upon what basis do you make most of your decisions—the practical or abstract possibilities?	*Epistemology Sort* __Sensors/Uptime __Intuitors/ Downtime
6. When you think about things or make decisions, do you tend to operate in black-and-white categories or does your mind go to the steps and stages that lie in between? Which do you value most?	*Perceptual Style* __ Black-White __ Continuum
7. When you look at a problem, do you tend first to consider the worst case scenario or the best? The problems and difficulties or the opportunities and positive challenges?	*Attribution Style* __ Optimist __ Pessimist
8. As you begin to think about some of your mental constructs, your ideas of success and failure, of love and forgiveness, of relationships and work, of your personal qualities... do you find the representations of what you know permanent or unstable? How can you tell? Think about something that you know without a doubt—about yourself. Now think of something that you know but with doubts and questions...	*Durability* __ Impermeable __ Permeable

9. When you think about the kind of places where you can study or read, can you do this everywhere or do you find that some places seem too noisy or have too many of some other stimuli? Describe your favorite environment for concentrating on something? How distractible do you find yourself generally in life?	*Focus Quality* __ Screening __ Non-Screening
10. When you think about a subject (whether a problem or not), do you first think about causation, source, and origins (why), or do you think about use, function, direction, destiny (how)?	*Philosophical Direction* __ Origins/Why __ Solutions/How
11. When you think about reality, do you tend to think about it as something permanent and solid made up of things or do you think of it as a dance of electrons, fluid, ever-changing, made up of processes?	*Reality Structure Sort* __ Aristotelian-Static __ Non-Aristotelian Process
12. When you think about communicating with somebody, what do you tend to give more importance to *what* they say or how they say it? When you communicate, do you pay more attention to the words and phrases that you use or to your tone, tempo, volume, eye contact, etc.? When you hear someone say something that seems incongruent with how they express it, and you don't know which message to go with, which do you tend to favor as the more 'real' message?	*Channel Sort* __ Communication __ Verbal/Digital __ NonVerbal/ Analogue __ Balanced
13. When you feel threatened, or challenged, by some stress... do you immediately respond, on the emotional level, by wanting to get away from it or to go at it? Invite the person to tell you about several specific instances when he or she faced a high stress situation. Do you detect a "go at" or "go away from" response to it?	*Emotional Coping* __ Passivity __ Aggressive
14. Where do you put most of your attention or reference: on yourself or on others (or something external to yourself)?	*Frame of Reference* __ Self-Reference __ Other-Reference
15. Think about an event in a work situation that once gave you trouble... What experience surrounding work would you say has given you the most pleasure or delight...? How do you normally feel while at work? When you make a decision, do you rely more on reason and logic or personal values or something else?	*Emotional State* __ Associated __ Dissociated
16. When you come into a new situation, do you usually act quickly after sizing it up or do you do a detailed study of all the consequences before acting?	*Somatic Response* __ Active __ Reflective __ Inactive

17. What leads you to *accept* the believability of a thing? Something about it *looks right* (V^+), *sound right* (A^t), *makes* sense (A_d), feels right (K^+) to you?	*Convincer Sort* __ Looks Right __ Sounds Right __ Feels Right __ Makes Sense
18. When you think about a time when you experienced an emotional state (positive or negative), does that bleed over and affect some or all of your other emotional states, or does it stay pretty focused so that it relates to its object?	*Emotional Direction* __ Uni-directional __ Multi-directional
19. When you think about a situation at work or in your personal affairs that seem risky or involving the public's eye, what thoughts-and-feelings immediately come to mind?	*Emotional Exuberance* __ Desurgency __ Surgency
20. What do you want in a job (relationship, car, etc.)? What do you want to do with your life?	*Motivation Direction* __ Toward Values __ Away From
21. Why did you choose your car? (or job, town, etc.).	*Conation Adaptive* __ Options __ Procedures
22. Do you like to live life spontaneously as the spirit moves you or according to a plan? Regarding doing a project together, would you prefer we first outline and plan it out in an orderly fashion or would you prefer to just begin to move into it and flexibly adjust to things as we go?	*Adaptation Style* __ Judging __ Perceiving
23. How did you get up this morning? What did you say to yourself just before you got up?	*Modal Operators* __ Necessity __ Possibility
24. What would you find as really important in how you choose to spend your next two week vacation? What kinds of things, people, activities, etc. would you want present for you to evaluate it as really great? Tell me about your favorite restaurant.	*Preference Sort* __ People __ Place __ Things __ Activity __ Information
25. Tell me about a goal that you have set and how did You go about making it come true? If you set a goal today to accomplish something of significance, how would you begin to work on it?	*Adapting to Expectation* __ Perfection __ Optimizing __ Skepticism

26. What do you tend to primarily concern yourself with—the price, convenience, time, or quality, or some combination of these when you consider making a purchase?	*Value Buying* __ Cost __ Convenience __ Quality __ Time
27. When you think about having and owning responsibility for something in a work situation or personal relationship, what thoughts and emotions occur to you? Has someone ever held you responsible for something that went wrong that felt very negative to you? What positive experiences can you remember about someone holding you responsible for something?	*Responsibility* __ Over-Responsible __ Under-Responsible
28. When you think about meeting someone new, do you immediately have a sense of trust and openness to the person, or thoughts and feelings of distrust, doubt, questions, jealousy, insecurity, etc.?	*People Convincer* __ Distrusting __ Trusting
29. When you feel the need to recharge your batteries, do you prefer to do it alone or with others?	*Battery Rejuvenation* __ Extrovert __ Ambivert __ Introvert
30. a) Do you know what you need in order to feel and function more successfully at work? b) Do you know what someone else needs in order to feel and function more successfully? c) Do you find it easy or not to tell a person that?	*Affiliation Sort* __ Independence __ Team Player __ Manager
31. How do you typically communicate in terms of placating, blaming, computing, distracting, and leveling?	*Communication Stances* __ Blamer __ Placator __ Distracter __ Computer __ Leveler
32. When you come into a situation, how do you usually respond? Do you respond a) with a sense of feeling and acting congruent and harmonious with your thoughts-and-feelings or, do you respond with a sense of not feeling or acting congruent and harmonious with your thoughts and feelings? b) Do you respond with a sense of cooperation with the subject matter, or a feeling of disagreement? c) Or, do you prefer to go above the immediate context and have thoughts about the situation?	*General Response* __ Congruent __ Incongruent __ Competitive __ Cooperative __ Polarity __ Meta

33. When you come into a situation, do you usually act quickly after sizing it up or do you engage in a detailed study of all of the consequences, and then act, or how do you tend to typically respond?	*Somatic Response* __ Active __ Reflective __ Both __ Inactive
34. Tell me about a work situation (or environment) in which you felt the happiest, some one-time-event.	*Work Preference* __ Things __ Systems __ People __ Information
35. How would you evaluate your work as of today? How would you evaluate things in your relationship? How do you know the quality of your work? Upon what basis do you say that?	*Comparison* __ Quantitative __ Qualitative
36. What source of knowledge do you consider authoritative and most reliable? From where would you gather reliable information that you can trust? When you decide that you need to do something where do you get the information to do it from?	*Knowledge Source* __ Modeling __ Conceptualizing __ Experiencing __Authorizing
37. If, in the process of studying something, you had to break off your study and leave it, would this settle well or feel very disconcerting? When someone begins a story but doesn't complete it, how do you feel about that? When you get involved in a project, do you find yourself more interested in the beginning, middle, or end of the project? What part of a project do you enjoy most?	*Closure* __ Closure __ Non-Closure
38. When you think about going out into a social group or out in public, how do you generally handle yourself? Do you really care about your social image and want to avoid any negative impact on others so that they recognize your tact, politeness, social graces, etc.? Or do you not really care about any of that and just want to "be yourself," natural, forthright, direct, transparent, etc.?	*Social Presentation* __ Shrewd/Artful __ Genuine/Artless
39. Evaluate your motives in interacting with others in terms of your motivational preferences between Power (dominance, competition, politics), Affiliation (relationship, courtesy, cooperation) and Achievement (results, goals, objectives) and using 100 points as your scale, distribute those hundred points among these three styles of handling 'power'.	*Hierarchy Dominance* __ Power __ Affiliation __ Achievement
40. As you think about this X (a thing, person, event, experience, etc.) what do you evaluate as valuable, important, or significant about this?	*Value Sort* List Values

241

41. Can someone 'tell' you something? How do you think and feel when you receive 'instructions?' How well can you 'tell' or 'order' yourself to do something and you carry it out without a lot of internal resistance about it?	*Temper to Instruction* __ Strong-Will __ Complaint
42. Do you think of your value as a person as conditional or unconditional? When you esteem yourself as valuable, worth-while having dignity, etc. do you do it based upon something or do you base it upon the fact of your humanity or that God made you in his image and likeness?	*Self-esteeming* __ Unconditional __ Conditional
43. As you think about some of the things that you can do well and that you know, without a doubt, you can do well and may even take pride in your ability to do them well, make a list of those items. How confident do you feel about your skill in doing these things?	*Self-Confidence* __ High Self-confidence __ Low Self-confidence
44. How do you experience yourself in terms of your mind, emotions, body, roles?	*Self-Experience* __ Mind __ Emotions __ Body — Roles
45. When you think about how well or how poorly you live up to your ideals and in actualizing your ideal self, do you feel pretty integrated, congruous, doing a good job in living true to your values and visions or do you feel torn, conflicted, un-integrated, incongruous?	*Self-Integrity* __ Conflicted __ Integrated
46. Where do you put most of your attention—on the past, present, or future? Or, have you developed an atemporal attitude so that you don't attend to 'time' at all?	*Time Tenses* __ Past __ Present __ Future
47. Do you represent 'time' as coming into you and intersected with your body, or outside of yourself and body?	*Time Experience* __ In "Time" __ Through "Time"
48. Do you represent 'time' as coming into you and intersected with your body, or outside of yourself and body?	*Time Access* __ Sequential __ Random
49. When you think about some difficulty arising in everyday life, a disappointment, problem, frustrating difficulty that will block your progress, etc., what usually comes to mind? How do you typically respond to internal needs or external hardships?	*Ego Strength Sort* __ Unstable __ Stable

Appendix C

The NLP Eye Access Chart And Representation System Predicates

As people represent information internally, they move their eyes, even though they may do it ever so slightly. Following someone's eye movements can allow you to know what sense modality a person may use at a given time to represent information. It is important to calibrate a persons organizations before making assumptions. With a "normally" organized right-handed person, the following describes the general pattern of eye accessing cues.

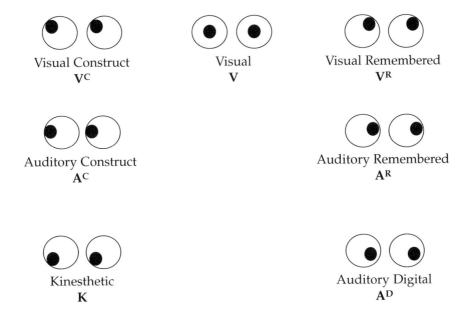

Visual Construct	Visual	Visual Remembered
V^C	V	V^R

Auditory Construct
A^C

Auditory Remembered
A^R

Kinesthetic
K

Auditory Digital
A^D

Predicates—words in language that indicate specific sensory modalities Representational Systems (RS):

Visual: see, view, observe, witness, sight, spot, look, glimpse, glance, peer, peek, peep, survey, eye, examine, inspect, gaze, stare, glare, pale, find, read, show, etc.

Auditory: listen, hear, overhear, sound, quiet, ask, beg, ring, chime, yell, scream, sing, speak, talk, shout, whisper, groan, moan, whine, buzz, call, click, etc.

Kinesthetic: bite, burst, bend, bind, break, fall, catch, fight, go, grasp, grab, hold, hit, climb, run, struggle, throw, walk, jump, push, feel, grip, handle, sense, impact, move, etc.

Unspecified: seem, be, aware, have, think, believe, allow, become, be able, have to, must, shall, know, do, make, understand, create, contemplate, ponder, desire, appreciate, sense etc.

Appendix D

Hierarchy Of Language On The Scale
Of Specificity & Abstraction

The Chunking Up Process

World of Meta-Level Abstractions
(the Kantian Categories)
(The Meta Meta-Programs & Meta-St)

Agreement Frame-of-Reference

↑

"What does that meaning mean to you? What idea, example describes this?"

"For what purpose...?"

"What intention do you have in this...?"
"What does this mean to you?"

↑

When mediating, chunk up to get agreement. Chunk-up until you get a nominalization.

The Structures of Intuition.
Deductive Intuition: the ability to take a general principle & chunk down to apply & relate to specific situations.

Inductive Intuition: the ability to chunk-up to find meanings, connections & relationships between the small pieces.

The Chunking Down Process:

↓

"What examples/references?"

"What specifically do you mean...?"
(Use any meta-model specificity question)

↓

More and More Specific Details & Distinctions

The World of Submodalities

High-level Abstractions
control lower-level ideas,
representations, understandings

The Big Picture
The World of Abstractions

↑

The language *mechanism* that moves us upward into higher level abstractions—*the Milton Model.*

Using intuiting to gather/process information live here in the world of the big chunks and into "Trance"

↑

Existence

↑

Economy

↑

Business

CEO

↑

Marketing *Managers*—Finance Managers

Managers

↑

Unit Managers

↑

Supervisors

↑

Administrative Support

The language *mechanism* that enables us to move down the scale into Specificity—*the Meta Model.* Those who gather information by Sensing live here. We come out of trance when we move here.

(Edited from Hierarchy of Ideas
Copyright 1987-1996, Tad James)

Appendix E

Meta-Programs in Five Categories and Meta Meta-Programs

Processing Cognitive/Perceptual	Feeling Emotional/Somatic	Choosing Conative/Willing	Responding Outputting-Behaving	Conceptualizing/Semanticizing Kantian Categories
#1 Chunk Size General/Specific Detail/Global/Dissociated	#13 Emotional Coping Passivity/Aggression	#20 Motivation Direction Toward/Away From Approach/Avoidance	#29 Battery Rejuvenation Extrovert/Ambivert/Introvert	#40 Values List of Values
#2 Relationship Matching/Mismatching Same/Difference	#14 Frame of Reference Internal/External Self-Referent/Other-Referent	#21 Conation Adaptation Options/Procedures	#30. Affiliation/Management Independent/Team Player/Manager	#41 Temper to Instruction Strong-Will/Compliant
#3 Rep. system VAKO A_d	#15 Emotional State Associated/Dissociated Feeling/Thinking	#22 Adaptation Judging/Perceiving Controlling/Floating	#31 Communication Stance Blamer/Placator/Distracter/Computer/Leveler	#42 Self-Esteem High SE/Low SE
#4 Info. Gathering Uptime/Downtime	#16 Somatic Responses Active/Reflective/Inactive	#23 Modal Operators Necessity/Possibility/Desire Stick/Carrot	#32 General Response Congruent/Incongruent Competitive/Cooperative; Polarity/Meta	#43 Self-Confidence Specific Skills...
#5 Epistemology Sort Sensors/Intuitors	#17 Convincer/Believability Looks, Sounds, Feels Right Makes Sense	#24 Preference People/Place/Things/Activity/Information	#33 Somatic Response Active/Reflective/Both/Inactive	#44 Self-Experience Body/Mind/Emotions/Roles
#6 Perceptual Categ. Black-White/Continuum	#18 Emotional Direction Uni-directional/Multi-directional	#25 Adapting to Expectations Perfection/Optimitizing/Skepticism	#34 Work Preference Things/Systems/People/Information	#45 Self-Integrity Conflicted Incongruity/Integrated Harmony

#46 "Time" Tenses
Past/Present/Future

#47 "Time" Experience
In "Time"/Through "Time"

#48 "Time" Access
Sequential/Random

#49 Ego Strength
Stable/Unstable

#50. Morality
Strong/Weak Superego

#51 Causational Sort
*Causeless/Linear CE/
Multi-CE/Personal CE/
External CE/Magical/
Correlational*

#35 Comparison
Quantitative/Qualitative

#36 Knowledge Source
*Modeling/Conceptualizing
Experiencing/Authorizing*

#37 Completion/Closure
Closure/Non-Closure

#38 Social Presentation
Shrewd-Artful/Genuine-Artless

#39 Hierarchical Dominance Sort
Power/Affiliation/Achievement

#26 Value Buying
*Cost/Convenience/Quality/Time
Timidity/Boldness*

#27 Responsibility
*Over-Resp./Under-Respons.
Balanced*

#28 People Convincer Sort
Distrusting/Trusting

#7 Scenario Thinking
*Best/Worst
Optimists/Pessimists*

#19 Emotional Exuberance
Desurgency/Surgency

#8 Durability
Permeable/Impermeable

#9 Focus Quality
Screeners/Non-Screeners

#10 Philosophical Direction
Why/How Origins/Solutions

#11 Reality Structure Sort
*Aristotelian/Non-Aristotelian
Static/Process)*

#12 Communication Channel Sort
Verbal-Digital/Non-Verbal-Analogue/Balanced

Appendix F

Meta-Programs As A Sorting Grid

The "Mental" Meta-Programs

#1. Chunk Size:
General/Specific; Global/Detail
__ **S**pecific Sorting/**G**lobal Sorting (Detail/General)
__ **A**bducting
Contexts:
__ Work/Career   __ Relationships
__ Intimates   __ Hobbies/Recreation
__ Sports   __Other:_____
__ **H**igh/**M**edium/Low level   __ Driver MP: **Yes**/**No**

#2. Relationship Sort: *Matching/Mismatching; Sameness or Difference/Opposite; Agree/Disagree*
__ **S**ameness or Matching/**D**ifference or Mismatching
Contexts:
__ Work/Career   __ Relationships
__ Intimates   __ Hobbies/Recreation
__ Sports   __ Other: _____
__ **H**igh/**M**edium/Low level   __ Driver MP: **Yes**/**No**

#3. Representational System Sort: *Visual/Auditory/Kinesthetic/Auditory-digital*
__ **V**isual/**A**uditory/**K**inesthetic
Contexts:
__ Work/Career   __ Relationships
__ Intimates   __ Hobbies/Recreation
__ Sports   __ Other:_____
__ **H**igh/**M**edium/Low level   __ Driver MP: **Yes**/**No**
__ Cross Modalities: V-A, V-K, K-V, etc.

#4. Information Gathering Style: *Uptime/Downtime*
__ **D**owntime/**U**ptime
Contexts:
__ Work/Career   __ Relationships
__ Intimates   __ Hobbies/Recreation
__ Sports   __ Other:_____
__ **H**igh/**M**edium/Low level   __ Driver MP: **Yes**/**No**

#5. Internal Perceiving Processes: *Sensors/Intuitors*
__ Sensor Inputting/Intuitor Inputting
Contexts:
__ Work/Career   __ Relationships
__ Intimates   __ Hobbies/Recreation
__ Sports   __ Other:_____
__ High/Medium/Low level   __ Driver MP: **Yes/No**

#6. Perceptual Categories Sort: *Black-and-white vs. Continuum*
__ Black-and-white/Continuum Thinking
Contexts:
__ Work/Career   __ Relationships
__ Intimates   __ Hobbies/Recreation
__ Sports   __ Other:_____
__ High/Medium/Low level   __ Driver MP: **Yes/No**

#7. Scenario Thinking Style: *Best vs. Worst Scenario Thinking; Optimists/Pessimists*
__ Optimists, Best Case/Pessimists, Worst Case
Contexts:
__ Work/Career   __ Relationships
__ Intimates   __ Hobbies/Recreation
__ Sports   __ Other:_____
__ High/Medium/Low level   __ Driver MP: **Yes/No**

#8. Perceptual Durability Sort: *Permeable/Impermeable*
__ Permeable Sorting/Impermeable Sorting
Contexts:
__ Work/Career   __ Relationships
__ Intimates   __ Hobbies/Recreation
__ Sports   __ Other:_____
__ High/Medium/Low level   __ Driver MP: **Yes/No**

#9. Focus Sort: *Screeners/Non-screeners*
__ Non-screening Sort/Screening Sort
Contexts:
__ Work/Career   __ Relationships
__ Intimates   __ Hobbies/Recreation
__ Sports   __ Other:_____
__ High/Medium/Low level   __ Driver MP: **Yes/No**

#10. Philosophical Direction: *Why/How; Origins/Solution Process*
__ Why - Origins/How - Function
Contexts:
__ Work/Career   __ Relationships
__ Intimates   __ Hobbies/Recreation
__ Sports   __ Other:_____
__ High/Medium/Low level   __ Driver MP: **Yes/No**

#11. Reality Structure Sort: *Aristotelian/Non-Aristotelian (Static/Process)*
__ **A**ristotelian Static/**N**on-Aristotelian Process Sorting
Contexts:
__ Work/Career   __ Relationships
__ Intimates   __ Hobbies/Recreation
__ Sports   __ Other:_____
__ **H**igh/**M**edium/Low level   __ Driver MP: **Yes**/No

#12. Communicational Channel Sort: *Verbal/Non-Verbal/Balanced*
__ **V**erbal- Digital/**N**on-Verbal- Analogue/**B**alanced
Contexts:
__ Work/Career   __ Relationships
__ Intimates   __ Hobbies/Recreation
__ Sports   __ Other:_____
__ **H**igh/**M**edium/Low level   __ Driver MP: **Yes**/No

The "Emotional" Meta-Programs

#13. Emotional Coping Style or Stress Response Pattern:
Passivity/Aggression/Dissociated
__ **P**assive/**A**ggressive
Contexts:
__ Work/Career   __ Relationships
__ Intimates   __ Hobbies/Recreation
__ Sports   __ Other:_____
__ **H**igh/**M**edium/Low level   __ Driver MP: **Yes**/No

#14. Frame of Reference or **Authority Sort:** *Internal/External; Self-Referent/*
Other-Referent
__ **O**ther Referencing/**S**elf Referencing (External/Internal Frames)
__ **B**alanced in both other-referencing and self-referencing
__ Other-Referencing with Self-referencing check
__ Self-Referencing with Other-referencing check
Contexts:
__ Work/Career   __ Relationships
__ Intimates   __ Hobbies/Recreation
__ Sports   __ Other:_____
__ **H**igh/**M**edium/Low level   __ Driver MP: **Yes**/No
__ If Other-Referencing: referencing off of who or what?
Reference person or group?

#15. Emotional State Sort: *Associated/Dissociated; Feeling/Thinking*
__ **A**ssociated/**D**issociated (Thinking/Feeling)
Contexts:
__ Negative Emotions   __ Positive Emotions
__ Present   __ Past   __ Future
__ Work/Career   __ Relationships
__ Intimates   __ Hobbies/Recreation
__ Sports   __ Other:_____
__ **H**igh/**M**edium/Low level   __ Driver MP: **Yes**/No

#16. Somatic Response Sort: *Active/Reflective/Inactive*
__ Inactive/**Reflective**/**Active**
Contexts:
__ Work/Career   __ Relationships
__ Intimates   __ Hobbies/Recreation
__ Sports   __ Other:_____
__ High/Medium/Low level   __ Driver MP: Yes/No

#17. The Convincer Or Believability Sort: *Representation of Acceptance of Persuasion Looks, Sounds, or Feels Right and/or Makes Sense*
__ Looks right/**S**ounds right/**F**eels right/**M**akes Sense
Contexts:
__ Work/Career   __ Relationships
__ Intimates   __ Hobbies/Recreation
__ Sports   __ Other:_____
__ High/**M**edium/**L**ow level __ Driver MP: Yes/No
__ **Process**:
    __ **Automatic**
    __ **Repetition**
    __ **Time Period**
    __ **Never** (almost never)

#18. Emotional Direction Sort: *Uni-directional/Multi-directional*
__ Uni-directional/**Multi-directional**/**Balanced**
Contexts:
__ Work/Career   __ Relationships
__ Intimates   __ Hobbies/Recreation
__ Sports   __ Other:_____
__ High/**M**edium/**L**ow level __ Driver MP: Yes/No

#19. Emotional Intensity/Exuberance Sort: *Desurgency/Surgency; Timidity/Boldness*
__ Desurgency/**Surgency**/**Balanced**
Contexts:
__ Work/Career   __ Relationships
__ Intimates   __ Hobbies/Recreation
__ Sports   __ Other:_____
__ High/**M**edium/**L**ow level __ Driver MP: Yes/No

The "Volitional" Meta-Programs

#20. Direction Sort: *Toward and Away From, Past Assurance/Future Possibilities;*
Approach/Avoidance
__ Toward/**A**way From (Approach/Avoidance)
__ Toward & **A**way from Equally
__ Toward with some Away From
__ **A**way from with some Toward
Contexts:
__ Work/Career   __ Relationships
__ Intimates   __ Hobbies/Recreation
__ Sports   __ Other:_____
__ High/**M**edium/Low level   __ Driver MP: **Yes/No**

#21. Conation Choice in Adapting: *Options/Procedures*
__ Procedure/**O**ption/**B**oth Option-Procedure
Contexts:
__ Work/Career   __ Relationships
__ Intimates   __ Hobbies/Recreation
__ Sports   __ Other:_____
__ High/**M**edium/Low level   __ Driver MP: **Yes/No**

#22. Adaptation Sort: *Judging/Perceiving, Controlling/Floating*
__ Judging-controlling/**P**erceiving-floating
Contexts:
__ Work/Career   __ Relationships
__ Intimates   __ Hobbies/Recreation
__ Sports   __ Other:_____
__ High/**M**edium/Low level   __ Driver MP: **Yes/No**

#23. Reason Sort of Modal Operators: *Necessity/Possibility/Desire Stick—*
   Carrot
__ Possibility/Necessity/**D**esire/**I**mpossibility
Contexts:
__ Work/Career   __ Relationships
__ Intimates   __ Hobbies/Recreation
__ Sports   __ Other:_____
__ High/**M**edium/Low level   __ Driver MP: **Yes/No**

#24. Preference Sort: *Primary Interest—People/Place/Things/Activity/Information*
__ People/**P**laces/**T**hings/**A**ctivity/**I**nformation
__ Combinations of such:
Contexts:
__ Work/Career   __ Relationships
__ Intimates   __ Hobbies/Recreation
__ Sports   __ Other:_____
__ High/**M**edium/Low level   __ Driver MP: **Yes/No**

#25. Goal Sort—Adapting to Expectations:
  Perfection/Optimization/Skepticism
  __ Perfectionistic/Optimizing/Skepticism
Contexts:
  __ Work/Career   __ Relationships
  __ Intimates   __ Hobbies/Recreation
  __ Sports   __ Other:_____
  __ High/Medium/Low level __ Driver MP: Yes/No

#26. Value Buying Sort: *Cost/Convenience/Quality/Time*
__ Cost/**Convenience**/Quality/Time
Contexts:
__ Work/Career   __ Relationships
__ Intimates   __ Hobbies/Recreation
__ Sports   __ Other:_____
__ High/Medium/Low level __ Driver MP: Yes/No

#27. Responsibility Sort: *Over-Responsible/Under-Responsible*
__ Over-responsible/Under-responsible/**Balanced**
Contexts:
__ Work/Career   __ Relationships
__ Intimates   __ Hobbies/Recreation
__ Sports   __ Other:_____
__ High/**Medium**/Low level __ Driver MP: Yes/No

#28. People Convincer Sort: *Distrusting/Trusting*
__ Distrust/Trust Orientation
Contexts:
__ Work/Career   __ Relationships
__ Intimates   __ Hobbies/Recreation
__ Sports   __ Other:_____
__ High/Medium/Low level __ Driver MP: Yes/No

The External "Response" Meta-Programs

#29. Rejuvenation of Battery Sort: *Extrovert, Ambivert, Introvert*
__ Extrovert/Introvert/**A**mbivert
Contexts:
__ Work/Career	__ Relationships
__ Intimates	__ Hobbies/Recreation
__ Sports	__ Other:_____
__ High/**M**edium/Low level	__ Driver MP: **Yes**/No

#30. Affiliation & Management Sort: *Independent/Team Player/Manager*
__ Management/Independent/**D**ependent/Potential Manager/**T**eam Player
Contexts:
__ Work/Career	__ Relationships
__ Intimates	__ Hobbies/Recreation
__ Sports	__ Other:_____
__ High/**M**edium/Low level	__ Driver MP: **Yes**/No

#31. Communication Stance Sort: *Basic Communication Modes*
__ Blamer/**Placator**/Computer/**D**istracter/**Leveler**
Contexts:
__ Work/Career	__ Relationships
__ Intimates	__ Hobbies/Recreation
__ Sports	__ Other:_____
__ High/**M**edium/Low level	__ Driver MP: **Yes**/No

#32. General Response Style: *Congruent/Incongruent/Competitive/*
Cooperative/Polarity/Meta
__ Congruity/Incongruity/Competitive/**C**ooperative/**P**olarity/**M**eta
Contexts:
__ Work/Career	__ Relationships
__ Intimates	__ Hobbies/Recreation
__ Sports	__ Other:_____
__ High/**M**edium/Low level	__ Driver MP: **Yes**/No

#33. Somatic Response Style: *Active/Reflective/Both/Inactive*
__ Active/**R**eflective/**B**oth
Contexts:
__ Work/Career	__ Relationships
__ Intimates	__ Hobbies/Recreation
__ Sports	__ Other:_____
__ High/**M**edium/Low level	__ Driver MP: **Yes**/No

#34. Work Preference Sort: *Things/Systems/People/Information*
__ Things/**S**ystems/**P**eople/**I**nformation
Contexts:
__ Work/Career	__ Relationships
__ Intimates	__ Hobbies/Recreation
__ Sports	__ Other:_____
__ High/**M**edium/Low level	__ Driver MP: **Yes**/No

#35. Comparison Sort: *Quantitative/Qualitative*
__ Quantitative Sorting/Qualitative S.
Contexts:

__ Work/Career	__ Relationships
__ Intimates	__ Hobbies/Recreation
__ Sports	__ Other:_____
__ High/**Medium**/Low level	__ Driver MP: **Yes**/No

#36. Knowledge Sort: *Modeling/Conceptualizing/Demonstrating/*
Experiencing/Authorizing
__ Modeling/Conceptualizing/
Demonstrating/Experiencing/
Authorizing
Contexts:

__ Work/Career	__ Relationships
__ Intimates	__ Hobbies/Recreation
__ Sports	__ Other:_____
__ High/**Medium**/Low level	__ Driver MP: **Yes**/No

#37. Completion/Closure Sort: *Closure/Non-Closure*
__ Closure/Non-Closure
Contexts:

__ Work/Career	__ Relationships
__ Intimates	__ Hobbies/Recreation
__ Sports	__ Other:_____
__ High/**Medium**/Low level	__ Driver MP: **Yes**/No

#38. Social Presentation: *Shrewd & Artful/Genuine & Artless*
__ Shrewd & Artful/Genuine & Artless
Contexts:

__ Work/Career	__ Relationships
__ Intimates	__ Hobbies/Recreation
__ Sports	__ Other:_____
__ High/**Medium**/Low level	__ Driver MP: **Yes**/No

#39. Hierarchical Dominance Sort: *Power/Affiliation/Achievement*
__ Power/**Affiliation**/Achievement/Balanced
Contexts:

__ Work/Career	__ Relationships
__ Intimates	__ Hobbies/Recreation
__ Sports	__ Other:_____
__ High/**Medium**/Low level	__ Driver MP: **Yes**/No

The **Meta** *Meta-Programs*

#40. Value Sort: *Emotional needs/Belief Systems*
__ **T**oward Values/**A**way From Values
List of:
Contexts:

__ Work/Career	__ Relationships
__ Intimates	__ Hobbies/Recreation
__ Sports	__ Other:_____
__ **H**igh/**M**edium/Low level	__ Driver MP: **Y**es/**N**o

#41. Temper to Instruction Sort: *Strong-Will/Compliant*
__ **S**trong-willed/**C**ompliant
Contexts:

__ Work/Career	__ Relationships
__ Intimates	__ Hobbies/Recreation
__ Sports	__ Other:_____
__ **H**igh/**M**edium/Low level	__ Driver MP: **Y**es/**N**o

#42. Self-Esteem Sort: *Conditional/Unconditional*
__ **C**onditional SE/**U**nconditional SE
Contexts:

__ Work/Career	__ Relationships
__ Intimates	__ Hobbies/Recreation
__ Sports	__ Other:_____
__ **H**igh/**M**edium/Low level	__ Driver MP: **Y**es/**N**o

#43. Self-Confidence Sort: *High/Low*
__ **L**ow Self-Confidence/**H**igh Self-Confidence
Contexts:

__ Work/Career	__ Relationships
__ Intimates	__ Hobbies/Recreation
__ Sports	__ Other:_____
__ **H**igh/**M**edium/Low level	__ Driver MP: **Y**es/**N**o

__ Self-Confidences in what specifically?

#44. Self-Experience Sort: *Mind/Emotion/Body/Role*
__ **M**ind/**E**motion/**W**ill/**B**ody/**R**ole/**P**osition/**S**pirit
Contexts:

__ Work/Career	__ Relationships
__ Intimates	__ Hobbies/Recreation
__ Sports	__ Other:_____
__ **H**igh/**M**edium/Low level	__ Driver MP: **Y**es/**N**o

#45. Self-Integrity: *Conflicted Incongruity/Harmonious Integration*
__ Incongruency /Congruency
Contexts:

__ Work/Career	__ Relationships
__ Intimates	__ Hobbies/Recreation
__ Sports	__ Other:_____
__ High/**Medium**/Low level	__ Driver MP: Yes/No

#46. "Time" Tenses Sort: *Past/Present/Future*
__ Past/Present/Future/Atemporal
Contexts:

__ Work/Career	__ Relationships
__ Intimates	__ Hobbies/Recreation
__ Sports	__ Other:_____
__ High/**Medium**/Low level	__ Driver MP: Yes/No

#47. "Time" Experience: *In "Time"/Through "Time"; Sequential Versus Random Sorting*
__ In "Time"/Through "Time" (Random/Sequential)
Contexts:

__ Work/Career	__ Relationships
__ Intimates	__ Hobbies/Recreation
__ Sports	__ Other:_____
__ High/**Medium**/Low level	__ Driver MP: Yes/No

#48. "Time" Access Sort: *Random/Sequential*
__ Random Accessing/Sequential Accessing
Contexts:

__ Work/Career	__ Relationships
__ Intimates	__ Hobbies/Recreation
__ Sports	__ Other:_____
__ High/**Medium**/Low level	__ Driver MP: Yes/No

#49. Ego Strength Sort: *Unstable/Stable*
__ Unstable/Stable
Contexts:

__ Work/Career	__ Relationships
__ Intimates	__ Hobbies/Recreation
__ Sports	__ Other:_____
__ High/**Medium**/Low level	__ Driver MP: Yes/No

#50. Morality Sort: *Weak/Strong Super-ego*
__ Unconscientious/Conscientious—
Weak/Strong Super-ego
Contexts:

__ Work/Career	__ Relationships
__ Intimates	__ Hobbies/Recreation
__ Sports	__ Other:_____
__ High/**Medium**/Low level	__ Driver MP: Yes/No

#51. Causation Sort: *Causeless, Linear Cause Effect (CE), Multi-CE, Personal CE, External CE, Magical, Correlational*
__ **C**auseless/**L**inear, **M**ulti, **P**ersonal, **E**xternal, **Ma**gical, **Cor**relational
Contexts:
__ Work/Career   __ Relationships
__ Intimates   __ Hobbies/Recreation
__ Sports   __ Other:_____
__ **H**igh/**M**edium/**L**ow level   __ Driver MP: **Y**es/**N**o

Appendix G

There Is No "Is"

Did you notice that we wrote this book using the General-semantic extensional device called **E-Prime** (except for quotes from others)? We did.

E-what? **English**-*primed* of the "to be" verb family of passive verbs (is, am, are, was, were, be, being, been). Invented by D. David Bourland, Jr. and popularized by Bourland and Paul Dennithorne Johnston in *To Be or Not: An E-Prime Anthology*, E-Prime and E-Choice empowers people to not fall into the "is" traps of language.

The "is" traps? Yes, Alfred Korzybski (1941/1994) warned that *the "is" of identity* and *the "is" of predication* present two dangerous linguistic and semantic constructions that map false-to-fact conclusions. The first has to do with identity—how we identify a thing or what we identify ourselves with and the second with attribution, how we frequently project our "stuff" onto others or onto things without realizing it.

Identity as "sameness in all respects," does not even exist. It can't. At the sub-microscopic level, everything involves a "dance of electrons" always moving, changing, and becoming. So no thing can ever "stay the same" even with itself. So nothing "is" in any static, permanent, unchanging way. Since nothing exists as eternal, but since everything continually changes, then nothing "is." To use "is" mis-speaks, mis-evaluates, and mis-maps reality. To say, "She is lazy..." "That is a stupid statement..." falsely maps reality. And Korzybski argued that unsanity and insanity ultimately lie in *identifications.*

Predication refers to "asserting" something. So to say, "This is good," "That flower is red," "He is really stupid!" creates a language structure which implies that something "out there" contains these qualities of "goodness," "redness," and "stupidity." The "is" suggests that such things exist *independent of the speaker's experience.* Not so. Our descriptions speak primarily about our internal experience indicating our judgments and values. More accurately we could have said, "I evaluate as good this or that," "I see that flower as red," "I think of him as suffering from stupidity!"

"Is" statements falsely distract, confuse logical levels, and subtly lead us to think that such value judgments exist outside our skin in the world "objectively." Wrong again. The evaluations (good, red, stupid) function as definitions and interpretations in the speaker's mind.

The "to be" verbs dangerously presuppose that "things" (actual events or processes) stay the same. Not! These verbs invite us to create mental representations of fixedness so that we begin to set the world in concrete and to live in "a frozen universe." These verbs code the dynamic nature of processes statically. "Life is tough." "I am no good at math."

Do these statements not sound definitive? Absolute? "That's just the way it is!" No wonder Bourland calls "is" "am" and "are," etc. *"the deity mode."* "The fact is that this work is no good!" Such words carry a sense of completeness, finality, and time-independence. Yet discerning the difference between the map and the territory tells us that these phenomenon exist on different logical levels. Using E-Prime (or E-Choice) reduces slipping in groundless authoritarian statements which only closes minds or invites arguments.

If we confuse the language we use in describing reality (our map) with reality (the territory), then we *identify* differing things. And that makes for unsanity. **There "is" no is.** "Is" non-references. It points to nothing in reality. It operates entirely as an irrational construction of the human mind. Its use leads to semantic mis-evaluations.

Conversely, writing, thinking, and speaking in E-Prime contributes to *"consciousness of abstracting"* (conscious awareness) that we make maps of the world which inherently differ from the world. E-Prime enables us to think and speak with more clarity and precision as it forces us to take first-person. This reduces the passive verb tense ("It was done." "Mistakes were made."). It restores speakers to statements, thereby contextualizing statements. E-Prime, by raising consciousness of abstracting, thereby enables us to index language. Now I realize that the person I met last week, Person $_{last\ week}$, "is" not equal in all respects to the person that now stands before me, Person $_{this\ week}$. This assist me in making critical and valuable distinctions.

E-Choice differs from E-Prime in that with it one uses *the "is" of existence* (e.g. "Where is your office?" "It is on 7th. Street at Orchard Avenue."), *the auxiliary "is"* (e.g. "He is coming next week.") and *the "is" of name*, (e.g. "What is your name?" "It is Michael." "My name is Bob."). Though we wrote this in E-Prime, we have decided to begin to use E-Choice so as to avoid some circumlocutious phrases that we have used in the past(!).

Reference: Hall (1995) "Elevating NLP to E-Prime" (Feb. 1995), *Anchor Point*.

Appendix H

Meta-Programs To Come

In order to not leave the impression that we have exhausted all possible meta-programs with these 51, we would call your attention to Woodsmall's (1988) work wherein he included a section that he playfully entitled, *"Wyatt Woodsmall's Meta Programming Cookbook."* Or, "Everything you ever wanted to know about sorting principles and were afraid to ask." There he enumerated not only Leslie and Richard's original meta-programs for therapy, and his expanded version, but multiple other sources and lists of meta-programs.

Within those lists we have identified additional ones that seem most promising to us. We have named the sort in bold with its distinctions in italic.

- **State**: *Primary/Meta Aware* (Very similar to the meta-states model)
- **Memory:** *Reliving/Meta Aware*
- **Rule Structure:** *my rules for me; my rules for me/my rules for you; no rules for me/my rules for you; my rules for me/your rules for you* (Source: Roger Bailey)
- **Context:** High/Low (sources: Edward Hall, Gregory Bateson, p. 99)
- **Harmony:** *Moving Away from Disharmony/Moving away from Harmony/Toward Harmony/Toward Disharmony*
- **Mental Development:** *Noise/Correlations (patterns)/Regularities/Laws/Counter Examples/Synthesis*
- **Mental Ordering:** *Thesis/Antithesis/Synthesis*
- **Tangibility Order:** *Concrete (connected, undifferentiated, sensuous)/Abstract (unconnected)*
- **Cosmos Order**: *Messy/Unmessy/Fussy!*
- **Eschatological:** *Life after death/No life after death; Heaven/Hell/Reincarnation/Limbo/Extinction*
- **Kolb Learning Styles:** *Concrete/Abstract Conceptualization/Active Experimentation/Reflective Observation/Accommodator/Diverger/Assimilator/Converger*
- **Gardner Multiple Intelligences:** *Linguistic, Logical-Mathematical/Spatial, Musical, Body-Kinesthetic/Intra-Personal/Inter-Personal*
- **Learning type:** *One Time Learning/Reinforcement Learning*)
- **Ambiguity Types:** *Novel/Complex/Insolvable.*
- **Risk Tasking:** *Safety (no RT)/Cautious (some RT)/Challenging (high level RT)/Fools (total RT)*
- **Time Nature:** *Compressed Time/Expanded Time*
- **Memory Playback:** *Continuous Real Time/Continuous Skip Time*
- **Memory Evaluation:** *Original Criteria/Present Day Criteria*

About the Authors

L. Michael Hall, Ph.D. earned his doctorate in Cognitive-Behavioral Psychology wherein he developed an extended meta-model using the formulations of General-Semantics. Dr. Hall has also authored numerous articles and books in NLP and General-Semantics. In 1994, he developed the Meta-States Model, and thereafter focused much of his work since that time on exploring logical levels and reflexivity in his workshops and training. His Myers Briggs Type Indicator - ENTJ (as of 1993.) You can reach him at: 1904 N. 7th. Street, Grand Junction Colorado, 81501-7418. Email: NLPMetaStates@OnLineCol.com.

In 1996/97 Michael has worked with *Edit Rodas Haskell* of NLP Center of Texas doing numerous trainings: 4600 Post-Oak Place, Suite 204, Houston, TX. 77027. Telephone Number: (970) 245-3235

Bob G. Bodenhamer, D.Min. directs NLP of Gastonia, North Carolina for many years where he has provided NLP training at Gaston College and has had an NLP Therapy Practice. Dr. Bodenhamer studied under, and received NLP and Time Line Therapy™ certification from, Dr. Tad James. He has served as a pastor in several churches. The National Board for Certified Counselors (Provider #5724) has approved NLP of Gastonia to offer continuing education activity. His Myers Briggs Type Indicator - ENTJ. You can reach him at 1516 Cecelia Drive, Gastonia, NC. 28054. Telephone Number: (704) 864-3585
Email: Bodenhamer@aol.com.

For more information on other books and trainings, see our Web Site:
http://members.aol.com/bodenhamer/bob.html

Bibliography

Bandler, Richard and Grinder, John (1975). *The Structure of Magic, Volume I: A Book About Language and Therapy*. Palo Alto, CA: Science & Behavior Books.

Bandler, Richard and Grinder, John (1976). *The Structure of Magic, Volume II.* Palo Alto, CA: Science & Behavior Books.

Bandler, Richard and Grinder, John (1979). *Frogs into Princes: Neuro-Linguistic Programming*. Moab, UT: Real People Press.

Bandler, Richard and Grinder, John (1982). *Reframing: Neuro-Linguistic Programming and the Transformation of Meaning*. Ut: Real People Press.

Bandler, Richard (1985). *Magic in Action.* Moab, UT: Real People Press.

Bandler, Richard (1985). *Using Your Brain for a Change: Neuro-Linguistic Programming.* Moab UT: Real People Press.

Bateson, Gregory (1979). *Mind and Nature: A Necessary Unity.* New York: Bantam.

Bateson, Gregory (1972). *Steps to an Ecology of Mind*. New York: Ballantine.

Beattie, Melody (1987). *Codependent No More*. New York: Harper & Row.

Bodenhamer, Bob G. (1993). *Advanced Communication Course: From Neuro-Linguistic Programming.* Gastonia, NC: NLP of Gastonia.

Bodenhamer, Bob G. (1995)."NLP Manual For Practitioners," Unpublished training manual. Gastonia, NC: NLP of Gastonia

Bodenhamer, Bob G.; Hall, Michael L (1997a) *Time-Lining: Advanced Patterns in "Time" Processes.* Grand Jct. CO: ET Publ.

Bourland, David D. Jr. and Johnston, Paul Dennithorne (1991). *To Be or Not: an E-Prime Anthology*. San Francisco, CA: International Society for General Semantics.

Bourland, David. D. Jr., Johnston, Paul Dennithorne; and Klein, Jeremy (1994). *More E-prime: To Be or Not II.* Concord, CA: International Society for General Semantics.

Branden, Nathaniel (1969). *The Psychology of Self-Esteem.* New York: Bantam Books.

Briggs, Katharine C., Myers, Isabel Briggs (1943/1987). *Myers-Briggs Type Indicator.* Palo Alto, CA: Consulting Psychologists Press, Inc.

Brunner, Jerome (1990). *Acts of Meaning.* Cambridge, MA: Harvard University Press.

Cade, Brian, and O'Hanlon, William H. (1993) *A Brief Guide to Brief Therapy.* New York: W.W. Norton and Company.

Cattell, Heather Kirkett (1989). *The 16PF: Personality in depth.* Champaign, IL: Institute for Personality and Ability Testing, Inc.

Charvet, R. Shelle. (1995). *Words that Change Minds: Mastering the Language of Influence.* Debuque, IA: Kendall/Hunt Publishing.

Dilts, Robert (1990). *Changing Belief Systems with NLP.* Cupertino, CA: Meta Publications

Dilts, Robert B., Epstein, Todd, Dilts, Robert W. (1991). *Tools for Dreamers: Strategies for Creativity and the Structure of Innovation.* Cupertino, CA: Meta Publications.

Dobson, James (1970). *Dare to Discipline.* Wheaton, IL: Tyndale House Publications.

Ellis, Albert and Harper, Robert A. (1976). *A New Guide to Rational Living.* Englewood Cliffs, NJ: Prentice-Hall, Inc.

Erickson, E. H. (1959). "Identity and the life cycle: Selected Paper." *Psychological Issue Monograph Series I* (No. 1). NY: International Universities Press.

Erickson, E. H. (1968). *Identity, Youth and Crisis.* NY: W.W. Norton.

Grinder, Michael (1989). *Righting the Educational Conveyor Belt.* OR: Metamorphous Press. Inc.

Hall, Michael L. (1987). Monograph: "Fight/Flight Patterns in Human Patterns of Communicating, Responding," Grand Jct. Co. ET Publ.

Hall, Michael L. (1989). "E-Prime in NLP" *Anchor Point, The International Journal for Effective NLP Communicators,* Feb. 1995.

Hall, Michael L. (1990). Monograph: *How to Read a Person (Almost) Like a Book.* Grand Jct. CO: ET Publ.

Hall, L. Michael (1995). *Meta-States: A New Domain of Logical Levels, Self-Reflexiveness in Human States of Consciousness.* Grand Junction, CO: ET Publ.

Hall, L. Michael (1996a). *Dragon Slaying: Dragons to Princes.* Grand Jct. CO: ET Publ.

Hall, L. Michael (1996b). *The Spirit of NLP: The Process, Meaning and Criteria for Mastering NLP.* Carmarthen, Wales: Anglo-American Book Company.

Hall, Michael L. (1996c). *Becoming a Ferocious Presenter.* Grand Jct. CO: ET Publications

Hall, Michael L. (1996d). *Languaging: the Linguistics of Psychotherapy.* Grand Jct. CO: ET Publ.

Hall, L. Michael (1997a). *Neuro-Linguistic Programming: Going Meta into Logical Levels.* Grand Jct. CO: ET Publ.

Hall, L. Michael (1997b). *Meta-State Journal: Patterns Volume I.* Grand Jct. CO: ET Publications

Huxley, Aldous (1954). *The Doors of Perception and Heaven and Hell.* NY: Harper & Row

Jacobson, Sid (1996). *Solution States: A Course in Solving Problems in Business with the Power of NLP.* Carmarthen, Wales: Anglo-American Book Company.

James, Tad; Woodsmall, Wyatt. (1988). *Time Line Therapy and the Basis of Personality.* Cupertino, CA: Meta Publications.

James, Tad. (1990). Tad James' Master Track Audio Tape Series on Meta-Programs.

James, William (1890). *Principles of Psychology: Volume I.* NY: Holt.

Jung, Carl (1923/1971). *Psychological Types.* MA: Princeton University Press.

Kohlbert, L. A. (1964). "Development of moral character and moral ideology". In M.L. Hoffman & L.W. Hoffman (Eds.), *Review of Child Development Research* **(Vol. 1)**. NY: Russell Sage Foundation.

Kohlbert, L. A. (1980). *The Meaning and Measurement of Moral Development.* Worcester, MA: Clark University Press.

Kolb, David A. (1981). *Learning Style Inventory.* Boston: McBer & Company Training Resources Group.

Korzybski, Alfred (1941/1994). *Science and Sanity: An Introduction to Non-Aristotelian Systems and General Semantics,* (*5th. ed.*). Lakeville, CN: International Non-Aristotelian Library Publishing Co.

Laborde, Genie Z. (1984). *Influencing with Integrity.* Palo Alto, CA: Syntony Publishing Co.

Lakoff, George (1987). *Women, Fire, and Dangerous Things: What Categories Reveal About the Mind.* Chicago: University of Chicago Press.

Lewis, Bryon A., Pucelik, R. Frank (1982). *Magic Demystified: A Pragmatic Guide to Communication and Change.* Portland, OR: Metamorphous Press, Inc.

Lloyd, Carl (1989). Unpublished dissertation, "The Impact of Role-Expectation Cognitions Upon Test-Taking." University of Texas at Arlington.

Maslow, Abraham H. (1954/1970). *Motivation and Personality.* New York: Harper & Row.

McClelland, D., Atkinson, J.W., Clark, R.A., & Lowell, E.L. (1953). *The Achievement Motive.* NY: Appleton-Century-Crofts.

McConnell, James V. (1977). *Understanding Human Behavior.* (2nd. edition). NY: Holt, Rinehart and Winston.

Mehrabian, Albert (1976). *Public Places and Private Spaces.* NY: Basic Books, Inc.

May, Rollo (1989). *The Art of Counseling.* NY: Gardner Press.

Miller, George (1956). "The magical number seven, plus or minus two: Some limits on our capacity to process information." *Psychological Review, 63,* pp.81-97.

Minninger, Joan (1988). *Make Your Mind Work for You.* Emmaus, PA: Rodale Press.

Munshaw, Joe; Zink, Nelson (1997). "What's A Map?" *Anchor Point 11: #5* (pp. 31-36).

O'Connor, Joseph; McDermott, Ian (1995). "Patterns of Influence: Review Article." *NLP World: The Intercultural Journal on the Theory and Practice of NLP.* Orzens, Switzerland. pp 75-80.

O'Connor, Joseph; Seymour, John (1990). *Introducing Neuro-Linguistic Programming: the New Psychology of Personal Excellence.* Great Britain: Mandala.

Piaget, J. (1932). *The Moral Judgment of the Child.* London: Routledge & Kegan Paul.

Piaget, J. (1951). *Play, Dreams and Imitation in Childhood.* NY: W. W. Norton.

Piaget, J. (1954). *The Construction of Reality in the Child.* NY: Basic Books.

Reese, Edward; Bagley, Dan, III. (1988). *Beyond Selling: How to Maximize Your Personal Influence.*

Robbie, Eric (1988). "Meta Program Detection." Unpublished Handout.

Robbie, Eric (1987). "Sub-Modality Eye Accessing Cues." *Journal of NLP International. Vol. 1*, N. 1. (January, 1987). pp 15-24. Jacksonville, FL. NLP International.

Robbins, Anthony (1991). *Awaken the Giant Within: How to Take Immediate Control of Your Mental, Emotional, Physical, and Financial Destiny.* N.Y: Simon and Schuster.

Robbins, Anthony (1986). *Unlimited Power: The New Science of Personal Achievement.* NY: Simon and Schuster.

Rooney, Gene; Savage, John S. (1989). *Neurological Sorts and Belief Systems.* Reynoldsburg, OH: L.E.A.D. Consultants, Inc.

Satir, Virginia (1972). *Peoplemaking.* Palo Alto, CA: Science and Behavior Books, Inc.

Schultz, D. (1990). *Theories of Personality.* Pacific Grove, CA: Brooks/Cole.

Seligman, Martin, E.P. (1975). *Helplessness: On Depression, Development, and Death.* San Francisco: Freeman.

Seligman, Martin E.P. (1991). *Learned Optimism.* New York: Alfred A. Knopf.

Taylor, Robert M., Johnson, Roswell H. (1986). *Taylor-Johnson Temperament Analysis.* Los Angeles, CA: Psychological Publications, Inc.

Woodsmall, Wyatt L. (1988). *Metaprograms.* Vienna, VA: Advanced Behavioral Modeling.

Yeager, Joseph (1985). *Thinking About Thinking with NLP.* Cupertino, CA: Meta Publications

Index

Glossary of NLP Terms

Accessing Cues: The ways we tune our bodies by breathing, posture, gesture and eye movements to think in certain ways.

As-If Frame: Pretending that some event has happened, so thinking "as if" it had occurred, encourages creative problem-solving by mentally going beyond apparent obstacles to desired solutions.

Analogue: Continuously variable between limits, like a dimmer switch for a light. An analogue submodality varies like light to dark, while a digital submodality operates as either off or on, e.g. we see a picture in either an associated or dissociated way.

Anchoring: The process by which any stimulus or representation (external or internal) gets connected to and so triggers a response. Anchors occur naturally and intentionally (as in analogue marking). The NLP concept of anchoring derives from the Pavlovian stimulus-response reaction, classical conditioning. In Pavlov's study the tuning fork became the stimulus (anchor) that cued the dog to salivate.

Association: This refers to mentally seeing, hearing, and feeling from inside an experience. Associated contrasts with dissociated. In dissociation, you see a young you in the visual image. Generally, dissociation removes emotion from the experience while in association we experience the information emotionally.

Auditory: The sense of hearing, one of the basic Representation Systems.

Behavior: Any activity we engage in, micro like thinking, or macro like external actions.

Beliefs: Thoughts, conscious or unconscious, which have grown up into through into a generalization about causality, meaning, self, others, behaviors, identity, etc. Beliefs address the world and operating in it. Beliefs guide us in perceiving and interpreting reality. Beliefs relate closely to values. NLP has several belief change patterns.

Calibration: Becoming tuned-in to another's state via reading non-verbal signals previously observed and calibrated.

Chunking: Changing perception by going up or down levels and/or logical levels. Chunking up refers to going up a level (inducing up, induction). It leads to higher abstractions. Chunking down refers to going down a level (deducing, deduction). It leads to more specific examples or cases.

Complex Equivalence: A linguistic distinction wherein someone makes two statements to mean the same thing, e.g. "He is late; he doesn't love me."

Congruence: A state wherein one's internal representation work in an aligned way. What a person says corresponds with what s/he does. Both their non-verbal signals and their verbal statements match. A state of unity, fitness, internal harmony, not conflict.

Conscious: Present moment awareness. Awareness of seven +/- two chunks of information.

Content: The specifics and details of an event, answers *what?* and *why?* Contrasts with process or structure.

Context: The setting, frame or process in which events occur and provides meaning for content.

Cues: Information that provides clues to another's subjective structures, i.e. eye accessing cues, predicates, breathing, body posture, gestures, voice tone and tonality, etc.

Deletion: The missing portion of an experience either linguistically or representationally.

Digital:	Varying between two states e.g. a light switch—either on or off. A digital submodality: color or black-and-white; an analogue submodality: varying between dark and bright.
Dissociation:	Not "in" an experience, but seeing or hearing it from outside as from a spectator's point of view, in contrast to association.
Distortion:	The modeling process by which we inaccurately represent something in our neurology or linguistics, can occur to create limitations or resources.
Downtime:	Not in sensory awareness, but "down" inside one's own mind seeing, hearing, and feeling thoughts, memories, awarenesses, a light trance state with attention focused inward.
Ecology:	The question about the overall relationship between idea, skill, response and larger environment or system. Internal ecology: the overall relationship between person and thoughts, strategies, behaviors, capabilities, values and beliefs. The dynamic balance of elements in a system.
Elicitation:	Evoking a state by word, behavior, gesture or any stimuli. Gathering information by direct observation of non-verbal signals or by asking meta-model questions.
Empowerment:	Process of adding vitality, energy, and new powerful resources to a person; vitality at the neurological level, change of habits.
Eye Accessing Cues:	Movements of the eyes in certain directions indicating visual, auditory or kinesthetic thinking (processing).
Epistemology:	The study of how we know what we know. NLP as an epistemology.
First Position:	Perceiving the world from your own point of view, associated, one of the three perceptual positions.
Frame:	Context, environment, meta-level, a way of perceiving something (as in Outcome Frame, "As If" Frame, Backtrack Frame, etc.).

Future Pace: Process of mentally practicing (rehearsing) an event before it happens. One of the key processes for ensuring the permanency of an outcome, a frequent and key ingredient in most NLP interventions.

Generalization: Process by which one specific experience comes to represent a whole class of experiences, one of the three modeling processes in NLP.

Gestalt: A collection of memories connected neurologically based on similar emotions.

Hard Wired: Neurologically based factor, the neural connectors primarily formed during gestation, similar to the hard wiring of a computer.

Incongruence: State wherein parts conflict and war with each other, having reservations, not totally committed to an outcome, expressed in incongruent messages, signals, lack of alignment or matching of word and behavior.

Installation: Process for putting a new mental strategy (way of doing things) inside mind-body so it operates automatically, often achieved through anchoring, leverage, metaphors, parables, reframing, future pacing, etc.

Internal Representations: Patterns of information we create and store in our minds, combinations of sights, sounds, sensations, smells and tastes.

Kinesthetic: Sensations, feelings, tactile sensations on surface of skin, proprioceptive sensations inside the body, includes vestibular system or sense of balance.

Leading: Changing your own behaviors after obtaining rapport so another follows, an acid test for high level of rapport.

Logical Level: A higher level, a level *about* a lower level, a meta-level that drives and modulates the lower level.

Loops: A circle, cycle, a story, metaphor or representation that goes back to its own beginning, so that it loops back (feeds back) onto itself. An open loop: a story left unfinished. A closed loop: finishing a story. In strategies: loop refers to getting hung up in a set of procedures that have no way out, the strategy fails to exit.

Map of Reality: Model of the world, a unique representation of the world built in each person's brain by abstracting from experiences, comprised of a neurological and a linguistic map, one's internal representations (IR).

Matching: Adopting facets of another's outputs (behavior, words, etc.) to enhancing rapport.

Meta: Above, beyond, about, at a higher level, a logical level higher.

Meta-Model: A model with 11 (or 12) linguistic distinctions that identifies language patterns that obscure meaning in a communication via distortion, deletion and generalization. 11 (or 12) specific challenges or questions by which to clarify imprecise language (ill-formedness) to reconnect it to sensory experience and the deep structure. Meta-modeling brings a person out of trance. Developed, 1975, by Richard Bandler and John Grinder. Basis of all other discoveries in NLP.

Meta-Programs: The mental/perceptual programs for sorting and paying attention to stimuli, perceptual filters that govern attention, sometimes "neuro-sorts," or meta-processes.

Meta-States: A state about a state, bringing a state of mind-body (fear, anger, joy, learning) to bear upon another state from a higher logical level, generates a gestalt state—a meta-state, developed by Michael Hall.

Mismatching: Offering different patterns of behavior to another, breaking rapport for the purpose of redirecting, interrupting, or terminating a meeting or conversation, mismatching as a meta-programs.

Modal Operators:	Linguistic distinctions in the meta-model that indicate the "mode" by which a person "operates"—the mode of necessity, impossibility, desire, possibility, etc., the predicates (can, can't, possible, impossible, have to, must, etc.) that we utilize for motivation.
Model:	A description of how something works, a generalized, deleted or distorted copy of the original.
Modeling:	A process of observing and replicating the successful actions and behaviors of others, the process of discerning the sequence of IR and behaviors that enable someone to accomplish a task, the basis of accelerated learning.
Model of the World:	A map of reality, a unique representation of the world via abstraction from our experiences, the total of one's personal operating principles.
Multiple Description:	The process of describing the same thing from different viewpoints.
Neuro-Linguistic Programming:	The study of excellence, a model of how people structure their experience, the structure of subjective experience, how humans become *programmed* in their thinking-emoting and behaving in their very *neurology* by the various *languages* they use to process, code and retrieve information.
Nominalization:	A linguistic distinction in the meta-model, a hypnotic pattern of trance language, a process or verb turned into an (abstract) noun, a process frozen in time.
Outcome:	A specific, sensory-based desired result, should meet the well-formedness criteria.
Pacing:	Gaining and maintaining rapport with another by joining their model of the world by saying which fits with and matches their language, beliefs, values, current experience, etc., crucial to rapport building.

Parts:	Unconscious parts, sub-personalities created through some Significant Emotional Experience (SEE), disowned and separated functions that begin to take on a life of their own, a source of intra-personal conflict when incongruous.
Perceptual Filters:	Unique ideas, experiences, beliefs, values, meta-programs, decisions, memories and language that shape and color our model of the world.
Perceptual Position:	Our point of view, one of three positions: first position—associated, second position—from another person's perspective, third position—from another other position.
Physiological:	The physical part of the person.
Predicates:	What we assert or predicate about a subject, sensory based words indicating a particular Representational Systems (visual predicates, auditory, kinesthetic, unspecified).
Preferred System:	The RS that an individual typically uses most in thinking and organizing experience.
Presuppositions:	Ideas that we have to take for granted for a communication to make sense, assumptions, that which "holds" (position) "up" (sup) a statement "ahead of time" (pre).
Rapport:	A sense of connection with another, a feeling of mutuality, a sense of trust, created by pacing, mirroring and matching, a state of empathy or second position.
Reframing:	Taking a frame-of-reference so that it looks new or different, presenting an event or idea from a different point of view so it has a different meaning; content or context reframing, a change pattern.
Representation:	An idea, thought, presentation of sensory-based or evaluative based information.
Representation System (RS):	How we mentally code information using the sensory systems: Visual, Auditory, Kinesthetic, Olfactory, and Gustatory.

Requisite Variety:	Flexibility in thinking, emoting, speaking, behaving; the person with the most flexibility of behavior controls the action; the Law of Requisite Variety.
Resources:	Any means we can bring to bear to achieve an outcome: physiology, states, thoughts, strategies, experiences, people, events or possessions.
Resourceful State:	The total neurological and physical experience when a person feels resourceful.
Satir Categories:	The five body postures and language styles indicating specific ways of communicating: leveler, blamer, placator, computer and distracter, developed by Virginia Satir.
Second Position:	Perceiving the world from another's point of view, in tune with another's sense of reality.
Sensory Acuity:	Awareness of the outside world, of the senses, making finer distinctions about the sensory information we get from the world.
Sensory-Based Description:	Information directly observable and verifiable by the senses, see-hear-feel language that we can test empirically, in contrast to evaluative descriptions.
State:	Holistic phenomenon of mind-body-emotions, mood, emotional condition, sum total of all neurological and physical processes within individual at any moment in time.
Strategy:	A sequencing of thinking-behaving to obtain an outcome or create an experience, the structure of subjectivity ordered in a linear model of the TOTE.
Submodality:	Distinctions within each RS, qualities of internal representations, the smallest building blocks of thoughts, characteristics in each system.
Synesthesia:	Automatic link from one RS to another, a V-K synesthesia involves seeing-feeling without a moment of consciousness to think about it, automatic program.

Third Position:	Perceiving the world from the viewpoint of an observer's position, one of the three perceptual positions, where you see both yourself and another.
Time-line:	A metaphor describing how we store our sights, sounds and sensations of memories and images, a way of coding and processing the construct "time."
Unconscious:	Everything not in conscious awareness, minor Representational Systems.
Universal Quantifiers:	A linguistic term in the meta-model for words that code things with "allness" (every, all, never, none, etc.), a distinction that admits no exceptions.
Unspecified Nouns:	Nouns that do not specify to whom or to what they refer.
Unspecified Verbs:	Verbs that have the adverb deleted, delete specifics of the action.
Uptime:	State where attention and senses directed outward to immediate environment, all sensory channels open and alert.
Value:	What is important to you in a particular context? Your values (criterion) are what motivate you in life. On the end of all motivational strategies you will find a kinesthetic. This kinesthetic is an unconscious value.
Visual:	Seeing, imagining, the RS of sight.
Visualization:	The process of seeing images in your mind.
Well-Formedness Condition:	The criteria that enable us to specific an outcome in ways that make it an achievable and verifiable, powerful tool for negotiating win/win solutions.

The Anglo American Book Company Ltd
Crown Buildings,
Bancyfelin,
Carmarthen SA33 5ND
Wales.
Telephone: 01267 211880 / 211886

We trust you enjoyed this title from our range of bestselling books for professional and general readership. All our authors are professionals of many years' experience, and all are highly respected in their own field. We choose our books with care for their content and character, and for the value of their contribution of both new and updated material to their particular field. Here is a list of all our other publications:

Figuring Out People
    by Bob G. Bodenhamer & L. Michael Hall   Paperback   £12.99

Gold Counselling: *A Practical Psychology with NLP*
    by Georges Philips   Paperback   £14.99

Grieve No More, Beloved: *The Book of Delight*
    by Ormond McGill   Paperback   £9.99

Influencing With Integrity
    by Genie Z. Laborde   Paperback   £12.50

Living Organisations: *Beyond the Learning Organisation*
    by Lex McKee   Hardback   £14.99

The New Encyclopedia of Stage Hypnotism
    by Ormond McGill   Hardback   £29.99

The POWER Process: *An NLP Approach to Writing*
    by Sid Jacobson & Dixie Elise Hickman   Paperback   £12.99

Scripts & Strategies in Hypnotherapy
    by Roger P. Allen   Paperback   £19.99

Seeing the Unseen: *A Past Life Revealed through Hypnotic Regression*
    by Ormond McGill   Paperback   £14.99

Solution States: *A Course in Solving Problems in Business Using NLP*
    by Sid Jacobson   Paperback   £12.99

The Spirit of NLP: *The Process, Meaning and Criteria for Mastering NLP*
    by L. Michael Hall   Paperback   £12.99

Time-Lining: *Patterns for Adventuring in "Time"*
    by Bob G. Bodenhamer & L. Michael Hall   Paperback   £14.99